Quaker Records of Southern Maryland

Births, Deaths, Marriages, and Abstracts from the Minutes

1658-1800

Henry C. Peden, Jr., M.A.

WILLOW BEND BOOKS
2006

WILLOW BEND BOOKS
AN IMPRINT OF HERITAGE BOOKS, INC.

Books, CDs, and more—Worldwide

For our listing of thousands of titles see our website
at
www.HeritageBooks.com

Published 2006 by
HERITAGE BOOKS, INC.
Publishing Division
65 East Main Street
Westminster, Maryland 21157-5026

Copyright © 1992 Henry C. Peden, Jr.

All rights reserved. No part of this book may be reproduced or transmitted in any form or by any means, electronic or mechanical, including photocopying, recording or by any information storage and retrieval system without written permission from the author, except for the inclusion of brief quotations in a review.

International Standard Book Number: 978-1-58549-215-9

CONTENTS

FOREWORD v

Map of QUAKER MEETINGS IN SOUTHERN MARYLAND vi

WEST RIVER MONTHLY MEETING REGISTER BIRTHS AND DEATHS, 1655 - 1800 1

MARRIAGES 13

CLIFTS MONTHLY MEETING REGISTER, 1662 - 1782 51

MONTHLY MEETING MINUTES, 1677 - 1771 67

BIRTHS AND DEATHS OF SANDY SPRING MONTHLY MEETING 86

INDEX 95

FOREWORD

Quakers (or The Society of Friends) first settled in Southern Maryland in 1658 and established meetings at West River, Severn, South River and Herring Creek in Anne Arundel County, at Pickawaxon and Patuxent in Charles County, and at the Clifts in Calvert County. For a while Baltimore County was included until the formation of Gunpowder Monthly Meeting in 1737 to include the Patapsco Meeting and Gunpowder Meeting. Monthly Meetings were later established at Indian Spring in Prince George's County and at Sandy Spring in what is now Montgomery County (see map). However, records for all meetings are not extant. For more information on the history and availability of all Quaker records in Maryland one should consult Phebe R. Jacobsen's *Quaker Records in Maryland* (Publication No. 14, Hall of Records Commission, Annapolis, Maryland, 1966), and Eleanor P. Passano's *An Index to the Source Records of Maryland* (Baltimore: Genealogical Publishing Company, 1967 reprint).

Information for this book has been taken from extant Quaker records of Southern Maryland prior to 1800 at the Maryland State Archives (and in some cases to 1815 if the children's dates of birth started prior to 1800 and ended thereafter) as follows, with the microfilm number shown:

(1) West River Monthly Meeting Register, beginning in 1655. (M545A).

(2) Clifts Monthly Meeting Register, 1662-1782. (M545).

(3) West River Monthly Meeting Minutes, beginning in 1698. Included are "Galloway Births, 1689-1709." (M637).

(4) Minutes of Monthly Meetings Held at the Clifts, West River, Herring Run, and Indian Spring from 1677 to 1771. (M605).

(5) Records of Births, Deaths and Membership of Sandy Spring Monthly Meeting, beginning in 1730. (M667).

(6) Marriage Certificates of West River, Herring Run, and Indian Spring Meetings, beginning in 1682. [This appears to include marriages of all the meetings within the Monthly Meeting.] (M639).

Henry C. Peden, Jr.
Bel Air, Maryland
February 29, 1992

QUAKER RECORDS OF SOUTHERN MARYLAND

WEST RIVER MONTHLY MEETING REGISTER
BIRTHS AND DEATHS, 1655-1800.

William Coale, Jr., son of William and Ester, of Anne Arundel County, b. 21st day of 7th month, 1655.
Edward Talbott, son of Richard and Elizabeth, of Anne Arundel County, b. 6th day of 9th month [November], 1658.
Joanna Hooker, dau. of Thomas and Joan, of Anne Arundel County, b. 15th day of 1st month, 1660/1.
Samuel Galloway, son of Richard and Hannah, of Anne Arundel County, b. 7th day of 8th month, 1659.
Thomas Hooker, Jr., son of Thomas and Joan, b. 13th day of 5th month, 1660/1.
Richard Galloway, son of Richard and Hannah, b. 28th day of 11th month, 1663.
Mary Ann Hooker, dau. of ---- and Joan, b, 31st day of 6th month, 16--.
Samuel Coale, son of William and Elizabeth, b. 9th day of 2nd month, 1676.
Hannah Coale, dau. of William, b. 20th day of 9th month, 1669.
Joan Hooker, wife of Thomas, d. 12th day of 12th month, 1675/6.
Rebecka Billingsley, dau. of Francis and Susanna, b. 23rd day of 3rd month, 1677.
Mary Ann Hooker, dau. of Joan, d. 2nd day of 7th month, 1678.
Sophia Elizabeth Richardson, dau. of William and Elizabeth, d. 2nd day of 7th month, 1678.
Cassandra Skipwith, dau. of George and Elizabeth, b. 29th day of 8th month, 1678.
Joseph Richardson, son of William and Elizabeth, b. 3rd day of 2nd month, 1678.
Johannes Hillen, son of Johannes and Joanna, b. 1st day of 11th month, 1679/80.
Artridge Giles, dau. of John and Mary, b. 4th day of 6th month, 16--.
George Skipwith, son of George, b. 7th ----.
Sopphira [Sophia] and Elizabeth Richardson, daus. of William and Elizabeth, of Anne Arundel County, b. 2nd day of 5th month, 1680, 2 or 3 hours with night. Sophia being first born.
Deborah Hillen, dau. of Johannes and Joanna, b. 26th day of 12th month, 1681/2.
Richard Talbott, son of Edward and Elizabeth, of Anne Arundel County, b. 6th day of 12th month, 1680.
Richard Talbott, son of Edward and Elizabeth, d. 26th day of 9th month, 1681.
John Hillen, of Anne Arundel County, d. 14th day of 5th month, 1682[?].
Edward Talbott, son of Edward and Elizabeth, b. 3rd day of 10th month, 1682.
Elizabeth Arnell, dau. of Richard and Martha Arnalld [sic], b. 29th day of 10th month, 1682.
Richard Arnald, d. in 3rd month, 1683.

QUAKER RECORDS OF SOUTHERN MARYLAND

William Coale, son of William and Elizabeth, relict of George Skipwith, b. 17th day of 2nd month, 1686.
Samuel Chew, son of Samuel and Ann, b. 28th day of 3rd month, 1683.
Ann Chew, dau of Samuel and Ann, b. 2nd day of 5th month, 1686.
John Chew, son of Samuel and Ann, b. 8th day of 2nd month, 1687, Calvert County.
Samuel Harrison, son of Richard and Elizabeth, b. 1st day of 5th month, 1679.
Sarah Harrison, dau, of Richard and Elizabeth, b. 27th day of 12th month, 1680.
Elizabeth Harrison, dau. of Richard and Elizabeth, b. 27th day of 8th month, 1682.
Mary Harrison, dau. of Richard and Elizabeth, b. 10th day of 8th month, 1683, m. to Samuel Chew, and d. 4th day of 6th month, 1725.
Richard Harrison, son of Richard and Elizabeth, b. 3rd day of 12th month, 1686.
Elizabeth Harrison, dau. of Richard and Elizabeth, b. 4th day of 10th month, 1688, Calvert County.
Elizabeth Harrison, wife of Richard, d. 6th day of 1st month, 1693/4, said Elizabeth being delivered of a boy, 27th day of 12th month, 1693, which said boy his life was spent before born into world, which was named Josiah.
Hannah Sarson, dau. of Edward and Mary, b. 23rd day of 5th month, 16--.
Elizabeth Sarson, b. 12th day of 8th month, 1683[?], Anne Arundel County.
Nehemiah Birckhead, son of Nehemiah and Elizabeth, b. 17th day of 8th month, 1683, Anne Arundel County.
Margaret Birckhead, dau. of Nehemiah and Elizabeth, b. 10th day of 6th month, 1685, Anne Arundel County.
Samuel Galloway, son of Samuel and Sarah, b. 16th day of 8th month, 1682.
Hannah Galloway, dau. of Samuel and Sarah, b. ----.
Sarah Galloway, d. 2nd day of 11th month, 1685.
Richard Galloway, son of Samuel and Ann, b. 5th day of 11th month, 1689, and d. 16th day of 8th month, ----.
Peter Galloway, son of Samuel and Ann, b. in year 1691 and d. 7 weeks[?] old.
John Galloway, son of Samuel and Ann, b. 14th day of 11th[?] month, 1692, and d. at 10 months and 2 weeks old.
John Galloway, son of Samuel and Ann, b. 6th day of 12th month, 1693.
Ann Galloway, dau. of Samuel and Ann, b. 11th day of 2nd month, 1695, Anne Arundel County.
Gorg [George] Skipwith, of Anne Arundel County, d. 18th day of 10th month, 1683.
Elizabeth Skipwith, dau. of Gorg [George] and Elizabeth, d. 1st day of 10th month, 1684.
Gorg [George] Skipwith, son of Gorg [George] and Elizabeth, d. in 10th month, 1694.
William Coale, son of William and Elizabeth, d. 11th day of 7th month, 1687.

WEST RIVER MONTHLY MEETING - BIRTHS AND DEATHS

William Richardson, Sr., d. 2nd day of 9th[?] month, 1697.
William Richardson and Margaret Smith m. 15th day of 5th month, 1689.
William Richardson, son of William and Margaret, b. 1st day of 5th month, 1690, and d. 22nd day of 12th month, 1731/2.
Elizabeth Richardson, son of William and Margaret, b. 31st day of 5th month, 1692 [1693?].
Samuel Richardson, son of William and Margaret, b. 14th day of 3rd month, 1694, and d. 16th day of 8th month, 1697.
Sophia Richardson, dau. of William and Margaret, b. 7th day of 3rd month, 1696.
Sarah Richardson, dau. of William and Margaret, b. 26th day of 9th[?] month, 1698.
Joseph Richardson, son of William and Margaret, b. 31st day of 11th month, 1701/2.
Elizabeth Richardson Sr., d. 1st day of 11th month, 1703/4.
Samuel Richardson, son of William and Margaret, b. 13th day of 7th month, 1703.
Daniell Richardson, son of William and Margaret, b. 25th day of 10th month, 1705, and d. 9th day of 8th month, 1756.
Richard Richardson, son of William and Margaret, b. in 12th month, 17--.
Nathan Richardson, son of William and Margaret, b. in 4th month, 17--, Anne Arundel County.
Thomas Richardson, son of William and Margaret, b. 20th day of 9th month, 1715.
Samuel Richardson, son of William and Margaret, b. 24th day of 2nd[?] month, 1722.
John Richardson, first son of Daniell and Elizabeth, b. 3rd day of 7th month, and d. about 4 months later.
Leurania Richardson, dau. of Daniell and Elizabeth, b. 22nd day of 11th month, 1693.
Daniell Richardson, son of Daniell and Elizabeth, b. 3rd day of 6th month, 1695/6.
John Richardson, son of Daniell and Elizabeth, b. 12th day of 1st month, 1697/8, and d. 21st day of 2nd month, 1702 [1722?].
Samuel Thomas and Mary Hutchins m. 15th day of 3rd month, 1688, Anne Arundel County.
Sarah Thomas, dau. of Samuel and Mary, b. last day of 1st month, 1689.
Samuel Thomas, 1st son of Samuel and Mary, b. 1st day of 12th month, 1690.
Samuel Thomas, 2nd son of Samuel and Mary, b. 11th day of 1st month, 1693, Anne Arundel County.
Philip Thomas, son of Samuel and Mary, b. 1st day of 1st month, 1694.
John Thomas, son of Samuel and Mary, b. 15th day of 2nd month, 1697.
Elizabeth Thomas, dau. of Samuel and Mary, b. 28th day of 10th month, 1698.
Mary Thomas, dau. of Samuel and Mary, b. 6th day of 9th month, 1700.
Samuel Thomas, 3rd son of Samuel and Mary, b. 12th day of 9th month, 1702, and d. 3rd day of 2nd month, 1708.

Above Sarah, after living with her husband Joseph Richardson between 19 and 20 years, d. 29th day of 11th month, 1724.
Joseph Richardson, husband to above Sarah, d. 18th day of 6th month, 1748, in 71st year.
Samuel Robinson, son of Daniell and Sarah, b. 14th day of 10th month, 1704.
Elizabeth Robinson, dau. of Daniell and Sarah, b. 28th day of 10th month, 1705.
Sarah Robinson, dau. of Daniell and Sarah, b. 27th day of 7th month, 1708.
Mary Waters, dau. of John and Elizabeth, b. 18th day of 9th month, 168[?].
Elizabeth Waters, dau. of John and Elizabeth, b. 21st day of 8th month, 1689, and d. 3rd day of 3rd month, 1699.
Margaret Waters, dau. of John and Elizabeth, b. 24th day of 12th month, 1692.
John Waters [Watters], son of John and Elizabeth, b. 10th day of 5th month, 1696.
William Waters [Watters], son of John and Elizabeth, b. 14th day of 5th month, 1699.
Joseph Watters, son of John and Elizabeth, b. 8th day of 10th month, 17--, and d. in 12th month, 1764.
Mary Webster, d. 9th day of 6th month, 1769.
Children of Gerrard and Margaret Hopkins: Elizabeth Hopkins, b. 16th day of 1st month, 1703/4; Joseph Hopkins, b. 2nd day of 9th month, 1706; Gerrard Hopkins, b. 7th day of 1st month, 1709; Phillip Hopkins, b. 9th day of 1st month, 1711; Samuel Hopkins, b. 16th day of 11th month, 1713; Richard Hopkins, d. 15th day of 10th month, 1715; William Hopkins, b. 8th day of 6th month, 1718; John Hopkins, b. 30th day of 8th month, 1720.
Elizabeth Hill, d. 27th day of 2nd month, 1772, age 69[?].
Gerrard Hopkins, son of Gerrard and Margaret, d. 3rd day of 7th month, 1777, age 68.
Cassander Talbott, dau. of John and Mary, b. 2nd day of 2nd month, 1708.
Elizabeth Laurence, dau. of Benjamin and Rachel, b. 8th day of 10th month, 1702.
Benjamin Laurence, son of Benjamin and Rachel, b. 27th day of 11th month, 1704.
Sophia Laurence, dau. of Benjamin and Rachel, b. 2nd day of 4th month, 1707.
John Laurence, son of Benjamin and Rachel, b. 11th day of 9th month, 1709.
Levin Laurence, son of Benjamin and Rachel, b. 6th day of 1st month, 1711 [1721?].
Margarett Laurence, dau. of Benjamin and Rachel, b. 17th day of 11th month, 1716 [1726?].
Children of William and Elizabeth Coale: Elizabeth Coale, b. 3rd day of 10th month, 1692; Mary Coale, b. 24th day of 10th month, 1694; William Coale, b. 11th day of 2nd month, 1697; Hannah Coale, b. 14th day of 5th month, 1699; Samuel Coale, b. 4th day of 6th month, 1701; Priscilla Coale, b. 5th day of 8th month, 1703;

WEST RIVER MONTHLY MEETING - BIRTHS AND DEATHS

Thomas Coale, b. 28th day of 1st month, 1705; Sarah Coale, b. 25th day of 12th month, 1706/7; Ann Coale, b. 10th day of 6th month, 1709.
Sarah Miles, dau. of Thomas and Ruth, b. 11th day of 11th month, 1705.
Thomas Miles, son of Thomas and Ruth, b. 5th day of 11th month, 1707.
Elizabeth Miles, dau. of Thomas and Ruth, b. 3rd day of 7th month, 1710.
Ruth Miles, mother of above children, d. 15th day of 1st month, 1714.
Jonathan Hanson, son of Jonathan and Kezia, b. 10th day of 9th month, 1710.
Margaret Hanson, dau. of Jonathan and Mary, b. 3rd day of 4th month, 1719, and d. in 6th month, 1721.
Mary Hanson, dau. of Jonathan and Mary, b. 19th day of 12th month, 1720.
Mordaca Hanson, son of Jonathan and Mary, b. 10th day of 4th month, 1723.
Samuel Richardson, son of Joseph and Sarah, b. 6th day of 5th month, 1706.
Joseph Richardson, 2nd son of Joseph and Sarah, b. 19th day of 7th month, 1708.
Mary Richardson, dau. of Joseph and Sarah, b. 13th day of 7th month, 1710.
William Richardson, 3rd son of Joseph and Sarah, b. 26th day of 10th month, 1712.
Phillip Richardson, 4th son of Joseph and Sarah, b. 29th day of 1st month, 1715.
Elizabeth Richardson, 2nd dau. of Joseph and Sarah, b. 18th day of 1st month, 1716/7.
Sarah Richardson, 3rd dau. of Joseph and Sarah, b. 3rd day of 3rd month, 1719.
John Richardson, son of Joseph and Sarah, b. 19th day of 1st month, 1720/1.
Richard Richardson, son of Joseph and Sarah, b. 5th day of 3rd month, 1723, and d. at his brothers Thomas Coale at Bush River on 22nd day of 7th month, 1736, and bur. at plantation of John Crockett, late of Bush River, Baltimore County.
Priscilla Hill, dau. of Henry and Mary, b. 9th day of 3rd month, 1718.
Mary Coale, wife of Thomas Coale, and dau. of Joseph and Sarah Richardson, d. 18th day of 12th month, 1741/2, and bur. at plantation of John Crockett, late of Bush River in Baltimore County.
Joseph Birckhead, son of Nehemiah and Margaret, b. 25th day of 11th month, 1714.
Margaret Birckhead, dau. of Nehemiah and Margaret, b. 12th day of 1st month, 1715.
Nehemiah Birckhead, father of above children, d. 11th day of 1st month, 1719.
Joseph Birckhead, d. 4th day of 11th month [January], 1739/40, aged 25 years, about 3:30 p.m.
Aaron Hawkings, son of Thomas and Elizabeth, b. 11th day of 1st month, 1706.
Joseph Hawkings, son of Thomas and Elizabeth, b. 19th day of 4th month, 1708.
Ruth Hawkings, dau. of Thomas and Elizabeth, b. 7th day of 11th month, 1713/4.
Deborah Moore, dau. of Mordecai and Deborah, b. 2nd day of 4th month, 1705, at South River in Maryland.

QUAKER RECORDS OF SOUTHERN MARYLAND

Hannah Moore, dau. of Mordecai and Deborah, b. 18th day of 8th month, 1706, d. 26th day, and was bur. 27th day by her brother and sister, Mordecai and Elizabeth, at West River burying place in Maryland.
Mary Moore, dau. of Mordecai and Deborah, b. 29th day of 6th month, 17--, at house of our dear brother and sister Hill at Philadelphia.
Heather [Hesther?] Moore, dau. of Mordecai and Deborah, b. 30th day of 6th month, 1710, at South River.
Elizabeth Moore, dau. of Mordecai and Deborah, b. 11th day of 8th month, 1712, at South River, and was bur. 1st day of 10th month, 1718, at West River.
Rachel Moore, dau. of Mordecai and Deborah, b. 4th day of 8th month, 1714.
Samuel Galloway, son of Richard and Hannah, d. at London in 2nd month of 1702, and was bur. there in Friends Burying Ground in Bunhill [Bunfield?].
Ann Galloway, widow of above Samuel, d. 20th day of 1st month, 1722/3.
Richard Galloway, son of above Samuel, d. last day of 12th month, 1730/1.
Thomas Sprigg m. Elizabeth Galloway, dau. of Richard and Sophia Galloway, 14th day of 12th month, 1737.
Thomas Sprigg, d. 29th day of December, 1780, aged about 67 years last November and was bur. in his garding [garden].
Elizabeth Galloway, dau. of Richard and Sophia, b. 16th day of 11th month, 1721.
Richard Sprigg, son of Thomas and Elizabeth, b. 16th day of 12th month, 1739.
Sophia Sprigg, dau. of Richard and Margaret, b. 21st day of 4th month, 1766.
Rebeckah Sprigg, dau. of Richard and Margaret, b. 6th day of 10th month, 1767.
Elizabeth Sprigg, dau. of Richard and Margaret, b. 25th day of 8th month, 1770.
Margaret Sprigg, dau. of Richard and Margaret, b. April 15, 1772, and d. about 3 months after.
Henrietta Sarah Sprigg, dau. of Richard and Margaret, b. July 2, 1775.
Margaret Sprigg, dau. of Richard and Margaret, b. 14th day of 2nd month, 1779.
Richard Galloway, Sr., b. 28th day of 11th month, 1663, and d. 27th[?] day of 8th month, 1736, and was bur. in grave yard at West River Meeting.
William Richardson, Sr., son of William and Elizabeth, b. 26th day of 6th month, 1668, d. 13th day of 5th month, 1744, and was bur. at West River Meeting Grave Yard on 15th day of 5th month, 1744.
Thomas Richardson, son of William and Margaret, d. 14th day of 4th month, 1745, at his house on eastern shore in Kent County, and was bur. ----.
Samuel Richardson, son of Richard and Margaret, b. 6th day of 2nd month, 1732.
Sophia Richardson, dau. of Richard and Margaret, b. 9th day of 4th month, 1735.
William Richardson, son of Nathan and Elizabeth, b. 27th[?] day of 9th month, 1736.
Joseph Cowman, son of Joseph and Sarah, b. 8th day of 8th month, 1732.
Ann Cowman, dau. of Joseph and Sarah, b. 1st day of 8th month, 1733.

WEST RIVER MONTHLY MEETING - BIRTHS AND DEATHS

Mary Cowman, dau. of Joseph and Sarah, b. 24th day of 12th month, 1735.
John Cowman, son of Joseph and Sarah, b. 24th day of 4th month, 1737.
Gerrard Hopkins, son of Philip and Elizabeth, b. 5th day of 4th month, 1737.
Richard Hopkins, 2nd son of Philip and Elizabeth, b. 7th day of 11th month, 1738/9.
Elizabeth Hopkins, dau. of Philip and Elizabeth, b. 23rd day of 11th month, 1740/1.
Philip Hopkins, 3rd son of Philip and Elizabeth, b. 25th day of 10th month, 1742/3.
William Richardson, son of Nathan and Elizabeth, b. 7th day of 9th month, 1735.
Elizabeth Richardson, dau. of Nathan and Elizabeth, b. 26th day of 10th month, 1740.
Nathan Richardson, son of Nathan and Elizabeth, b. 26th day of 6th month, 1744.
Elizabeth Richardson, wife of Nathan, d. 10th day of 5th month, 1746, and was bur. at Bush River at burial place of her father, John Crockett.
Children of Philip and Ann Thomas: Samuel Thomas, b. June 12, 1725, around 8 p.m.; Philip Thomas, b. July 3, 1727, around 5:30 a.m.; Mary Thomas, b. January 1, 1731; Elizabeth Thomas, b. March 8, 1732/3; Richard Thomas, b. July 17, 1736; John Thomas, b. August 26, 1743, around 6 a.m.
John Thomas above m. Sarah Murray, August 23, 1777, and their dau. Ann Thomas was b. July 6, 1778.
Philip Thomas, son of John and Sarah, b. July 29, 1782.
Samuel Hopkins, son of Philip and Elizabeth, b. 16th day of 5th month, 1745, around 7 a.m.
Nehemiah Birckhead, son of John and Christian, b. 29th day of 10th month, 1746.
Margaret Moore, 1st child of Mordecai and Elizabeth, b. at her father's house, near London Town in Maryland, 14th day of 11th month, 1740.
Mary Moore, 2nd child of Mordecai and Elizabeth, b. 13th day of 9th month, 1743, near London Town.
Richard Moore, 3rd child of Mordecai and Elizabeth, b. 2nd day of 8th month, 1745, near London Town.
Samuel Preston Moore, 4th child of Mordecai and Elizabeth, b. 10th day of 7th month, 1747, near London Town.
Daniell Richardson, son of Nathan and Hannah, b. 1st day of 12th month, 1749/50.
Margaret Thomas, wife of John, d. 16th day of 3rd month, 1806.
Elizabeth Brooke, wife of Basil, d. 17th day of 8th month, 1794, around 11 a.m.
Basil Brooke, d. 22nd day of 8th month, 1794, a few minutes after sunset.
Ann Galloway, dau. of Joseph and Ann, b. 5th day of 7th month, 1750.
Philip Thomas, son of Philip, Jr. and Ann, b. 27th day of 11th month, 1756.
Ann Thomas, dau. of Philip, Jr. and Ann, b. 21st day of 6th month, 1758, and d. 4th day of 7th month, 1760.
Margaret Hopkins, dau. of Gerrard and Mary, b. last day of January, 1731.
Gerrard Hopkins, b. 25th day of 6th month, 1732.

QUAKER RECORDS OF SOUTHERN MARYLAND

Mary Hopkins, dau. of Gerrard and Mary, b. 11th day of 9th month, 1734.
Sarah Hopkins, b. 20th day of 7th month, 1737.
Richard Hopkins, 2nd son of Gerrard and Mary, b. 7th day of 12th month, 1739, and died soon after.
Elizabeth Hopkins, b. 3rd day of 9th month, 1741.
Rachel Hopkins, b. 30th day of 10th month, 1742.
Joseph Hopkins, b. 11th day of 11th month, 1744.
Richard Hopkins, b. 20th day of 1st month, 1747.
Hannah Hopkins, b. 29th day of 6th month, 1749.
Elisha Hopkins, b. 15th day of 10th month, 1752.
Ezekiel Hopkins, son of Johns and Mary, b. 11th day of 3rd month, 1747.
Johns Hopkins, son of Johns and Mary, b. 8th day of 5th month, 1751.
Samuel Hopkins, son of Johns and Elizabeth, b. 3rd day of 2nd month, 1759.
Philip Hopkins, son of Johns and Elizabeth, b. 24th day of 9th month, 1760.
"The other of Johns Hopkins children on other side of book" [sic].
Elizabeth Richardson, dau. of Richard and Elizabeth, b. 14th day of 9th month, 1756.
Richard Richardson, son of Richard and Elizabeth, b. 8th day of 1st month, 1758, and d. 17th day of 1st month, 1775.
Mary Richardson, dau. of Richard and Elizabeth, b. 20th day of 4th month, 1760.
Ann Thomas Richardson, dau. of Richard and Elizabeth, b. 5th day of 2nd month, 1763.
John Thomas Richardson, son of Richard and Elizabeth, b. 20th[?] day of 5th month, 1765.
William Richardson, son of Richard and Elizabeth, b. 14th day of August, 1767.
Joseph Richardson, son of Richard and Elizabeth, b. ----.
Rebekah Richardson, dau. of Richard and Elizabeth, b. ----.
Joseph Richardson, son of William and Anne, b. 24th day of 9th month, 1744.
Ann Richardson, dau. of William and Anne, b. 29th day of 7th month, 1747.
Richard Hopkins, son of Johns and Elizabeth, b. 2nd day of March, 1762.
Mary Hopkins, dau. of Johns and Elizabeth, b. 7th day of 1st month [January], 1764.
Margaret Hopkins, dau. of Johns and Elizabeth, b. 20th day of 2nd month, 1766.
Richard Cowman, son of Joseph and Elizabeth, b. 17th day of 1st month, 1755.
Joseph Cowman, 2nd son of Joseph and Elizabeth, b. 13th day of 4th month, 1757.
Elizabeth Cowman, dau. of Joseph and Elizabeth, b. 1st day of 7th month, 1759.
Samuel Cowman, b. 26th day of 7th month [July], 1762.
John Cowman, b. 30th day of 3rd month [March], 1765.
Sarah Cowman, dau. of Joseph and Elizabeth, b. 16th day of 11th month, 1769.
Gerrard Hopkins, son of Johns and Elizabeth, b. 24th day of 10th month, 1769.

WEST RIVER MONTHLY MEETING - BIRTHS AND DEATHS

Elizabeth Hopkins, dau. of Johns and Elizabeth, b. ٤---.
Evan Hopkins, son of Johns and Elizabeth, b. 30th day of November, 1772.
Ann Hopkins, dau. of Johns and Elizabeth, b. 26th day of February 1775.
Rachel Hopkins, dau. of Johns and Elizabeth, b. 7th day of September, 1777.
Sarah Hill, Sr., d. in February, 1755, in 83rd year of her age.
Margaret Richardson, d. in February, 1756, in 84th year of her age.
Sarah Hill, wife of Joseph, d. 11th day of January, 1761.
Daniel Richardson, d. in August, 1756.
Margaret Richardson, wife of Richard, d. 1760.
Richard Richardson, d. 25th day of 2nd month, 1761.
Joseph Hill, d. 25th day of 10th month, 1761, at age 56.
Sophia Galloway, d. 27th [29th?] of 1st month[?], 1781, in her 85th year.
Ephraim Gover, son of Robert and Sarah, b. 5th day of 11th month, 1744.
Sarah Gover, dau. of Robert and Sarah, b. 28th day of 1st month, 1745.
Mary Gover, dau. of Robert and Sarah, b. 25th day of 6th month, 1746.
Rachel Gover, dau. of Robert and Sarah, b. 14th day of 3rd month, 1747.
Ephraim Gover, son of Robert and Sarah, b. 10th day of 10th month, 1748.
Hannah Gover, dau. of Robert and Sarah, b. 5th day of 8th month, 1750.
William Gover, son of Robert and Sarah, b. 18th day of 2nd month, 1752.
Robert Gover, son of Robert and Sarah, b. 17th day of 10th month, 1753.
Jean Gover, dau. of Robert and Sarah, b. 3rd day of 3rd month, 1755.
Margarett Gover, dau. of Robert and Sarah, b. 23rd day of 3rd month, 1757.
Elizabeth Gover, dau. of Robert and Sarah, b. 22nd day of 9th month, 1759.
Joseph Cowman, son of John and Sarah, b. 9th day of 8th month, 1758.
Mary Cowman, dau. of John and Sarah, b. 18th day of 4th month, 1760.
Garrard Cowman, son of John and Sarah, b. 6th day of 5th month, 1762.
John Cowman, son of John and Sarah, b. 10th day of 4th mnonth, 1764.
Sarah Cowman, dau. of John and Sarah, b. 9th day of 2nd month, 1764.
Margaret Cowman, dau. of John and Sarah, b. 22nd day of 5th month, 1769.
Ann Cowman, dau. of John and Sarah, b. 24th day of 7th month, 1771.
Elizabeth Cowman, dau. of John and Sarah, b. 12th day of 3rd month, 1774.
Richard Cowman, son of John and Sarah, b. 13th day of 9th month, 1777.
Joseph Hill, Jr., 1st child of Henry and Mary, b. at West River in month of May, 1750.
Henrietta Hill, dau. of Henry and Mary, b. same place, 24th day of 12th month, 1751.
Philip Thomas, son of Samuel and Mary, d. 23rd day of 11th month, 1762, aged 68[?] years.
Ann Thomas, widow of above Philip, d. 22nd day of 5th month, 1771, in her 71st year.

Margaret Harris, wife of William and mother of this family, d. 23rd day of -- month, 1766, and was bur. in Friends burying place near Clifts the 7th day of same month, in 56th year of her age.
William Harris, son of Samuel and Rachel, b. 26th day of -- month, 1772.
Samuel Harris, son of Samuel and Rachel, b. 17th day of 9th month, 1774.
Children of Samuel and Sarah Plummer: Ruth Plummer, b. 10th day of 3rd month, 1725; Thomas Plummer, b. 8th day of 7th month, 1726; Joseph Plummer, b. 3rd day of 5th month, 1728; Samuel Plummer, b. 30th day of 8th month, 1730; Casander Plummer, b. 3rd day of 7th month, 1731/2 [sic]; Sarah Plummer, b. 30th day of 6th month, 1734; Abraham Plummer, b. 16th day of 5th month, 1736; Rachel Plummer, b. 16th day of 12th month, 1738; Ursula Plummer, b. 16th day of 1st month, 1742; Elizabeth Plummer, b. 29th day of 3rd month, 1744; Anna Plummer, b. 26th day of 8th month, 1747; Susannah Plummer, b. 16th day of 10th month, 1751.
John Hutchinson Garretson, son of Cornelius and Priscilla, b. 20th day of 5th month [May], 1764.
Thomas Garretson, son of Cornelius and Priscilla, b. 8th day of 9th month, 1765.
James Brooke, son of Basil and Elizabeth, b. 5th day of 5th month [May], 1766.
Ann Robertson, dau. of William and Elizabeth, b. 6th day of 1st month, 1772.
Samuel Robertson, son of William and Elizabeth, b. 9th day of 5th month, 1774.
William Richardson, son of Joseph and Rebecca, b. 30th day of 12th month, 1722.
Richard Richardson, son of Joseph and Rebecca, b. 24th day of 7th month, 1725.
Mary Richardson, dau. of Joseph and Rebecca, b. March 5, 1727.
Joshua Hopkins, son of Johns and Catty, of Philadelphia, b. 27th day of 12th month, 1779, about 6 o'clock in the morning.
Joseph Hopkins, son of Johns and Catty, b. 16th day of 8th month, 1782, around 1 a.m.
Ann Thomas Chew, dau. of Samuel and Mary, d. 22nd day of 5th month [May], 1777, and was bur. at West River grave yard.
Isaac Howell Hopkins, son of Elisha and Hannah, b. 31st day of 3rd month, 1781.
Deborah Hopkins, dau. of Elisha and Hannah, b. 8th day of 7th month, 1782.
Samuel Hance, son of Benjamin and Sarah, b. 12th day of 3rd month, 1781.
Thomas Cleverly Hance, son of Benjamin and Sarah, b. 27th day of 9th month, 1782.
Ann Hance, dau. of Benjamin and Sarah, b. 7th day of 6th month, 1784.
Children of Gideon and Elizabeth Dare: Sarah Dare, b. 9th day of 2nd month, 1776; Priscilla Dare, b. 17th day of 9th month, 1777; Thomas Cleaverly Dare, b. 28th day of 10th month, 1779; Henry Dare, b. 18th day of 10th month, 1781; Elizabeth Dare, b. 6th day of 9th month, 1783; Gideon Dare, b. 8th day of 3rd month, 1786; William Dare, b. 18th day of 12th month, 1787.
Children of John and Johannah Plummer: Jerom Plummer, b. 3rd day of 1st month, 1774; Gerrard Plummer, b. 7th day of 9th month, 1775; Mary Plummer, b. 13th day

WEST RIVER MONTHLY MEETING - BIRTHS AND DEATHS

of 3rd month, 1777; Ann Thomas Plummer, b. 12th day of 1st month, 1779; John Plummer, b. 20th day of 4th month, 1781; Joseph Plummer, b. 4th day of 10th month, 1783.

Children of Richard Thomas, Jr. and Deborah Elizabeth: Thomas Thomas, b. 1st day of 8th month, 1784; Frederick Augustus Thomas, b. 27th day of 9th month, 1788; Mary Thomas, b. 18th day of 10th month, 1791; Sarah Thomas, b. 26th day of 4th month, 1794.

Children of Bernard and Sarah Gilpin: Sarah Gilpin, b. 30th day of 5th month, 1794; Elizabeth Gilpin, b. 21st day of 11th month, 1795; Ann Robinson Gilpin, b. 1st day of 7th month, 1797; Thomas Gilpin, b. 10th day of 2nd month, 1799; Samuel Gilpin, b. 28th day of 3rd month, 1801; Hannah Gilpin, b. 20th day of 5th month, 1803; Lydia Gilpin, b, 16th day of 4th month, 1805.

Isaac Howell Hopkins, son of Joseph and Elizabeth, b. 19th day of 12th month, 1770.

Patience Hopkins, dau. of Joseph and Elizabeth, b. 5th day of 11th month, 1771.

Gerrard Hopkins, son of Joseph and Elizabeth, b. 22nd day of 1st month, 1775.

Hannee and Mary Hopkins, twin daus. of Joseph and Elizabeth, b. 12th day of 4th month, 1777.

Joseph and Elizabeth Hopkins, twins of Joseph and Elizabeth, b. 10th day of 3rd month, 1781.

Margaret Hopkins, dau. of Joseph and Elizabeth, b. 2nd day of 3rd month, 1779.

Isaac Gray Hopkins, son of Joseph and Elizabeth, b. 16th day of 6th month, 1783.

Priscilla Hopkins, dau. of Joseph and Elizabeth, b. 24th day of 10th month, 1785.

Mary Hopkins, dau. of Joseph and Elizabeth, b. 9th day of 4th month, 1788.

Samuel Hopkins, son of Joseph and Elizabeth, b. 9th day of 4th month, 1790.

Sarah Hopkins, dau. of Joseph and Elizabeth, b. 3rd day of 8th month, 1792.

Elizabeth Snowden, dau. of Philip and Patience, b. 8th day of 10th month, 1792.

Samuel Snowden, son of Philip and Patience, b. 13th day of 1st month, 1794.

Children of Thomas and Ann Norris: Mary Ann Norris, b. 4th day of 10th month, 1793; Robert Norris, b. 30th day of 4th month, 1795; John Norris, b. 14th day of 10th month, 1796; Sarah Norris, b. 31st day of 1st month, 1799; Elizabeth Norris, b. 13th day of 2nd month, 1802.

Samuel Elliott and Mary Richardson, dau. of Richard and Elizabeth, m. November 12, 1780, at West River.

John Elliott, son of Samuel and Mary, b. November 2, 1781.

Elizabeth Richardson, d. 27th day of 5th month, 1782.

Joseph Richardson, son of William and Margaret, d. 4th day of 11th month, 1782, age 81 years, at 1:20 a.m., and was interred by his daughter in Johns Hopkins burying ground at South River.

Elizabeth Richardson, dau. of Richard and Elizabeth, b. 14th day of 9th month, 1756, and d. 20th day of 3rd month, 1762.

QUAKER RECORDS OF SOUTHERN MARYLAND

Richard Richardson, son of Richard and Elizabeth, b. 8th day of 1st month, 1758, and d. January 17, 1775, around 3 p.m., in his 16th year.
Mary Richardson, dau. of Richard and Elizabeth, b. 20th day of 4th month, 1760.
Ann Thomas Richardson, dau. of Richard and Elizabeth, b. 5th day of 2nd month, 1763.
John Thomas Richardson, b. 14th day of 5th month, 1765.
William Richardson, b. 14th day of 8th month, 1767.
Joseph Richardson, b. 17th day of 7th month, 1770.
Rebekah Richardson, b. 26th day of 8th month, 1772.
Deborah Snowden Richardson, b. 11th day of 8th month, 1775.
"This ends manuscript of West River Meeting begun in Volume 14, Number 2" [sic].
ADDITIONAL BIRTHS:
Damaris Hooker, dau. of Thomas and Joan, b. 29th day of 11th month, 1667.
William Coale, son of William and Hannah, b. 20th day of 8th month, 1667.
Elizabeth Giles, dau. of John and Mary, of Ann---, b. 7th day of -- month, 1668.
Nathaniel Giles, son of John and Mary, b. 10th day of 1st month, 1677.
John Giles, Jr., son of John and Mary, b. 7th day of 11th month called January, 1670.
Jacob Gilles [Giles?], son of John and Mary, b. 11th day of 4th month [June], 1673.
William Richardson, Jr., son of William and Elizabeth, of Anne Arundel County, b. 26th day of 6th month [August], 1668.
Daniel Richardson, son of William and Elizabeth, b. 3rd day of 1st month [March], 1670.
Benjamin Hooker, son of Thomas and Joan, b. 15th day of 11th month, 1670.
Joseph Richardson, son of William and Elizabeth, b. 13th day of 3rd month, 1671.
Elizabeth Skipwith, dau. of George and Elizabeth, b. 18th day of 9th month [November], 1670.
Elizabeth Coale, dau. of William and Elizabeth, b. 30th day of 6th month [August], 1671.
Phillip Coale, son of William and Elizabeth, b. 6th day of 7th month [September], 1673.
Sophia Elizabeth Richardson, dau. of William and Elizabeth, b. 4th day of 5th month [July], 1675.
Mary Ann Hooker, dau. of Joan Hooker, b. 31st day of 6th month, ----.

QUAKER MARRIAGES OF SOUTHERN MARYLAND

MARRIAGES, 1682-1800

Nehemiah Birkhead, m. **Elizabeth Sloper**, ---- 1682. Witnesses: Abraham Birkhead, Ann Birkhead, Abraham Birkhead, Jr., Richard Pernall, Bartholemy Watts, Richard Hall, John Wilson, Robard ----, Richard Harrison, Samuell Chew, Francis Holland, Jr., Job Evans, Elizabeth Hall, Richard Beckworth, Joseph Chew, William Dorrumple, Moses Wilson, William B----, Robart Arme [?], Ann Chew, Jr., Ann Chew, Sr., Elizabeth Hall, Sarah Beckworth, Elizabeth Harrison, Levey Hall, Elizabeth B----.

Joseph Chew, of Calvert County, m. 17th day of 9th month, 1685, to **Mary Smith**, of said county, of the meeting at the house of Richard Johns, Calvert County, married at the house of Ann Chew in Herring Creek, Anne Arundel County. Witnesses: Ann Chew, Alse Smith, Thomas Smith, William Chew, Joseph Smith, Benjamin Chew, Elizabeth Harrison, Margret Gill, Francis Hollond, Sarah Hollond, Margret Smith, Sarah Smith, Ann Chew, Jr., Margret Hollond, Caleb Chew, John Chew, Richard Harrison, Thomas Evernden, William Richardson, Edward Talbott, Thomas ----, John Willson, John Hurle, Samuell Galloway, Mordicai More, John Talbott, William Cole, Humphry Cole, William Cole, Jr., William Richardson, Jr., Phillip Cole, John Wilson, Moses Wilson, Elizabeth Cole, Elizabeth Hollond, Ann Birkhead, Mary Birkhead, Hannah Wilson, Rachel Hall, Elizabeth Cole, Jr., Faith Gong [Yong?].

Richard Galloway, m. 10th day of 10th month called December, 1686, to **Elizabeth Lawrence**, widow, Anne Arundel County, at William Richardson's house near West River. Witnesses: Samuel Galloway, Sr., William Cole, Jr., Edward Talbott, Phillip Cole, Samuel Coale, Richard Harrison, William Richardson, Sr., William Richardson, Jr., M. Moone, Joseph Chew, William Edmonson, Thomas Hooker, Umphrey ---- [Hooker?], John Belt, John Flud [?], Joseph Richardson, Solloman Sparrow, Joseph Willumes [?], Elizabeth Lawrence, Elizabeth Talbot, Elizabeth Coal, Elizabeth Carter, Elizabeth Belt, Elizabeth Richardson, Sarah Thomas, Elizabeth Lockwood, Sarah Hooker, Millesson Batty, Mary Nighton, Elizabeth Knighton, Mary Giles, Janes Hollon, Elizabeth Vreily [?].

Richard Tayller, of Anne Arundel County, m. 7th day of 6th month commonly called August, 1687, to **Ann Trasey**, of Anne Arundel County, at William Richardson's at West River. Witnesses: William Richardson, Sr., Ed. Talbott, Samuell Thomas, John Belt, Mahlon Radriffe [?], Daniell Richardson, Edward Selby, Jr., Samuell Galloway, John Larking, John Giles, John Talbott, William Coale, Jr., William Richardson, Jr., Philip Coale, Joseph Richardson, Walter Smith, Elizabeth Tailler, Charity Tydings, Elizabeth Richardson, Millessent Battee, Sarah Thomas, Sarah Moors, Sophia Richardson, Samuell Coale.

Samuell Thomas, of Anne Arundel County, m. 15th day of 3rd month commonly called May, 1688, to **Mary Hutchins**, of Calvert County, at the home of Samuell Thomas, of Anne Arundel County. Witnesses: Francis Hutchins, Margaret Evans,

QUAKER RECORDS OF SOUTHERN MARYLAND

Job Evans, Margarett Tench, Grace Scrivener, Elizabeth Coale, Sarah Hooker, Elizabeth Smith, Thomas Smith, Philip Cole, Samuell Coale, Samuel Lane, Benjamin Scrivener, William Coale, Jr., William Richardson, Elizabeth Richardson, Richard Galloway, Elizabeth Galloway, William Richardson, Jr., Joseph Heathcote, Mary Knighton, Elizabeth Battee, Joseph Richardson, Joseph Hanslap, Solomon Sparrow, Sophia Richardson, Francis Hanslap.

Richard Letton, of Anne Arundel County, m. April 18, 1689, to **Honor Durdin,** of Anne Arundel County, widow, at Ann Lambot's, widow, at South River. Witnesses: John Belt, William Richardson, Solloman Sparrow, Richard Galloway, Thomas Witchell, John Durden, Mathers Hodges [?], Elizabeth Whely [Phelys?], John Gray, Robert Ward, John Moale, Robart Sample, Joseph Willames, William Barross [?], John Camton[?], John Fairbrother, Gabrill Parrot, Jr., Joseph Burton, Charles Loyd, Elizabeth Richardson, Elizabeth Bolden, Ann Lambart, Honour Maryarty, Margret Maryarte, Jane Fairbrother.

William Cole, Jr., planter, of Anne Arundel County, m. 30th day of 5th month commonly called July, 1689, to **Elizabeth Sparrow,** of the Clifts in Calvert County, at Richard Johns' house at the Clifts. Witnesses: Richard Johns, Solomon Sparrow, William Coale, Richard Galloway, Edward Talbott, William Richardson, Phil. Coale, Thomas Sparrow, Abra. Johns, Samuell Coale, Samuell Constable, George Royston, John Austin, Francis Bilingsly, Robert Johnson, Robert Harper, Christr. Harris, John Pardo, Richard Giles, John Talbott, Fras. Hutchins, Margt. Hutchins, Elizabeth Hutchins, William Holyday, William Chew, Hanah Everest, John Cutting [Catling?], Thomas Everest, William Edmondson, Mary Webb, Margt. Kidd, Elizabeth Mears, Hesther Pardo, Thomas S----, Elizabeth Johns, Elizabeth Coale.

William Richardson, Jr., of Anne Arundel County, m. 16th day of 5th month commonly called February, 1689, to **Margaret Smith,** of Calvert County, at the house of her mother Alece Smith. Witnesses: Alse Smith, Thomas Smith, Nathan Smith, Sarah Smith, Richard Harrison, Joseph Chew, John Talbott, Daniell Richardson, Joseph Richardson, Elizabeth Smith, Elizabeth Benson, Samuell Harrison, Sarah Harrison, Elizabeth Talbott, William Coale, William Coale, Jr., Job Evans, Philip Coale, Ann Birckhead, Richard Galloway, Elizabeth Skipwith, Ann Chew, Solomon Sparrow, Elizabeth Sparrow. Sarah Moores, Mary Sarson, Elizabeth Smith, Thomas Evernden, Margreat Evans, Frances Billingsly, Humphrey Hodges, George Rosyton, Richard Johns, George Cole.

Thomas Witchell, of Anne Arundel County, m. 10th day of 3rd month commonly called November, 1690, to **Mary Serson,** widow, of Anne Arundel County. Witnesses: William Richardson, Samuell Thompson, Humphrey Hodges, Soloman Sparrow, John Eliey, Fardinando Battee, Samuell Galloway, Sr., Thomas Lincecom, Richard Latten, Robert Woard, Nor. Witchell, Jean Witchell, Elizabeth Taler, Jane Lincecom, Mary Tomass, Ann Galloway, Ann Eliey, Ivanna [?] Word, Ann Burges, Honer Lettle.

QUAKER MARRIAGES OF SOUTHERN MARYLAND

Solomon Sparrow, of Anne Arundel County, son of Thomas, deceased, and Elizabeth, m. 12th day of 6th month commonly called August, 1690, to **Sarah Smith**, dau. of Thomas, deceased, and Alce, of Calvert County, at the house of Alice Smith, widow and mother of said Sarah Smith. Witnesses: Thomas Smith, Nathan Smith, Samuell Galloway, Thomas Brooks, Thomas Tinch, Richard Johns, Richard Harrison, Samuel Young, William Coale, Jr., William Richardson, Jr., Richard Galloway, John Woodden, Joseph Chew, Abraham Johnes, Thomas Sparrow, William Richardson, Sr., Samuel Thomas, Will Chew, Samuell Harrison, Elizabeth Taylor, Alice Smith, Margarett Richardson, Elizabeth Harrison, Elizabeth Smith, Elizabeth Johnes, Ann Galloway, Elizabeth Cole, Margarett Tench, Elizabeth Smith, Grace Scrivener, Mary Smith, Elizabeth Galloway, Elizabeth Richardson, Elizabeth Galloway, Ann Birckhead, Elizabeth Chew, Mary Thomas, Sophia Richardson, Elizabeth Woodden, Elizabeth Benson, Ann Chew, Sarah Talbott.

William Chew, son of Samuel, deceased, and Ann, m. 20th day of 10th month commonly called December, 1690, to **Sydney Wynn**, both of Anne Arundel County, Maryland, dau. of Thomas and Martha, deceased, of Pennsylvania. They were married at home of William Richardson. Witnesses: Ann Chew, Joseph Chew, P--: Chew, John Chew, Caleb Chew, S--- Burges, John Meriton [?], William Holland, William Edmondson, William Coale, William Richardson, Jr., Robert Hartland [?], M. Moore, William Richardson, Sr., Solomon Sparrow, Samuel Galloway, Richard Galloway, Nicholas Delaplaine, Samuell Thomas, Joseph Richardson, Joseph Burges, Benjamin Burges, Joseph Hanslap, Elizabeth Richardson, Elizabeth Belt, Sarah Sparrow, Margaret Richardson, Frances Hanslap, Sop: Richardson.

Charles Gosidge, of Baltimore County, son of John and Ann, of Kingdom of England, deceased, m. 15th day of 12th month commonly called February, 1690, to **Ann Hawkins**, dau. of John and Mary, of Anne Arundel County. [Note: Gosidge signed his name Gorsuch]. Witnesses: William Richardson, Sr., Mord. Moor, Samuel Galloway, Job Evans, Samuel Thomas, Thomas Witchell, William Richardson, Jr., Ralph Jackson, Joseph Heathcote, John Eliey, Joseph Richardson, Elizabeth Richardson, Elizabeth Galloway, Elizabeth Talbott, Elizabeth Taylor, Elizabeth Battee, Elizabeth Woolding, Elizabeth Lockwood, Ann Galloway, Sarah Sparrow, Margaret Richardson, Mary Gresham, Richard Welsh, Mary Welsh, Honour Maryarty, Mary Witchell, Martha Heathcote, Fardinando Battee, John Larkin, Mathew Roorer [?], Sophia Richardson, Richard Galloway, Philip Coale, Benjamin Lawrence, Richard Wigg, Solomon Sparrow, Robert Lockwood, James Murry, Daniell Richardson, John Reston.

Daniell Richardson, of Anne Arundel County, son of William and Elizabeth, m. 4th day of 12th month commonly called February, 1691, to **Elizabeth Welsh**, dau. of John, deceased, and Mary, of Anne Arundel County, at home of William Richardson, Sr. Witnesses: James Ellis, Silvester Welsh, William Richardson, Jr., Richard Purnell, John Welsh, Joseph Richardson, John Welsh, Elizabeth Richardson, Mary Purnell, Sarah Welsh, Margarett Richardson, Sophia

QUAKER RECORDS OF SOUTHERN MARYLAND

Richardson, Elizabeth Talbott, Philip Coale, Samuell Coale, Richard Harrison, Elizabeth Harrison, Elizabeth Coale, Elizabeth Lockwood, M. Moore, Solomon Sparrow, Neh. Birkhead, John Belt, Fardinando Battee, Abraham Birkhead, Samuell Thomas, Richard Snowden, Dutton Lane, Samuel Galloway, Richard Galloway, Benjamin Eastipp, Richard Coale, Jr., Ann Chew, Jr., Ann Galloway, Mary Thomas, Sarah Sparrow, Elizabeth Woodden, Elizabeth Galloway, Elizabeth Lawremce, Elizabeth Battee, Elizabeth Lockwood, Mary Snowden, Mary Giles.

Benjamin Chew, of Anne Arundel County, m. 8th day of 10th month called December, 1692, to **Elizabeth Benson,** of Calvert County, at home of Richard Harrison, father-in-law of aforesaid Elizabeth Benson. Witnesses: Richard Harrison, Joseph Chew, William Chew, Jno. Chew, Caleb Chew, Samuel Harrison, Nathan Smith, Thomas Smith, William Richardson, Thomas Everden, Abraham Birkhead, Solomon Sparrow, Neh: Birkhead, Phillip Coale, Humphrey Hodges, Richard Purnell, Joseph Hanslap, Samuel Brothers, Richard Chester, Thomas Blake, Anne Chew, Elizabeth Harrison, Alce Smith, Elizabeth Smith, Mary Smith, Elizabeth Coale, Sr., Mary Purnell, Cassabdra Skipwith, Sarah Harrison, Rebecca Birkhead, Lydia Chew, Rebecca Mear.

Richard Harrison, of Calvert County, m. 7th day of 3rd month commonly called May, 1695, to **Elizabeth Hall,** at the house of Richard Harrison. Witnesses: Elisha Hall, Joseph Hall, Samuell Harrison, Sarah Harrison, Mary Harrison, Benjamin Hall, Sarah Hall, Aaron Hall, Benjamin Chew, Thomas Smith, Elizabeth Evans, Rachell Smith, Elizabeth Chew, Alice Smith, Ann Hall, Elizabeth Smith, Ann Short, Mary Biggs, Will Richardson, Jr., Christopher Mather [Mathew?], Robert Gover, Benjamin Leatherington, Neh. Birckhead, Elizabeth Cole, Elizabeth Suvy, Samuell Chew. Mary Deaver, Geo: Royston, James Stoddert, George Philips, Samuel Philips, Jr., Thomas Salmon, Jno. Chew, Thomas Evernden, Philip Coale.

Richard Galloway, of Anne Arundel County, m. 10th day of 10th month commonly called December, 1696, to **Elizabeth Lawrence,** widow, at the house of William Lawrence, near West River. Witnesses: Samuel Galloway, Sr., William Cole, Jr., Edward Talbott, Phillip Cole, Samuel Coale, Richard Harrison, William Richardson, Sr., William Richardson, Jr., M. Moore, Joseph Chew, William Edmondson, Thomas Hooker, Umphrey Hooker, John ----, John ----, Joseph Richardson, Solloman Sparrow, Joseph ----, Elizabeth Lawrence, Elizabeth Talbot, Elizabeth Coale, Elizabeth Carter, Elizabeth Belt, Elizabeth Richardson, Sarah Thomas, Elizabeth Lockwood, Sarah Hooker, Misleyson [?] Bally [?], Mary Neighbor, Elizabeth ----, Mary Gill, Jane Gollen, Elizabeth Presly.

Philip Coale m. 6th day of 2nd month called April,, 1697, to **Cassandra Skipwith,** at home of William Coale, Sr. in Anne Arundel County. Witnesses: Elizabeth Coale, Sr., William Coale, Jr., ---- Thomas, ---- Smith, Edward Tolbut, William Holland, John Harris, ---- Birckhead, ---- Huchens, Thomas Sparrow, Thomas Miles, Joseph Richardson, Robert Gover, Samuell Harrison, Richard ----, Sam Harrison, [il-

QUAKER MARRIAGES OF SOUTHERN MARYLAND

legible] ----den, Thomas Heigh [?], George Harris, Jos: Chew, William Chew, Elizabeth Smith, Elizabeth Coale, Alles Smith, Elizabeth Harrison, Elizabeth Johns, Sarah Harrison, Ann Chew, Elizabeth Chew, Margaret Holland, ---a Sparrow, Sop-- Richardson, Elizabeth Hutchins, Mary Biggs, Ann Burges, Elizabeth Thomas, Elizabeth Chew, Richard Harrison, William Richardson, Jr., Sol Sparrow, Jno. Scotte, amd James Heigh.

Robert Franklin, of Anne Arundel County, m. 19th day of 10th month commonly called October, 1697, to **Artheridge Giles**, of Anne Arundel County, at their meeting house at West River. Witnesses: John Giles, Jacob Giles, Solomon Sparrow, Samuell Thomas, Nath. Giles, Richard Wigg, Joseph Richardson, William Cole, Jr., William Richardson, Jr., Richard Galloway, Daniell Richardson, Jonathan Taylor, Henry Bayton, George Gray, Thomas Smith, Richard Harrison, Philip Cole, Thomas Eveston [Creston?], Benjamin Chew, Caleb Chew, Samuell Lane, Augustin Hawkins, George Burton, Dutton Lane, Jacob Hooker, Edward Parrish, John Parrish, Elizabeth Waters, Sarah Franklin, Sarah Clark, ---- Hawkings, ELizabeth Richardson, Sr., Sarah Sparrow, Elizabeth Richardson, Jr., Sarah Giles, Margaret Richardson, Elizabeth Galloway, Ann Galloway, Sophia Richardson, Elizabeth Battee.

John Parrish, son of Edward and Clare Parrish, of Anne Arundel County, m. 23rd day of 11th month commonly called January, 1700, **Sarah Horn**, widow, and dau. of Robert and Sarah Franklin, of Anne Arundel County, at the house of William Richardson. Witnesses: Robert Franklin, Richard Gott, Edward Parrish, William Parrish, Samuell Thomas, Samuell Galloway, Solomon Sparrow, William Richardson, William Coale, Daniell Richardson, Gerrard Hopkins, Benjamin Lawrence, Richard Galloway, Joseph Richardson, Nathaniel Giles, Sarah Willobee, Benjamin Welsh, Samuel Waters, Nathan Chandelee, Samuell Galloway, Jr., Artheridge Franklin, Elizabeth Gott, Sarah Horn, Margaret Horn, Elizabeth Waters, Mary Thomas, Sarah Sparrow, Elizabeth Richardson, Sarah Thomas, Elizabeth Coale, Jr., Margaret Richardson.

Benjamin Lawrence, son of Benjamin and Elizabeth Lawrence, of Anne Arundel County, m. 6th day of 11th month called January, 1701/2, to **Rachel Marriarte**, dau. of Edward and Honer, of Anne Arundel County, at Col. Thomas Tailor's. Witnesses: Thomas Miles, John Preston, John Talbot, Sarah ----, Mary Waters, Nath. Giels, Jacob Giels, William Richardson, Jr., Daniel Richardson, John Belt, John Giels, Sam Lane, Elizabeth Galloway, Mary Richardson, Elizabeth Huchens, Mary Thomas, Soph Sparrow, Sara Sparrow, Elizabeth Hutchins, Sara Giles, Richard Galloway, Edward Marriarte, William Coale, Sam. Galloway, Solo. Sparrow, Sam: Thomas, John Salkeld, Robert Roberts, Morda. Moore, William Richardson, Jos: Richardson, Gerr: Hopkins, Richard Johns.

Jacob Giles, of West River, Anne Arundel County, son of John and Mary Giles, of same place, deceased, m. 8th day of 11th month commonly called January, 1701, to **Elizabeth Arnell**, dau. of Richard and Martha, of aforesaid place, deceased, at

QUAKER RECORDS OF SOUTHERN MARYLAND

William Richardson's. Witnesses: Samuell Galloway, Mord. Moore, Richard Galloway, William Coale, Joseph Richardson, Thomas Miles, Samuell Galloway, Jr., John Reston, Dutton Lane, Gerrard Hopkins, Samuell Lane, Elizabeth Coale, Jr., Elizabeth Richardson, Jr., Elizabeth Richardson, Sr., Elizabeth Hutchins, Jr., Margaret Richardson, Margarett Hopkins, Sarah Lane, Sarah Sparrow, Mary Waters, Mary Harwood, Elizabeth Richardson, Jr., Sophia Richardson, John Salkeld, Edward Talbott, Sarah Giles, Sarah Thomas, Elizabeth Talbott, Margarett Waters, Philip Thomas, John Thomas, Solomon Sparrow, William Richardson, William Richardson, Jr., Samuell Waters, Robert Roberts, Samuell Thomas, Elizabeth Talbott, Elizabeth Waters, Nath. Giles, Artheridge Franklin, Robert Franklin, Mary Thomas, Elizabeth Hutchins, John Talbott.

Richard Bond, of Calvert County, m. on 24th day of 7th month called September, 1702, to **Elizabeth Chew**, of Anne Arundel County, at Herring Creek Meeting House in Anne Arundel County. Witnesses: Richard Harrison, Thomas Smith, Nathan Smith, Samuel Lane, William Richardson, Samuell Galloway, Samuell Chew, Neh: Birkhead, Richard Galloway, Samuell Gover, Aaron Hall, Elisha Hall, Phillip Coale, Sarah Lane, Sarah Sparrow, Margret Richardson, Elizabeth Smith, Mary Harrison, Elizabeth Harrison,, Ann Galloway, Elizabeth Coale, Margret Holland, Cassandra Coale, Ann Shorter [Shooter?], Elizabeth Waters.

Danell Robinson, of Calvert County, m. 13th day of 11th month called January, 1703, to **Sarah Neeves**, of Anne Arundel County, at Herring Creek Meeting House in Anne Arundel County. Witnesses: Hen: Child, Samuel Chew, Robert Roberts, Joseph Chew, Nat: Smith, El-- Hall, Jo. Willson, Richard Harrison, Samuel Harrison, [illegible] ----den, Samuel Chew, Jr., William Coale, Elizabeth Harrison, Elizabeth Coale, Elizabeth Chew, Elizabeth Bond, Pris: [?] Roberts, Morda. Moore, Samuel Galloway.

Thomas Miles, of Anne Arundel County, m. 27th day of 4th month commonly called June, 1704, to **Ruth Jones**, dau. of Joseph and Elizabeth, of Anne Arundel County, at William Richardson's. Witnesses: Jos. Jones, Jos. Jones, Sam Jones, Solo. Sparrow, Sam Thomas, Nat. Smith, Sam Galloway, Phillip Coale. Tho. Smith, William Coale, Richard Galloway, Jos. Richardson, John Preston, Rob. Franklin, John Talbot, Jr., William Richardson, William Richardson, Jr., Dan. Richardson, Benjamin Lawrence, Ed. Talbott, Elizabeth Jones, Elizabeth Talbot, Mary Thomas, Sa. Sparrow, Ann Galloway, Elizabeth Coale, Jr., Elizabeth Richardson, Sop. Sparrow, Mar. Richardson, Sar. Thomas, Elizabeth Talbott, Jr., Richard Galloway.

Joseph Jones, son of Griffith and Joane, of Philadelphia County, Pennsylvania, merchant, m. 8th day of 4th month, 1704, **Margaret Birckhead**, dau. of Nehemiah, of Anne Arundel County, Maryland, merchant, at Herring Creek, at the house of Richard Johns of Calvert County. Witnesses: Griffith Jones, Neh: Birckhead, Neh. Birckhead, Jr., Joseph Willex [Willcox?], Sol. Birckhead, Abra: Birckhead,

QUAKER MARRIAGES OF SOUTHERN MARYLAND

Rebeckah Birckhead, Mary Child, Ann Birckhead, Elizabeth Cole, Elizabeth Harrison, Margaret Holland, Margaret Johns, Margaret Kidd, Elizabeth Kingsbury, Deborah Lloyd, Samuel Jenings, Griffith Owen, Tho: Everden, Edward Shippen, Samuell Chew, Richard Harrison, Richard Gaul [?], Joseph Shippen, Robert Roberts, Hen: Child, Robert Harper, Richard Harrison, Jr.,Ann Shippen, Elza: Bond, Mary Harper, Elizabeth Johns, Cassandra Coale, William Holland, Isaac Norris, Elisha Hall, Samuell Harrison, Samuel Chew, Jr., Philip Coale, Richard Hill, Nath: Smith, Thomas Smith, Josias Towgood, Jno: Giles, Jam: Heath, Sarah Hall, Mary Waters, Mary Towgood, Sarah Giles.

Thomas Hawkines, son of John and Mary, of Anne Arundel County, m. 30th day of 5th month commonly called March, 1704, to **Elizabeth Giles**, dau. of Richard and Margaret Arnell, at William Richardson's. Witnesses: Samuel Thomas, Elizabeth Talbott, John Hawkines, John Talbott, Robert Franklin, Benjamin Welsh, Elizabeth Walters, Mary Thomas, Sarah Thomas, Ann Galloway, Mary Waters, Elizabeth Locked, Elizabeth Coale, Mary Withell, Elizabeth ----, Mary Snoden, Mar. Richardson, Sar. Lane. Sar. Sparrow, Sar. Hutchings, Eliza Gotte, Sam Galloway, Richard Galloway, William Coale, Rich Snowden, Gerr: Hopkins, Sam Gover, John Gale, Ffran. Butler, Jose: Richardson, Solo: Sparrow.

Richard Geist, of Baltimore County, m. 7th day of 10th month called December, 1704, to **Zipporah Murray**, of same county, at Baltimore Town, on the south side of Potaptico River. Witnesses: Hen: Child, Richard Snowden, Sr., Richard Snowden, Jr., Hezek. Linthicom, Ed: Davis, John Gale, Thomas Hooker, Jam: Steveison, Hen: Hall, John: Martin, John Hayse, Char. Gorsuch, Chris: Mather, John Wilmote, John: Tidings, Jo: Morray, Rich Cromwell, Keia Morray, Elizabeth Cromwell, Will: Cromwell, Tho: Cromwell, Ni: Hicksimons, Ruth Heathcote, Mary Cromwell, John Ashman, Sar. Bale, George Thorpe, Sam: Hooker, Tho: Rockhould, Tho: Randall, Rich. Snowden, Sar. Hooker, Sar: Lane, Mary Snowden, Eliza: Hayes, Eliza: Halle, Peshe: Lane.

John Tidings, of Anne Arundel County, son of Richard and Charity Tidings, late of Anne Arundel County, deceased, m. 16th day of 6th month commonly called August, 1705, to **Mary Ellis**, dau. of James and Mary, late of Anne Arundel County, at West River. Witnesses: Thomas Stockett, Phill: Dowell, William Richardson, Sam. Thomas, Rich Snowden, Rich Galloway, William Coale, Aron: Rawlings, John Gaile, Garr: Hopkins, John Talbott, Jr., William Richardson, Ed. Talbott, Sam. Waters, Rich: Snowden, Phillip Thomas, Mary Dowell, Eliz: Richardson, Sar. Giles, Jo. Belt, Eliz: Talbott, Jr., Marg: Richardson, Eliz: Lockwood, Ann Galloway, Mary Snowden, Mary Thomas, Rach: Lawrence, Marg. Hopkines, Eliz. Galloway, Mary Waters, Eliz: Richardson, Fran: Hutchins, Robert Roper.

Joseph Richardson, son of William and Elizabeth, of Anne Arundel County, deceased, m. 25th day of 8th month, 1705, to **Sarah Thomas**, dau. of Samuel and Mary, of Anne Arundel County, at West River. Witnesses: Samuel Galloway, William Richardson, Jr., Frances Wason, Thomas Smith, John Giles, Richard

QUAKER RECORDS OF SOUTHERN MARYLAND

Galloway, William Coale, John Preston, Solomon Sparrow, Gerard Hopkins, Lauriana Richardson, Margarett Richardson, Mary Smith, Elizabeth Hutchens, Jr., Elizabeth Richardson, Jr., Eliza Coale, Ann Galloway, Elizabeth Waters, Sarah Giles, Sarah Sparrow, Hanna Galloway, Margaret Hopkins, Elizabeth Hawkins, Jr., Philip Coale, Elizabeth [?] Smith, ---- Johns, Jno. Hutchins, Edward Talbott, John Talbott, Jr., Margaret Johns, Francis Hutchins, Prisilla Hutchins, Mary Hutchins, ---- Smith, Samuel Thomas, Mary Thomas, William Richardson, Daniell Richardson, John Talbott, Sr., Philip Thomas, John Thomas.

Thomas Carr, son of Walter and Lartha Carr, of Anne Arundel County, m. 22nd day of 9th month, 1705, to **Elizabeth Price**, dau. of Mordecai and Mary, of Anne Arundel County, at West River. Witnesses: Mary Thomas, Ann Gallaway, Deborah Moore, Elizabeth Hawkins, Sarah Sparrow, Elizabeth Waters, Hana Gallaway, Mary Huchins, Margaret Hopkins, Samuell Gallaway, Samuell Thomas, Richard Gallaway, John Hawkins [?], John Gale, Garard Hopkins, Joseph Richardson, Henry Child, Francis Wason, Beniamen Welch, John Chew, James Bales, Mordicai Price, Mary Price, Beniamen Capell, Stephen: Price, Robard Franklin, Artredge Franklin, Thomas Holand, Elizabeth Goot.

Richard Snowden, youngest son of Richard Snowden, Jr. and Mary, his wife, m. 19th day of 3rd month, 1709 commonly called May, to **Elizabeth Coale, Jr.**, dau. of William and Elizabeth, all now of Anne Arundel County, at West River. Witnesses: Nathan Smith, Thomas Preston, William Richardson, William Everest, Cadde. Edwards, John Talbott, William Ford, Elizabeth Wooden, Elizabeth Waters, Mary Lewin, Elizabeth Lockwood, Sarah Sparrow, Margt. Richardson, Sarah Lane, Sarah Richardson, Mary Witchell, Deborah Moore, Ann Galloway, Jr., Mary Galloway, Hanah Galloway, Phil. Thomas, William Richardson, Jr., William Harris, Joseph Smith, Edward Parrish, Samuel Battee, Jno. Crockett, Robert Roberts, Priscilla Johns, Gerrd. Hopkins, Fras. Hutchins, Mary Hutchins, Leonard Weyman, Mary Clark, Solom: Sparrow, Richard Galloway, Samuel Thomas, Mary Thomas, Elizabeth Talbott, Edmd. Waman, Leonard Waman, Jr., Richard Jones, Jr., Thomas Gassaway, Robert Saunders, Benjamin Harris, Samuel Galloway, Hen: Child, Morda. Moore, Aron Rawlings, Peter Galloway, John Galloway, Richard Moore, John Giles, Jos. Richardson, Richard Snowden, Jr., Elizabeth Snowden, Richard Snowden, Sr., Richard Snowden, Jr., William Coale, Mary Snowden, Elizabeth Coale, Elizabeth Johns, Prisa. Roberts, Mary Coale, William Coale, Jr., Samuel Coale, Dorcas Weyman, Deb: Linthycombe, Aquilla Johns, Margt. Hopkins, Richard Johns, Jr., Hanah Coale, Kinsey Johns, Isaac Johns, Hez: Linthycombe, Phil. Coale, Margt. Johns, Richard Galloway, Elizabeth Johns, Jr.

Joseph Smith, of Calvert County, son of Nathan and Elizabeth, m. 4th day of 3rd month commonly called May, 1710, to **Laurana Richardson**, of Anne Arundel County, dau. of Daniel and Elizabeth. Witnesses: William Coale, Samuel Galloway, John Giles, Edward Talbot, William Baldwin, Richard Bond, Richard Galloway,

QUAKER MARRIAGES OF SOUTHERN MARYLAND

Richard Jones [Sr.?], Joseph Richardson [Jr.?], Samuel Richardson, Thomas Sparrow, Solomon Sparrow, William Waters, Gerrd. Hopkins, Jno. Crocket, Benjamin Welsh, Robert Franklin, William Coale, Jr., Edward Parrish, Samuell Coale, Sophia Richardson, Sarah Giles, Sarah Sparrow, Margt. Richardson, Sarah Lane, Sarah Richardson, Elizabeth Coale, Elizabeth Parrish, Mary Snowden, Elizabeth Talbott, Jr., Cassandra Coale, Mary Thomas, Ann Galloway, Mary Towgood, Mary Witchell, Elizabeth Giles, Ann Galloway, Jr., Mary Coale, Sophia Giles, Hanah Coale, Elizabeth Waters, Artridge Franklin, Elizabeth Thomas, Elizabeth Wooden, Sarah Norris, Elizabeth Rigbie, Mary Clark, Mary Parrish, Susana Rawlings, Sarah Richardson, Jr., Nathan Smith, Elizabeth Smith, Daniel Richardson, Elizabeth Richardson, Nathan Smith, Jr., Elizabeth Talbott, Thomas Smith [Jr.?], John Richardson, Elizabeth Smith, Jr., Sarah Smith, William Richardson, Joseph Richardson, Sussana Smith, John Talbott, Philip Coale, William Richardson, Jr., Josias Towgood, Thomas Miles, Samuel Lane, John Galloway.

Thomas Holland, son of Anthony and Isabell, late of Anne Arundel County, deceased, m. 3rd day of 2nd month commonly called April, 1712, to **Margret Waters**, dau. of John, late of aforesaid county, deceased, and Elizabeth, his surviving wife, at West River Meeting House in Anne Arundel County. Witnesses: John Talbott, Sammuell Galloway, Morda. Moore, Samuel Thomas, Richard Galloway, Gerrd. Hopkins, William Coale, Richard Galloway, Samuell Thomas, Jr., Jos: Richardson, Jr., William Richardson, Jno. Crocket, Mary Thomas, Sarah Sparrow, Ann Galloway, Elizabeth Wooden, Deborah Moore, Mary Thomas, Mary Parrish, Elizabeth Coale, Mary Coale, Margt. Richardson, Elizabeth Richardson, Sophia Richardson, Ann Galloway, Jr., Jacob Holland, Elizabeth Waters, Mary Talbott, Nathaniell Giles, Elizabeth Norris, John Norris, Robert Franklin, John Giles, Jr., Hanah Norris, Sarah Norris, Elizabeth Parrish, Sarah Giles, Stephen Price, John Waters, William Waters.

Nehemiah Birckhead, of Anne Arundel County, m. on 24th day of 6th month, 1712, to **Margarett Johns**, of Calvert County, at Clifts Meeting House. Witnesses: John Clark, Francis Hutchens, Jon. Astin, Robert Harper, Benjamin Hance, Joseph Harris, Abram. Johns, Richard Johns, Robert Roberts, Richard Bond, Priscilla Johns, Richard Johns, Jr., Kensey Johns, M---- Hutchens, Jon. Wilson, Elizabeth Johns, Elizabeth Bond, Nathn. Giles, Thomas Preston, Ann Harris, Ann Young, George Harris, Mary Johns, Jon. Leach.

Richard Hall, son of Elisha and Sarah, of Calvert County, m. 4th day of 7th month called September, 1712, to **Mary Johns**, widow of Aquila, late of Calvert County, at the Clifts. Witnesses: Robert Harper, Jesse Bourne, Able Royston, Richard Johns, Thomas Chalkley, Robert Roberts, Kensey Johns, Isaac Johns, Priscilla Johns, Priscilla Roberts, Andrew Tanehill, Richard Johns, Jr., Jo. Wilson, Samuel Chew (of Maidstone), Elihu Hall, Samuel Harrison, Richard Harris, Jr., Elizabeth Harrison, Sarah Harrison.

QUAKER RECORDS OF SOUTHERN MARYLAND

Joseph Coleman, m. last day of 6th month, 1712, to **Mary Thomas**, both of Anne Arundel County, at the Clifts Meeting House, having appeared together in there usual meeting place in Prince George's County. Witnesses: Thomas Chalkley, Gerrard Hopkins, Richard Snowden, Jr., Benjamin Lawrence, Robert Franklin, Edward Talbott, Samuel Waters, Jeremiah Murdock, Jno. Jackson, Jno. Crocket, Thomas Plummer, Sr., Thomas Plummer, Jr., George Plummer, James Plummer, Mary Boyd, Sr., Sarah Green, Elizabeth White, Elizabeth Plummer, Thomasin Welsh, Fras. Duvall, Ruth Jackson, Edward Parrish, John Wesh, Ralph Somerfield, John Plummer, Jerom Plummer, Philemon Plummer, Morda. Moore, Elizabeth Burges, Deborah Moore, Fras. Hanslip, Ursulla Burges, Sussanah Hutchens, Burges Mitchell, Mord. Mitchell, Elizabeth Coats.

Jacob Duhataway, son of Jacob and Margaret, late of Anne Arundel County, deceased, m. 16th day of 9th month usually called November, 1712, to **Elizabeth Parrish**, dau. of Edward and Mary, of Anne Arundel County, now living, at meeting house at West River. Witnesses: John Hawkins, Samuell Galloway, Richard Galloway, William Coale, Richard Snowden Jr., M: Moore, Ralph Sumerfield, Joseph Coleman, Robert Franklin, Solomon Sparrow, Samuell Thomas, William Richardson, Gerrd. Hopkins, Jos: Galloway, Jos: Richardson, Samuell Coale, William Dowell, Samuell Thomas, Jr., Jno. Crocket, Ann Galloway, Mary Thomas, Margt. Richardson, Elizabeth Wooding, Deborah Moore, Sarah Richardson, Sarah Sparrow, Margt. Hopkins, Elizabeth Hopkins, Edward Parrish, Thomas Atkins, John Parrish, Sarah Parrish.

Isaac Johns, son of Richard and Elizabeth, of Calvert County, m. 25th day of 10th month, 1712, to **Ann Galloway**, dau. of Samuel and Ann, of Anne Arundel County, at West River Meeting House. Witnesses: Prisa. Johns, William Coale, Jr., Mary Coale. Solo: Sparrow, Sar: Sparrow, Richard Johns, Abra: Johns, Elizabeth Hopkins, Hanah Ford, Mary Galloway, Richard Galloway, William Coale, John Galloway, Petr: Galloway, Jos: Galloway, Richard Galloway, Elizabeth Coale, Margt. Hopkins, Gerd. Hopkins, Richard Galloway, Jr., Samuell Galloway, Ann Galloway, Richard Johns, Jr., Kensey Johns, Mary Thomas, Sr., Deborah Moore, Margt. Richardson, Sophia Richardson, Sarah Richardson, Constance Young, Debor: Moore, Jr., Mary Thomas, Jr., Rachell Lawrence, Cassandra Coale, Jr., Morda. Moore, Samuel Thomas, William Richardson, Samuel Chew (of Maidstone), Jno. Crockett, Robert Walker, Jos. Richardson, William Dowell, Thomas Preston.

Benjamin Ball, of Kent Island, m. 8th day of 5th month usually called July, 1714, to **Elizabeth Richardson**, dau. of William and Margaret, of Anne Arundel County. Witnesses: Fras. Hutchens, Margt. Hopkins, Hanah Coale, Jno. Richardson, Jos. Richardson, Samuel Richardson, Jos. Smith, Abra. Johns, Jno. Talbott, Samuel Harrison, John Giles, Richard Richardson, Kensey Johns, Isaac Johns, Constance Young, Elizabeth Bond, Jos. Smith, Lurania Smith, Richard Harrison, Elizabeth Chew, Susana Smith, Sarah Harrison, Elizabeth Chew, Sr., Ann Galloway,

QUAKER MARRIAGES OF SOUTHERN MARYLAND

Elizabeth Coale, Mary Thomas, Mary Witchell, Margt. Birckhead, Prisa. Johns, William Richardson, Mary Richardson, Thomas Ball, Ruth Richardson, Daniel Richardson, Joseph Richardson, Thomas Smith, Mary Smith, Sarah Richardson, Jr., Sarah Smith, Solomon Sparrow, Thomas Chalkley, M. Moore, Samuel Chew (of Maidstone), Sarah Thomas, Sarah Lane, Samuel Galloway, Richard Bond, Neh. Birckhead, Gerd. Hopkins, William Lovell [Dovell?], Jno. Crockett, Samuel Thomas, Richard Lane, Samuel Coale, William Coale, Jr., Jos. Galloway, John Giles, Jr., Jacob Giles, Richard Galloway, Mary Snowden, Elizabeth Snowden, Mary Coale, Elizabeth Thomas, Sarah Sparrow.

Thomas Miles, of Anne Arundel County, m. 23rd day of 10th month usually called December, 1714, to **Elizabeth White**, widow, of Prince George's County, at West River Meeting. Witnesses: Samuel Galloway, M. Moore, Richard Galloway, Samuel Thomas, William Richardson, John Giles, Solom: Sparrow, Gerd. Hopkins, Jos. Galloway, Jos. Richardson, John Ellis, Jno. Crockett, Ann Galloway, Deborah Moore, Sarah Sparrow, Mary Thomas, Margt. Richardson, Mary Snowden, Margt. Hopkins, Sophia Richardson, Constn. Young, Elizabeth Plummer, Hanah Coale, Rachel Clark, Mary Galloway, Ann Thomas, Sarah White, Samuel White, Mary Jones, Sarah Jones, Samuel Griffith, John Evans, Mareen Duvall, Thomas Evans.

Richard Galloway, Jr., m. 29th day of 7th month usually called September, 1715, to **Sophia Richardson**, dau. of William and Margaret, all of Anne Arundel County, at West River Meeting. Witnesses: Mary Thomas, Cassandra Coale, Elizabeth Wooding, Jr., Margt. Hopkins, Elizabeth Snowden, Mary Coale, Hanah Coale, Hanah Sumerfield, Mary Thomas, Jr., Elizabeth Thomas, Elenr. Smith, Elizabeth Talbott, Jr., Benjamin Lawrence, Daniel Richardson, Jno. Crockett, Thomas Gassaway, Samuel Harrison, Samuel Chew, Jr., John Chew, Samuel Thomas, Gerrd. Hopkins, Richard Johns, Jr., Richard Snowden, Samuel Chew (of Maidstone), Isaac Johns, J. Galloway, Ralph Sumerfield, William Coale, Richard Hill, Jos. Richardson, Samuel Richardson, Jos. Galloway, Jos. Smith, Richard Galloway, Samuel Lane, Richard Richardson, Richard Galloway, Jr., Sophia Galloway, Richard Galloway, William Richardson, Margt. Richardson, Samuel Galloway, Ann Galloway, Lucy Belt, Joseph Richardson, Sarah Richardson, Sarah Sparrow, Mary Chew, Elizabeth Chew, Elizabeth Coale, Elizabeth Talbott, Mary Smith, Joseph Smith, Laurana Smith, John Talbott, Phil. Coale.

Samuel Chew, son of Benjamin, deceased, and Elizabeth, surviving, m. 7th day of 8th month usually called October, 1715, to **Mary Galloway**, dau. of Samuel and Ann, all of Anne Arundel County, at West River Meeting. Witnesses: Richard Johns, Jr., Richard Richardson, Mary Witchell, Mary Coale, Richard Galloway, Jr., Sophia Galloway, Thomas Preston, Elizabeth Rigbie, Jos: Richardson, Hanah Coale, Jno. Crockett, Mary Chew, Elizabeth Chew, J. Galloway, Nath. Chew, Jos: Galloway, Richard Galloway, Elizabeth Coale, Kensey Johns, Isaac & Ann Johns, William Richardson, Robert Roberts, Samuel Thomas, Gerd. Hopkins, Mary Thomas, Samuel Galloway, Ann Galloway, Elizabeth Bond, Richard Galloway, Samuel

QUAKER RECORDS OF SOUTHERN MARYLAND

Harrison, Samuel Chew, Jr., John Chew, Elizabeth Johns, Jr., Ann Chew, Sarah Sparrow.

Peter Galloway, son of Samuel and Ann, of Anne Arundel County, m. 19th day of 11th month usually called January, 1715, to **Elizabeth Rigbie**, dau. of John and Elizabeth, late of said county, deceased, at West River. Witnesses: Joseph Richardson, John Crockett, ---- Jones, Jr., ---- Johns, ---- Galloway, Mary Coale, Hannah Coale, Sarah Sparrow, Elizabeth Coale, Sarah Lane, Mary Thomas, ---- Hopkins, William Richardson, Isaac Johns, Joseph Galloway, Richard Galloway, William Coale, Edward Parrish, Samuell Coale, Mord. Moore, Samuell Thomas, Gerrard Hopkins, George Westgarth, Samuell Galloway, Ann Galloway, Richard Galloway, John Galloway, Benjamin Lawrence, Lucey Belt, Richard Galloway, Jr., John Belt.

James Dickenson, son of William and Elizabeth, of Talbot County, m. 21st day of 9th month usually called November, 1717, to **Hannah Coale**, dau. of William and Elizabeth, of Anne Arundel County, at West River Meeting. Witnesses: Elizabeth Wartnaby, Mary Thomas, Mary Parish, Elizabeth Duhataway, Mary Hall, Sr., Rachel Lawrence, Ann Parish, Margt. Richardson, Sarah Galloway, Mary Chew, Elizabeth Hopkins, Sarah Lane, Samuel Thomas, William Richardson, Jamnes Elderton, Samuel Richardson, Daniel Richardson, Jr., Elizabeth Coale, Samuel Dickenson, Samuel Galloway, Richard Galloway, Elizabeth Troth, Ann Galloway, Gerd. Hopkins, Margtt. Hopkins, Robert Roberts, Peter Sharp, Abra. Johns, Richard Johns.

Richard Snowden, son of Richard and Mary, m. 19th day of 10th month, 1717 commonly called December, to **Elizabeth Thomas**, dau. of Samuel and Mary, both of Anne Arundel County, at West River. Witnesses: Richard Galloway, Peter Wills, Samuel Chambers, Richard Galloway, Jr., Benjamin Welsh, Nathan Rigbie, Aron Rawlings, Joseph Adams, Jos: Richardson, Jr., Jona. Newman, Samuel Richardson, Richard Hill, Solomon Sparrow, Jeames Carroll, Jona. Hanson, Edward Talbott, William Richardson, John Giles, James Edeetar [Eldeston?], Ann Galloway, Margt. Richardson, Mary Talbott, Rachel Welsh, Sarah Giles, Elizabeth Galloway, Elizabeth Wooden, Sarah Richardson, Sarah Sparrow, Sophia Galloway, Elizabeth Talbott, Casna. Rigbie, Elizabeth Coale, Casn. Smith, Mary Snowden, Mary Thomas, Sarah Richardson, Philip Thomas, Leonard Wayman, Samuell Thomas, Joseph Richardson, John Talbott, Francis Hutchins, John Welsh, Neh: Birckhead, John Thomas, William Coale, Sarah Coale, Jane Rutland.

John Galloway, son of Samuell and Ann, m. 31st day of 5th month usually called July, 1718, to **Mary Thomas**, dau. of Samuell and Mary, all of Anne Arundel County, at West River Meeting House. Witnesses: Joseph Richardson, Sollomon Sparrow, John Newman, Josh. Richardson, Jr., William Richardson, Hanah Rosenquest, Mary Snowden, Mary Crockett, Cassandra Smith, Elizabeth Wooden, Susanah Paca, Jon. Talbott, Jr., Sarah Lane, Mary Witchell, Margt. Richardson, Ann

QUAKER MARRIAGES OF SOUTHERN MARYLAND

Rawlings, Mary Hance, Priscilla Coale, Eliz. Hopkings, Margt. Hopkings, Elizabeth Brookes, Mary Brookes, Danll. Richardson, [Jr.?], Elizabeth Galloway, Sarah Sparrow, John Thomas, Pricilla Johns, Frances Hutchins, Frans. Hutchins, William Foard, Richard Johns, Lucey Belt, Sarah Galloway, Aquila Paca, Aron Rawlings, Gerrard Hopkings, Samuell Richardson, Abraham Johns, James Brooks, Casandra Coale, Moses Rawlings, Alexander Rosenquest, John Hawkings, Benjamin Whichcote, Samuell Galloway, Samuell Thomas, Ann Galloway, Mary Thomas, Richard Galloway, Peter Galloway, Philip Thomas, Joseph Galloway, Mary Chew, Elizabeth Snowden, Sarah Richardson, Samuell Thomas, Jr., Richard Galloway, Hannah Foard, Richard Galloway, [Jr.?], Samuell Chew (of Maidstone), Josh. Richardson, Richard Snowden, Margt. Birkhead.

Jonathan Hanson, of Baltimore County, son of Timothy and Barbara, late of Phildelphia County, Pennsylvania, m. 29th day of 5th month commonly called July, 1718, to **Mary Price**, dau. of Mordecai and Mary, late of Anne Arundel County, Maryland, at West River Meeting House. Witnesses: Margret Richardson, Mary Thomas, Sarah Giles, Sarah Lane, Sarah Sparrow, Elizabeth Wooden, Elizabeth Talbott, Elizabeth Watters, Elizabeth Talbott, Jr., Richard Galloway, Samuell Galloway, Samuell Thomas, Gerrard Hopkins, Aron Rawlings, Richard Galloway, Jr., John Hawkins, Robert Frankling, Benjamin Welsh, Solomon Sparrow, Samuell Richardson, William Richardson, John Talbott, Joseph Galloway, John Galloway, Joseph Richardson, Daniell Richardson, Jr., Thomas Wasson, Edward Parrish, Jr., John Elderton [Eccleston?], Samuel Harrison, Mordecai Price, Ezebn. Price, Benjamin Price, Edward Norris, Joseph Norris.

Richard Galloway, Sr., m. 30th day of 5th month commonly called July, 1719, to **Sarah Sparrow**, both of Anne Arundel County, at West River Meeting House. Witnesses: Mary Witchell, Elizabeth Snowden, Hanah Rosenquest, Elizabeth Talbott, Elizabeth Welsh, Sophia Galloway, Maru Parish, Ann Thomas, Gerrard Hopkins, Josh. Richardson, Sarah Richardson, Mary Hopkins, Elizabeth Hopkins, Gerrard Hopkins, Jr., Joseph Hopkins, Daniell Richardson, James Elderton, Lucey Belt, John Belt, Benjamin Lawrance, John Talbott, Turner Wootton, Zacha. Macubbine, Richard Snowden, Benjamin Lawrance, Jr., Isaac Johns, Kensey Johns, William Richardson, Solomon Sparrow, Beniamin Ball, Ruth Richardson, Mordecai Moore, Samuell Thomas, Henry Child, Mary Thomas, John Leeds [?], Richard Wigg, Thomas Smith, Margtt. Richardson, Sarah Lane, Elizabeth Ball, Joseph Smith, Samuell Richardson, Richard Richardson, Elizabeth Johns, Elizabeth Coale, Elizabeth Wooden, Mary Smith, Sarah Hollyday, Rachel Lawrance, Luranie Smith, Richard Galloway, Jr., John Galloway, Joseph Galloway, Richard Galloway, Ann Johns, Josh. Smith.

Henry Hill, Jr., son of Henry and Mary, m. 9th day of 1st month commonly called March, 1720/1, to **Sarah Galloway**, dau. of Samuel and Ann, both of Anne Arundel County, at West River Meeting House. Witnesses: Mary Galloway, Sarah Galloway, Sophia Galloway, Samuell Thomas, Mary Thomas, Margt. Hopkins, Margt.

QUAKER RECORDS OF SOUTHERN MARYLAND

Richardson, Elizabeth Chew, Sarah Harrison, Cassandra Rigbie, Cassandra Smith, Mary Moore, Elizabeth Hopkins, Sarah Richardson, Nathn. Rigbie, William Richardson, Samuell Harrison, Samuell Richardson, Jos. Richardson, Richard Johns, Jos. Cowman, Loyd Zachary, Henry Hill, Mary Hill, Ann Galloway, Jno. Galloway, Petr. Galloway, Jos. Galloway, Ann Johns, Levin Hill, Richard Galloway (of Cumberstone), Richard Galloway, Richard Galloway, Jr., Lucy Pardoe, Isaac & Ann Johns, Elizabeth Galloway, Mary Hill.

Levin Hill, son of Henry, m. 10th day of 11th month called January, 1722/3, to **Elizabeth Hopkins**, dau. of Gerrard, both of Anne Arundel County, at West River. Witnesses: Solomon Sparrow, Margt. Richardson, Joseph Richardson, Sarah Richardson, Elizabeth Snowden, John Giles, Jr., J. Richardson, Jr., Cassandra Rigbie, Ann Thomas, Sarah Galloway, Mary Thomas, Margt. Moore, Elizabeth Wooden, Richard Hall, Ann Rawlings, Richard Johns, Abra. Johns, Arthur Harris, Joseph Hill, Joseph Hopkins, Mary Gellis, Priscilla Roberts, Isaac Johns, Robert Roberts, Elizabeth Roberts, Henry Child, Deborah Hill, Henry Hill, Gerrard Hopkins, Margarett Hopkins, Mary Hill, Richard Hill.

John Giles, son of John, of Baltimore County, m. 8th day of 11th month called January, 1722, to **Cassandra Smith**, dau. of Nathan, late of Calvert County, deceased, at West River. Witnesses: Joseph Richardson, Richard Richardson, Samuel Chew (of Maidstone), Nat. Rigbie, John Galloway, Richard Galloway, Elizabeth Wooding, Elizabeth Watters, Elizabeth Talbott, Samuell Stockett, Laurania Smith, Robert Franklin, Mary Thomas, Richard Welsh, Sarah Franklins, Robert Franklins, John Giles, Sarah Giles, Sarah Galloway, Margt. Richardson, Betty Giles, Jacob Giles, Margt. Hopkins, Thomas Stockett, Robert Welsh, Hen. Child, William Richardson, Richard Galloway, Solomon Sparrow, Jos: Galloway, Richard Galloway (of Cumberstone), Ann Rawlings, Samuel Thomas, Jr., Sophia Galloway, Rachell Lawrence, Elizabeth Hopkins, Ann Chew, Rebekah Johnes.

Joseph Richardson, son of William and Margarett, of Anne Arundel County, m. 6th day of 1st month usually called March, 1722/3, to **Rebekah Johns**, dau. of Aquila and Mary, late of Calvert County, at Herring Creek in Anne Arundel County. Witnesses: Samuel Gover, Hannah Sumerfield, Elizabeth Gover, Joseph Hopkins, Elizabeth Smith, Sarah Bond, Elizabeth Brooke, Richard Johns, Aquila Johns, Samuel Harrison, Sarah Harrison, Elizabeth Bond, Sarah Hall, Elizabeth Hall, Ann Chew, Ann Chew, Richard Galloway, Sr., Richard Galloway, Mary Chew, Neh. Birckhead, Gerrard Ball, Henry Child, William Richardson, Margrett Richardson, Mary Hall, Richard Hall, Elizabeth Hall, Sarah Richardson, Daniel Richardson, Richard Richardson, Mary Hall, Jr., Kensey Johns, Isaac Johns, Margt. Hopkins, Robert Roberts, Joseph Richardson, Thomas Smith, Nathan Richardson, Elizabeth Johns, Abra. Johns, Solomon Sparrow.

Melchizdeck Murry, of Baltimore County, son of James and Jemina, late of Baltimore County, m. 13th day of 9th month called November, 1723, to **Sophia**

QUAKER MARRIAGES OF SOUTHERN MARYLAND

Giles, daughter of John and Sarah of Baltimore County, having laid their intentions of marriage before two public monthly meetings and a quarterly meeting, were married at their meeting house in Baltimore County. Witnesses: Sarah Parish, John Parish, Hannah Cromwell, Ruth Murray, Richard Taylor, Thomas Cear, John Fishman, John Cromwell, Edward Norris, Sarah Franklin, John Parish, William Parish, Zepporah Gist, Ann Magy Giles, Cassandra Giles, Nath. Giles, Oliver Cromwell, Jon. Hanson, John Giles, Betty Giles, John Giles, Jr., Jacob Giles.

Samuel Plummer, son of Thomas and Elizabeth, of Prince George's County, m. 4th day of 1st month called March, 1723/4, **Sarah Miles**, dau. of Thomas, of Prince George's County, having declared their intentions of marriage at two public meetings in Calvert and Anne Arundel Counties, were married at their meeting house in Prince George's County. Witnesses: Jerom Plummer, John Plummer, George Plummer, John Evans, Thomas Revets, Thomas Plummer, John Miles, Richard Johns, William Richardson, Daniel Richardson, Joseph Richardson, Sr., Thomas Plummer, Elizabeth Plummer, Thomas Miles, James Plummer, Philemon Plummer, Priscilla Plummer, Phebe Plummer, Micajah Plummer, Thomas Miles, Jr., Elizabeth White, Samuel White, Benjamin White.

Joseph Cowman, mariner, of City of London in Great Britain, m. 5th day of 1st month (March), 1723/4, to **Sarah Hill**, widow, of Anne Arundel County, at West River Meeting House in Anne Arundel County. Witnesses: Richard Galloway (of Cumberstone), John Galloway, Joseph Galloway, Richard Galloway, Richard Galloway, Jr., Isaac Johns, William Foard, John Hanbury, Richard Johns, Phillip Thomas, Hen: Child, Robert Roberts, William Richardson, William Richardson, Jr., Richard Snowden, Kensey Johns, Gerrard Hopkins, Richard Johns, Margt. Richardson, Mary Thomas, Jos: Richardson, Ann Thomas, Sarah Richardson, Ann Chew, Sarah Coale, Ann Rawlings, Margt. Hopkins, Solomon Sparrow, Nath. Tanner, Samuel Chew, Jr., John Thomas, Samuell Richardson, Richard Richardson, Tho: Warren, Joseph Richardson, John Hall.

John Steward, of Anne Arundel County, m. 3rd day of 1st month called March, 1723/4, to **Sarah Frankling**, dau. of Robert and Artridge, both of Anne Arundel County, at West River. Witnesses: Henry Child, William Richardson, Jno. Hanbury, Mary Thomas, Richard Galloway, Jos: Richardson, Sarah Richardson, Daniell Richardson, Anthony Gott, Edward Parrish, Mary Mackembine, Elizabeth Welsh, William Richardson, Gerrard Hopkins, Joseph Richardson, William Lotherington, William Ford, William Coale, Richard Johns, Margrett Richardson, Sophia Galloway, John Thomas, Robert Frankling, Artradge Frankling, Richard Frankling, John Frankling, William Parrish, Sarah Parrish, Margrett Holland, John Parrish, John Carr.

Richard Lewis, of Baltimore County, son of Richard and Elizabeth, late of England, m. 15th day of month called May, 1723, **Betty Giles**, dau. of John and Sarah, of Baltimore County, at their meeting house of the north side of the Patapsco in Baltimore County, having declared their intentions at two public meetings in Anne

Arundel County. Witnesses: John Galloway, William Richardson, Peter Galloway, George Walker, William Browen [Brewer?], S---- Parrish, Mary Hanson, Abra. Harrington, Jos. Jordan, Jonathan Hanson, Richard Tayler, Samuell Johnson, Philip Wilkinson, John Parrish, Elizabeth Parrish, John Giles, Sarah Giles, John Giles, Jr., Sophia Giles, Jacob Giles, Nath. Giles, Jr.

Mordecai Price, of Baltimore County, m. 28th day of 2nd month usually called April, 1724, **Elizabeth White**, dau. of Guy and Elizabeth, late of Prince George's County, at their meeting house in Prince George's County, having declared their intentions to marriage at two public meetings in Anne Arundel and Calvert Counties. Witnesses: Jos. Hopkins, James Plummer, Mareen Duvall, William Richardson, Zeporah Duvall, Sarah Wells, Thomas Plummer, Martha Evans, Sarah Coale, Hen: Child, Richard Galloway, Jr., Benja. White, John Miles, Sarah Plummer, Jerom Plummer, Elizabeth Plummer, Micajah Plummer, Ro--a Plummer, Thomas Miles, Samuell White, John Price, Elizabeth Carr, Sarah Price, William Coale, Sarah Coale.

Philip Thomas, of Anne Arundel County, m. 11th day of 6th month called August, 1724, to **Ann Chew**, dau. of Samuel, at Samuel Chew's house. Witnesses: Kensey Johns, Henry Child, Peter Sharp, Robert Roberts, Gerrard Hopkins, Elizabeth Johns, Sarah Hall, Mary Hall, Sarah Harrison, Mary Chew, Sarah Bond, Abraham Johns, Dorothy Brooks, Ann Chew, Ann Rawlings, Elizabeth Gover, Sarah Robertson, Mary Hall, Sarah Richardson, Ann Thomas, Sarah Locks, Margt. Birckhead, Thomas Smith, Ann Chew, Richard Galloway, William Richardson, Samuel Chew (of Maidstone), John Galloway, Margt. Richardson, Joseph Richardson, Richard Richardson, Daniel Richardson, Elizabeth Smith, Priscilla Johns, Richard Johns, Elizabeth Robertson, Margt. Hopkins, Mary Richardson, Samuel Chew, Mary Chew, Mary Thomas, Samuel Thomas, Jr., John Thomas, Elizabeth Snowden, Mary Galloway, Nath. Chew, Sarah Richardson, Samuel Harrison, Elizabeth Bond, John Chew, Elizabeth Holland, Samuel Chew, Elizabeth Birckhead, Rebekah Richardson.

Joseph Hill, m. 17th day of 7th month called September, 1724, to **Sarah Richardson**, both of Anne Arundel County, at West River. Witnesses: Samuell Thomas, Auther Harris, Samuell Richardson, Nathan Richardson, Thomas Richardson, Mary Galloway, Ann Johnes, Elizabeth Snowden, Mary Thomas, Elizabeth Galloway, Cassandra Rigbie, Ann [?] Coale, Richard Moore, Samuell Chew (of Medstone), Hen. Child, Nath. Chew, ---- Hall, John Galloway, Richard Snowden, Sarah Coale, Elizabeth Robertson, Samuell Harrison, Sarah Harrison, Mary Chew, Samuell Chew, Elizabeth Hall, Mary Chew, Ann Thomas, Ann Chew, Mary Hall, Sarah Richardson, Elizabeth Wooding, Mary Chew, Richard Wigg, Mary Moore, Henry Hill, William Richardson, Mary Richardson, Sarah Galloway, Elizabeth Ball, Daniell Richardson, Jos. Richardson [last six surnames are illegible].

QUAKER MARRIAGES OF SOUTHERN MARYLAND

Aquilla Massey, son of Jonathan, of Baltimore County, m. 7th day of ye month called January, 1724/5, to **Sarah Coale**, dau. of William, deceased, of Anne Arundel County, at West River Meeting House. Witnesses: Jos. Cowman, John Talbott, Jos. Richardson, Cassandra Talbott, Daniell Richardson, Solomon Sparrow, John Giles, Jr., Gilbert Crockett, Leonard Hopkins, Phillip Hopkins, ----Richardson, Priscilla Robers, Sarah Galloway, Sarah Coale, Jos. Galloway, Jos. Hopkins, Hen. Child, Elizabeth Snowden, Elizabeth Wooden, Mary Thomas, Margt. Richardson, Ann Thomas, Robert Franklin, William Coale, Thomas Coale. Richard Galloway, Richard Galloway, Jr., John Galloway, Gerrard Hopkins, Margt. Hopkins, Peter Galloway.

James Brookes, of Prince George's County, m. 1st day of the month called June, 1725, to **Deborah Snowden**, dau. of Richard, of Anne Arundel County, at home of Richard Snowden. Witnesses: Deborah Linthicum, Mary Flowlar [Fowler?], Elizabeth Clark, Elizabeth Johns, Elizabeth Birckhead, Margt. Birckhead, Mary Moore, Thomas Hewitt, Jos. Cowman, John Galloway, William Richardson, Margt. Preston, Margt. Moore, Mary Hill, Neh. Birckhead, John Thomas, Richard Johns, Abra: Johns, Samuell Richardson, Deborah Linthicum, Richard Galloway, Mary Wayman, Henry Hill, Rachell Welsh, Mary Witchell, Samuel Preston, Jos. Richardson, Daniell Richardson, Thomas Clark, Leon [?] Linthicum, James Brooke, Deborah Brooke, Richard Snowden, Elizabeth Smith, Mary Snowden, Dorothy Br--e, Ann Br---, Sarah Birckhead [next six surnames are illegible], Deborah Hill, Mary Gilliss, Elizabeth Hill, Margt. Richardson, Susanna Rawlins, Richard Moore, Ann Wayman, Edmund Wayman, Fraances Lay [?], Edward Gaither [?], Leonard Wayman, Thomas Linthicum, Giden Linthicum, Peter Galloway.

John England, of Cecil County, m. 10th day of 3rd month, 1727, to **Margaret Birkhead**, of Anne Arundel County, at Herring Creek Meeting. Witnesses: Neh. Birkhead, Sarah Birkhead, Neh. Birkhead, Jr., Elizabeth Birkhead, Fran. Birkhead, Henry Child, John Timmons [Simmons?], Benson Bond, Margtt. Timmons [Simmons?], Richard Johns, Abra. Johns, Joseph Birkhead, Margtt. Birkhead.

Joseph Hopkins, son of Gerrard and Margaret, m. 17th day of 6th month called August, 1727, to **Ann Chew**, dau. of John, deceased, and Elizabeth, both of Anne Arundel County, at Herring Creek. Witnesses: Ann Thomas, Henry Child, Richard Galloway, Jr., Margarett Richardson, Richard Galloway, Samuell Chew, Elizabeth Hill, Philip Hopkins, Samuell Chew, Samuell Harrison, Nath. Chew, Isaac Johns, Richard Johns, Gerrard Hopkins, Margarett Hopkins, Elizabeth Hall, Elihu Hall, Gerrard Hopkins, Jr., Sophia Galloway, Leaven Hill, Benjamin Chew, Sarah Harrison, Richard Richardson, Joseph Richardson, Elizabeth Birkhead, Nehemiah Birkhead, Francis Birkhead, Daniel Richardson, Richard Hall, Sarah Hall, Sarah Harrison, Mary Chew, William Richardson [last two names illegible].

Nathaniel Giles, of Baltimore County, m. 27th day of 1st month commonly called March, 1729, to **Elizabeth Welch**, widow, of Anne Arundel County, at West River.

QUAKER RECORDS OF SOUTHERN MARYLAND

Witnesses: Artridg Frankling, Rachel Giles, Richard Galloway, William Richardson, Peter Galloway, Artridg Franklin, Robert Frankling, Mary Talbott, Sarah Steward, Lucy [?] Talbott, Richard Welch, Elizabeth Wish [?], Joseph Galloway, Gerrard Hopkins, Richard Galloway (of Cumberstone), Sarah Galloway, Margtt. Richardson, Mary Thomas, Margtt. Hopkins, Sarah Coale, Hannah Foard, Elizabeth Galloway, Richard Galloway, Jr.

Samuel Wallis, son of Samuel, late of Calvert County, m. 23rd day of 2nd month called April, 1730, to **Cassandra Talbott**, dau. of John Talbott, late of Anne Arundel County, at West River. Witnesses: Henry Child, Wm. Richardson, Isaac Johns, Gered Hopkins, Richard Galloway, Jr., Joseph Galloway, James Elderton, Daniel Richardson, Nath. Richardson, Solomon Sparrow, Thomas Richardson, Richard Richardson, Joseph Richardson, Margt. Richardson, Mary Thomas, Margt. Hopkins, Hannah Ford, Mary Galloway, Margt. Cole, Elizabeth Galloway, Hannah Jenkinson, C. Benfield, Frances Benfield, Mary Talbott, Elizabeth Waters, Richard Galloway, Sarah Galloway, Artridge Frankling, Abraham Wallis, Sarah Steward, Atridge Frankling, Jr., Rachel Waters, George Harris.

Gerard Hopkins, Jr., of Anne Arundel County, m. 7th day of 3rd month called May, 1730, to **Mary Hall**, dau. of Richard, of Calvert County, at Herring Creek. Witnesses: Neh. Birckhead, Samuell Thomas, Jr., William Richardson, Daniell Richardson, Richard Johns (of Angelica), John Galloway, William Richardson, Jr., Elihu Hall, Henery Child, Casandare [Cassandra?] Coale, Mary Coale, Joseph Galloway, Samuell Gover, Mary Chew, Ann Thomas, Mary Chew, Elizabeth Birckhead, Elizabeth Gover, Elizabeth Gover, Gerrard Hopkins, Margt. Hopkins, Richard Hall, Mary Hall, Sarah Hall, Philip Hopkins, Elisha Hall, Richard Johns (of Fishing Creek), Isaac Johns, Ann Johne, Richard Johne, Levin Hill, Richard Johne, Samuel Chew (of Maidstone).

Richard Richardson, son of William and Margaret, m. 26th day of 3rd month commonly called May, 1730, to **Margaret Coale**, dau. of Willian and Elizabeth, deceased, both of Anne Arundel County, at West River. Witnesses: Ann Thomas, Margaret Thomas, Elizabeth Galloway, Ann Thomas, Elizabeth Richardson, Mary Galloway, Ann Galloway, Samuel Smith, Philip Hopkins, Joseph Yates, J. Richardson, Jr., John Coulston, Sophia Galloway, James Elderton, Nat. Rigbie, Casandra Rigbie, Gerrard Hopkins, Margaret Hopkins, Solomon Sparrow, Sarah Coale, Rebecca Richardson, Henery Child, Elizabeth Galloway, Jr., Elizabeth Wooden, Hanah Foard, Mary Richardson, Mary Thomas, Artridge Frankling, Peter Galloway, Joseph Cowman, William Richardson, Margaret Richardson, Joseph Richardson, Jr., Thomas Richardson, Sarah Galloway, William Coale, Daniel Richardson, Richard Galloway, Jr., Joseph Richardson, Joseph Hill, Sarah Hill, Nathan Richardson, William Richardson.

Edward Fell, of Baltimore County, m. 8th day of the month of October, 1730, to **Ann Thomas**, dau. of Samuel, of Anne Arundel County, at West River. Witnesses:

QUAKER MARRIAGES OF SOUTHERN MARYLAND

Sarah Galloway, Margt. Richardson, Rebekah Richardson, Ellen Fell, Elizabeth Galloway, Elizabeth Galloway, Anne Johns, Mary Galloway, Sarah Coale, Elizabeth Richardson, Elizabeth Crockett, Neh. Birkhead, Henry Child, William Richardson, Jr., Peter Galloway, Samuel Chew (of Maidstone), Jos: Cowman, John Rendell, Joseph Galloway, Richard Galloway (of Cumberstone), Daniell Richardson, Phillip Hopkins, Mary Thomas, Samuel Thomas, P: Thomas, John Thomas, William Fell, Elizabeth Snowden, Mary Galloway, Ann Thomas, Elizabeth Thomas, Joseph Richardson, Richard Richardson, John Galloway, Richard Johns.

Thomas Coale, of Baltimore County, m. 3rd day of the month called December, 1730, to **Mary Richardson**, dau. of Joseph, of Anne Arundel County, at West River. Witnesses: Margt. Richardson, Jos: Richardson, Jr., Elizabeth Richardson, Elizabeth Crockett, Mary Thomas, Mary Thomas, Margt. Hopkins, Margt. Richardson, Sarah Galloway, Sophia Galloway, Joseph Richardson, Richard Galloway, Jr., Sarah Richardson, Samuell Thomas, Jr., William Richardson, Sr., Gerrard Hopkins, Richard Galloway, Sarah Coale, Ann Fell, Jos: Richardson, Rebekah Richardson, Nathan Richardson, Margt. Thomas, P: Thomas, Richard Snowden, Jos: Snowden, Richard Richardson, Skipwith Coale, Cassandra Coale, Mary Coale, Edward Fell, Peter Galloway, Thomas Lane, Daniel Richardson.

Samuel Waters, Jr., son of Samuel and Jane, of Prince George's County, m. 4th day of 3rd month called May, 1732, **Artridge Frankling**, dau. of Robert, deceased, and Artridge, of Anne Arundel County, at West River. Witnesses: Margt. Richardson, Rebekah Richardson, Sophia Galloway, Elizabeth Galloway, Jr., Hanah Foard, Mary Parish, Margt. Hopkins, Mary Galloway, Elizabeth Crockett, Sarah Coale, Henry Child, Richard Galloway, Richard Galloway, Jr., William Foard, Jos: Richardson, William Coale, Phillip Hopkins, Thomas Richardson, Gerrard Hopkins, William Richardson, John Stewart, Jr., Artridg Frinklin, Richard Frinklin, John Frinklin, Jacob Frinklin, John Stewart, Elizabeth Warters, Mary Talbott, Isabell Frinklin, Lucy Talbott.

John Webster, of Baltimore County, m. 17th day of 2nd month called April, 1735, to **Mary Talbott**, of Anne Arundel County, at West River Meeting House. Witnesses: Sophia Galloway, Richard Galloway, Daniell Richardson, Jos. Watkins, E. Stringfellow, John Galloway, Jos. Galloway, Jr., William Thomas, Peter Galloway, Zachariah Maccubin, John Talbott, Edward Talbott, Nathan Richardson, Elizabeth Galloway, Mary Galloway, Ann Thomas, Margaret Thomas, Mary Chew, Richard Galloway, William Richardson, Gerrard Hopkins, Joseph Galloway, Sarah Watkins, ---- Watkins, Ann Watkins, Ann Galloway, Samuell Galloway, Sarah Stewart, J. Franklin, John Franklin, Sarah Cowman, Sarah Galloway, Mary Thomas, Margaret Richardson, Rebeckah Richardson, Elizabeth Galloway, Jr.

Nathan Richardson, son of William and Margrett, of Anne Arundel County, m. 30th day of 8th month, 1735, to **Elizabeth Crockett**, dau. of John and Mary, of Baltimore County, at their meeting house near Bush River in Baltimore County.

QUAKER RECORDS OF SOUTHERN MARYLAND

Witnesses: Martha Paca, Mary Galloway, Drucilla [Pricilla?] Paca, John Webster, Joshua Bond, Thomas Bond, Mary Webster, Edward Talbott, Frances Midelmore, Richard Richardson, John Crockett, Thomas Coale, Thomas Richardson, Aquilla Massey, William Dallam, Margrett Webster, James Isham, Richard Caswell, John Higginson, Mary Crockett, Gilbert Crockett, Agnes Crockett, Mary Crockett, Jr.
John Plummer, son of Francis Plummer of Prince George's County, m. **Rachell Miles**, dau. of Thomas Miles of Prince George's County, on 18th day of the month called May, 1736, at their meeting house. Witnesses: Sarah Coale, Eliner Duvall, Elizabeth Plummer, Elizabeth Duvall, Eliner Wells, Sarah Wells, Easter Hill, Mary Coale, Ruth Plummer, Ma. Plummer, Yates Plummer, Thomas Miles, William Coale, Samuell Duvall, John Lamar, Joseph Richardson, Maran Duvall, Samuell White, Benjamin White, Samuel Plummer, James Plummer, Jer. Plummer, Chs. Plummer, Gab. Plummer.
John Pierpont, son of Charles and Sidney, of Anne Arundel County, m. 10th day of 6th month called August, 1737, to **Ann Gassaway**, dau. of Nicholas and Elizabeth, of Anne Arundel County, at the meeting house near Elk Ridge in Anne Arundel County. Witnesses: Frans: Pairpoint, Nicholas Gassaway, Sidney Pairpoint, Cha;[?] Pairpoint, Elizabeth Richardson, Priscilla Dorsey, Margaret Richardson, Prudence Talbott, Elizabeth Talbott, Hannah Hammond, Vallin [?] Brown, Richard Richardson, Nathan Richardson, Caleb Dorsey, Jr., Edward Talbott, Thomas Colegate, Henry Pairpoint, Jr., Jos. Pairpoint, John Gassaway, Jr., Margt. Brown, Elizabeth Brown, Joshua Brown.
Jerom Plummer, m. 7th day of the month called June, 1737, to **Margaret Child, Jr.**, both of Anne Arundel County, at Herring Creek Meeting House. Witnesses: Samuel Harrison, Samuel Chew (of Wells?), Neh: Birckhead, Sarah Birckhead, Richard Hall, Joseph Richardson, Rebeckah Richardson, Richard Harrison, Gerrard Ball, Thomas Spigg [Sprigg], Philip Darnall, Henry Darnall, Ospon [?] Manner, Osborn Spigg [Sprigg], Thomas Harwood, Basil Waring, John Smith Prather, Henry Child, James Plummer, Micajah Plummer, Phebe Williams, Nathan Smith, William Wilson, Ruth Roberts, Rachel Wilson, Elizabeth Waters, Sarah Harrison, Sarah Lane.
Francis Pierpont, son of Charles, m. 19th day of 11th month called January, 1737, to **Sarah Richardson**, dau. of Joseph, both of Anne Arundel County, at their meeting house at West River. Witnesses: Joseph Galloway, Mary Chew, Elizabeth Chew, William Thomas, William Richardson, John Ijams, James Sanders, Jona. Rawlings, Richard Rawlings, Plummer Ijams, Rebekah Richardson, Daniell Richardson, Margt. Richardson, Thomas Coale, Sophia Galloway, Gerrard Hopkins, Margt. Hopkins, Joseph Cowman, Sarah Cowman, Elizabeth Coyl, Joseph Richardson, Mary Thomas, John Peirpoint, William Richardson, Sr., William Richardson, Jr., Phillip Richardson, Mary Galloway, Margt. Thomas, Sarah Galloway, Joseph Richardson.

QUAKER MARRIAGES OF SOUTHERN MARYLAND

Henry Hill, m. 14th day of November, 1738, to **Sarah Galloway,** both of Anne Arundel County, at the house of said Henry Hill. Witnesses: Mary Galloway, Margt. Hill, Ann Davidge, ELizabeth Chew, Samuell Ogle, Benjamin Tasker, Daniell Dulany, Betty Gilliss, Cassandra Giles, Joseph Cowman, Sarah Cowman, Thomas Sprigg, John Andrew, John Galloway, Edward Edwards, Sarah Giles, Henr: Mari: Dulany, Ann Tasker, Elizabeth Carpenter, Anne Tasker, James Sterling, Caleb Dorsey, Robert Davidge, Mary Chew, Thomas Ruley, Elizabeth Sprigg, Hannah Hill, Nathan Richardson, Richard Hill, Jr. Henry Hill, Jr., Henry Gilliss, Mary Moore, Rachel Moore, Safrettar [?] Moore, Morda. Moore, Gerrard Hopkins, Jr., Margt. Hopkins, Joseph Galloway, Benjamin Chew, Samuell Galloway, Sarah Hill, Mary Gilliss, Joseph Hill, Priscilla Dorsey, Elizabeth Hill, Mary Gilliss, Jr., Ezekiel Gilliss, Joseph Richardson, Rebekah Richardson, Daniel Richardson, Caleb Dorsey, Jr., Thomas Richardson.

Mordecai Moore, son of Richard, of Anne Arundel County, merchant, m. 9th day of 8th month, 1739, to **Elizabeth Coleman,** dau. of Joseph, of Prince George's County, Practitioner in Physick. Witnesses: Mary Sympson, Hanah Jenkinson, Joseph Cowman, Richard Galloway, Samuel Burgett, Anthony Beck, John Moss, Henry Perdue [Ferdue?], Richard Perdue [Ferdue?], Mary Hill, Mary Gillis, Ezekiel Gillis, Mary Gillis, Jr., Elizabeth Gillis, Ann Pead [Tead?], Jane Chambers, Elizabeth Chapman, Elizabeth Sprigg, Margt. Coleman, Fr. Warman, Deborah Hill, Mary Moore, Rachel Moore, Richard Hill, Richard Hill, Jr., Hannah Moore, Margt. Moore, Saphreateon Moore, Richard Moore, Thos: Moore, Chals: Moore.

Jerom Plummer, of Anne Arundel County, m. 11th day of 12th month commonly called February, 1741/2, to **Mary Harris,** of Anne Arundel County, at West River Meeting House. Witnesses: Joseph Richardson, Joseph Cowman, Joseph Galloway, Joseph Richardson, Daniel Richardson, Thomas Sprigg, Edward Ward, John Talbott, Edward Sprigg, William Richardson, Richard Richardson, Ann Harris, Sophia Galloway, Rebekah Richardson, Elizabeth Sprigg.

Richard Holland, son of Thomas, deceased, and Margaret, of Prince George's County, m. 14th day of 10th month, 1743, to **Ruth Plummer** dau. of Samuel and Sarah, of same county, at the meeting house in Prince George's County [Indian Spring]. Witnesses: Ann Plummer, Prisiller Plummer, Thomas Miles, George Parker, Mary Plummer, Mordecai Waters, William Piles, James Drane, Richard Piles, Samuel Plummer, Sr., Cassandri Holland, Mary Holland, Samuel Waters, Jr., Thomas Plummer, Joseph Plummer, Samuel Plummer, Jr., Yates Plummer, Ibeg. Plummer, George Plummer.

John Birckhead, of Anne Arundel County, m. 6th day of 12th month commonly called February, 1745/6, to **Christian Harris,** of Calvert County, at the house of John Wilkinson, in Calvert County. Witnesses: Richard Richardson, Aquila Johns, Joseph Richardson, Littleton Waters, Charles Grahame, Gerrard Ball, Philip Hopkins, Richard Hall, Henry Wilkinson, Benjamin Johns, Rachel Johns, Sarah Waters, William Harris, Jr., Priscilla Johns, Ann Birckhead, Elizabeth Harris,

QUAKER RECORDS OF SOUTHERN MARYLAND

Elizabeth Birckhead, Joseph Richardson, Rebekah Richardson, Elizabeth Hopkins, Richard Johns (of Angelica), Thomas Lingan, Samuel Robertson, Mary Richardson, John Wilkinson, Ann Wilkinson, Nehemiah Birckhead, Ann Richardson, Samuel Birckhead, Elizabeth Waters, Mathew Birckhead, Elizabeth Wilkinson, Mary Wilkinson, Anna Wilkinson, John Benjamin Wilkinson, William Richardson, Anna Harris.

Henry Hill, m. 12th day of 3rd month called May, 1748, to **Mary Thomas,** both of Anne Arundel County, at West River. Witnesses:Ann Harris, Margt. Johns, ---- Waring, Richard Johns (of Angelica), Thomas Sprigg, Joseph Richardson, Jr., Henry Gillis, John Weems [?], Margt. Talbott, Joseph Galloway, Joseph Cowman, John Talbott, Nathan Richardson, Richard Chew, Sophia Galloway, Frances Chew, Joseph Richardson, Daniel Richardson, Richard Thomas, Mary Hepburn [?], Mary Gillis, William ----, Elizabeth Sprigg, Betty Gillis, Nathan ----, Mary Crockett, Richard Richardson, Richard Richardson, [Jr.?], Joseph Hill, Philip Thomas, ---- Thomas, Sarah Hill, Margt. Richardson, Mary Thomas, Samuel Thomas, Jr., William Thomas, Philip Thomas, Jr., Elizabeth Thomas.

Joseph Galloway, m. 8th day of 6th month called August, 1749, to **Ann Harris,** both of Anne Arundel County, at West River Meeting House. Witnesses: William Coale, Jr., Samuel Coale, Richard Foard, Thomas Coale, Richard Thomas, P. Thomas, John Hepburn, John Talbott, Margt. Talbott, Thomas Sprigg, Nathl. Chew, Joseph Paris, John Ramsay, William Foard, Margaret Coale, Ann Coale, John Cowman, Benjamin Johns, Joseph Richardson, Rebekah Richardson, Joseph Hill, Gerrard Hopkins, Daniel Richardson, Philip Hopkins, Elizabeth Hopkins, Kensey Johns, Mary Thomas, Ann Thomas, Mary Hepburn, Margt. Richardson, Elizabeth Sprigg, William Thomas, John Thomas, Philip Thomas, Henry Hill, Gerrard Hopkins, Jr., Sarah Cowman, Joseph Cowman, Elizabeth Robertson, William Harris, Mary Plummer, Samuel Galloway, Richard Johns (of Angelica), Jerom Plummer, Samuel Robertson, Susanna Galloway, Ann Galloway, Ann Cowman, Mary Cowman, Joseph Galloway, Jr., Joseph Cowman, Jr., Daniel Robertson.

Johns Hopkins, m. 14th day of 9th month called November, 1749, to **Mary Crockett,** of Anne Arundel County, at West River. Witnesses: Joseph Galloway, Mary Owing, Ann Mersey, Elizabeth Sprigg, Gerrard Hopkins, Jr., Edward Sprigg, Margaret Hopkins, Mary Hopkins, Betty Gilliss, Henry Gilliss, Richard Johns, Joseph Cowman, Margt. Talbott, John Talbott, Joseph Richardson, Richard Richardson, Gerrard Hopkins, Margt. Richardson, Daniel Richardson, Philip Hopkins, Elizabeth Hopkins, Richard Richardson, Ann Richardson, Richard Hall, Sophia Galloway.

Israel Thompson, of Fairfax County, Virginia, m. 2nd day of 4th month called April, 1754, to **Ann Richardson,** of Frederick County, Maryland, at the Sandy Spring Meeting House in Frederick County. Witnesses: Basil Brook, Jonathan Massey, George Matthews, Edward Matthews, William Gates, John Bersher [?], Elizabeth

QUAKER MARRIAGES OF SOUTHERN MARYLAND

Walker, Sid [Lid?] Bell, Joseph Richardson, Ann Jeanes, Henry Boston [Bolton?], Elizabeth Thomas, Aquila Massey, Richard Thomas, James Brooke, Jr., Elizabeth Brooke, Sarah Richardson, Richard Waters, John Thomas, Roger Brooke, Phil: Thomas, Richard Brooke, Evan [?] Thomas, Edward Thompson, Joseph Richardson, Mary Wilkinson, Richard Johns, Deborah Brooke, Joseph Richardson, Samuel Richardson, Mary Thomas, Sophia Richardson, Samuel Thomas, Rachel Holland, Ann Holland, Sarah Holland, Elioner Owen, Aquilla Duvall, Sarah Duvall, Mary Aldrige, Ann Richardson, Sarah Richardson, Samuel Rogers, Thomas Davis, Jr., Jos. Gore [?], George Norman, Thomas Brooke.

Richard Richardson, of Anne Arundel County, m. 13th day of 8th month called August, 1754, to **Elizabeth Thomas**, at the house of Richard Snowden. Witnesses: Ann Hammond, Sarah Hopkins, John Hopkins, Gerrard Hopkins, Phil. Thomas, Evan Thomas, Jos. Cowman, Garrard Hopkins, Jr., Elizabeth Hall, Richard Johns, Samuel Snowden, Samuel Richardson, Philip Hopkins, John Thomas, Ann Crabb, Thomas Snowden, Margaret Contee, Sarah Thomas, Mary Snowden, Elizabeth Snowden, Elizabeth Thomas, Samuel Thomas, Elizabeth Cowman, Margaret Hopkins, Mary Hopkins, Ann Cowman, Joseph Richardson, Richard Snowden, Mary Hopkins, Sophiah Galloway, Samuel Thomas, Mary Thomas, Richard Thomas, John Cowman.

Joseph Cowman, of Anne Arundel County, m. 4th day of 4th month called April, 1754, to **Elizabeth Snowden**, dau. of Richard, at the house of Richard Snowden. Witnesses: Even [Evan] Thomas, Phil. Thomas, Elisha Harrison, Elizabeth Thomas, Elizabeth Thomas, Margarit Hopkins, Will. Thomas, Elizabeth Snowden, Elizabeth Thomas, Richard Thomas, Phil. Thomas, Gerrard Hopkins, Richard Thomas, Joseph Galloway, Samuel Snowden, Ann Cowman, John Cowman, John Snowden, Samuel Thomas, Samuel Galloway, Mary Snowden, Mary Thomas, John Thomas, Richard Snowden, Elizabeth Snowden, Mary Thomas, Thomas Snowden, Ann Crabb, Margaret Contee, Mary Hopkins, Tubman Lowes, Joseph Richardson, Henry Wright Crabb, John Contee, Adam Spencer, Gerrard Hopkins, Jr., Edmond Jenings, Johns Hopkins, Richard Brooke.

Philip Thomas, m. 30th day of 4th month called April, 1754, to **Ann Galloway**, both of Anne Arundel County, at West River. Witnesses: William Thomas, William Harris, Elizabeth Thomas, Rebekah Harris, Philip Thomas, Ann Thomas, Mary Plummer, William Tipple, Elizabeth Waring, Kensey Johns, Joseph Richardson, Rebekah Richardson, Sophia Galloway, Elizabeth Sprigg, Margaret Hopkins, Ann Cowman, Richard Richardson, Adam Spencer, Jr., Gerrard Hopkins, Samuel Robertson, Gerrard Hopkins, Daniel Richardson, James Maccubbin, Ann Galloway, Samuel Chew, Elizabeth Snowden, Phillip Hopkins, Sarah Chew, Mary Gassaway, Susanna Johns, Margaret Contee, Ann Johns, Joseph Cowman, Samuel Snowden, Margaret Johns, Philip Thomas, Joseph Galloway, John Cowman, Benjamin Harrison, Richard Thomas, John Thomas, Margaret Harris, Mary Thomas, Mary Hepburn, Elizabeth Snowden, Samuel Galloway, Richard Chew, John Hep-

QUAKER RECORDS OF SOUTHERN MARYLAND

burn, Jr., Mary Peisley, Catherine Payton, Richard Snowden, Anna Steward, John Hepburn, Sarah Robertson, Richard Johns.

Daniel Richardson, of Anne Arundel County, m. 12th day of 11th month called November, 1754, to **Margaret Hopkins**, dau. of Gerrard, at the house of Gerrard Hopkins. Witnesses: Rebekah Richardson, Elizabeth Hopkins, Elizabeth Sprigg, Richard Richardson, Thomas Sprigg, Mary Hopkins, Gerrard Hopkins, Jr., Sarah Hopkins, Phillip Hopkins, Johns Hopkins, Mary Hopkins, Joseph Hill, Gerrard Hopkins, Mary Hopkins, Joseph Richardson, Sophia Galloway, Sarah Hill, Elizabeth Hill, Cassandra Gaither, Martha Gambrill, Elenor Hood, Ruth Warfield, Anne Gambrill, Benjamin Gaither, Gass. Watkins, Thomas Richardson, Mary Wilkinson, William Hood, Anne Hammond, M. Gaither, Rachel Hopkins, Augt. Gambrill, Anne Hood, William Jiams [Ijams], Richard Sprigg, Edward Sprigg, Phillip Thomas, Jr., John Talbott, Ann Cowman, Ann Watkins, John Cowman, Rebekah Harris.

William Coale, of Baltimore County, m. 30th day of 12th month called December, 1756, to **Sarah Robertson**, of Calvert County, at the meeting house at Herring Creek. Witnesses: Sarah Ward, Phil. Thomas, Ann Harris, Sarah Harris, Sarah Birckhead, Neh. Birckhead, Mary Plummer, Rebekah Harris, C---- Birckhead, Georg Robertson, Nehemiah Birckhead, John Coale, Georg Robertson, Robert Ward, John Ward, William Coale, Samuel Robertson, Elizabeth Robertson, Elizabeth Ward, John Coale, Daniel Robertson, Sarah Sanders, Joseph Richardson, Sarah Gover, Mary Gover, John Cowman, Richard Johns, Elizabeth Sanders, Sarah Harrison, Susanna Harrison, Richard Hall, Neh. Birckhead, Jr., Elizabeth Sanders, Mary Harris, Elisha Harrison, Richard Richardson, William Robertson, Ri. Johns, John Birckhead, Henry Sanders, Richard Thomas.

John Cowman, of Anne Arundel County, m. 27th day of 9th month called Spetember, 1757, to **Sarah Hopkins**, dau. of Gerrard, of Anne Arundel County, at the house of Garrard Hopkins. Witnesses: Philip Hammond, Thomas Norris, Philip Coale, Edward Edwards, Joseph Hopkins, Richard Hopkins, John Wallis, Ezekiel Hopkins, John Hopkins, Jr., Benjamin Gaither, Edward Hall, Robert Harris, Richard Sprigg, Richard Snowden, Thomas Sprigg, Anna Mary Hammond, Ann Edwards, Rebekah Harris, Mary Wilkinson, Prissilla Ruley, Thomas Jones, Mary Gaither, Ann Hall, Elizabeth Richardson, Elizabeth Hall, John Thomas, Richard Thomas, Evan Thomas, Isaac Hall, Cornelus Garrison, Philip Thomas, Jr., Henry Sanders, Samuel Wallis, Thomas Richardson, Edward Sprigg, Sarah Cowman, Garrard Hopkins, Mary Hopkins, Mary Hopkins, Joseph Cowman, Elizabeth Hill, Elizabeth Hopkins, Margret Richardson, Elizabeth Cowman, Ann Cowman, Mary Gassaway, Mary Hopkins, Elizabeth Hopkins, Joseph Richardson, Rebekah Richardson, Johns Hopkins, Joseph Galloway, Richard Richardson, Thomas Gassaway, Elizabeth Sprigg.

QUAKER MARRIAGES OF SOUTHERN MARYLAND

Johns Hopkins, of Anne Arundel County, m.16th day of 2nd month called February, 1758, to **Elizabeth Thomas**, dau. of Samuel, at house of Samuel Thomas. Witnesses: Joseph Cowman, Mary Hopkins, Elizabeth Brooke, Evan Thomas, Richard Richardson, Samuel Snowden, Thomas Snowden, Samuel Thomas, Gerrard Hopkins, Sarah Richardson, John Snowden, Richard Thomas, John Thomas, Will [Witt?] Thomas, James Brooke, Roger Brook, Richard Brook, Basel Brook, John Cowman, Richard Thomas, William Richardson, Joseph Richardson.

Robert Pleasants, son of John, of Virginia, m. 7th day of 2nd month, 1760, to **Mary Hill**, widow of Henry Hill and dau. of Philip Thomas, of Maryland, at West River. Witnesses: Sophia Galloway, Richard Richardson, Mary Plummer, Joseph Cowman, Johns Hopkins, Samuell Waters, Yates Plummer, Mary Thomas, Joseph Galloway, John Thomas, John Waters, William Harris, Ann Hepburn, Joseph Richardson, Rebekah Richardson, William Thomas, Richard Thomas, John Thomas, Samuel Thomas, Mary Hepburn, Margret Thomas, Thomas Harris, John Cowman, Henry Wilson, Ann Harris, Rachel Plummer, Roger Brooke, Samuel Hopkins, Ann Richardson, Anna Steward, Mary Gassaway, Anna Robertson, Daniel Robertson, Sarah Harris, Elizabeth Hopkins, Robert Gover, Sarah Gover, Oliver Matthews, Ann Cowman, Ann More, Daniel Rawlings, Jr., Thomas Richardson, Rachel Hopkins.

John Harris, of Virginia, m. 11th day of 3rd month called March, 1760, to **Rachel Plummer**, dau. of Samuel and Sarah, of Prince George's County, at the meeting house in Prince George's County [Indian Springs]. Witnesses: Abraham Jones, Richard Richardson, Sarah Gover, Isaac Hague, Ann Richardson, Joseph West Hammond, Thomas Miles, Mahlon Janney, Margery Lyles, Rachel Jones, Susana Plummer, Joseph Richardson, Rebekah Richardson, Sarah Plummer, Ann Plummer, Jemima Plummer, Sarah Plummer, Zach. Lyles, John Thomas, Sarah Plummer, Ruth Holland, Cassandra Ballenger, Sarah Janney, Ursula Plummer, Joseph Plummer, Abraham Plummer, Elizabeth Plummer, Anna Plummer.

Isaac Webster, of Baltimore County, m. 1st day of 1st month called January, 1761, to **Sarah Richardson**, dau. of Joseph, of Frederick County, at Sandy Spring Meeting House. Witnesses: Thomas Riggs, Elisha Riggs, Samuel Brown [?], Charles Massey, Thomas Brooke, John Snowden, John Armitt, Jr., Basil Brooke, Joseph Hopkins, John Talbott, Richard Brooke, Samuel White, Jr., Roger Brooke, Joshua Warfield, James Brooke, Edward W---, Jr., Arnold Holland [?], Ephraim Bond [?], John Riggs, Joseph Richardson, Sarah Richardson, Sarah Plummer, Samuel Richardson, Samuel Thomas, Margrett Thomas, Evan Thomas, John Thomas, Richard Thomas.

Thomas Pleasants, of Goochland County, Virginia, m. 2nd day of 6th month called June, 1761, to **Elizabeth Brooke**, dau. of James, of Frederick County, Maryland, at Sandy Spring Meeting House. Witnesses: Roger Brooke, Richard Brooke, Basil Brooke, Thomas Brooke, James Brooke, Mary Brooke, Hannah Brooke, ---- [an illegible name due to part of page missing], Hannah Richardson, Samuel Chew,

QUAKER RECORDS OF SOUTHERN MARYLAND

Artridge Waters, Margret Mathews, Elizabeth Richardson, Samuel Richardson, John Thomas, Jr., John Snowden, Samuel Thomas, Samuel Waters, Richard Contee, Milcah Richardson, Hannah Richardson, Robert Ball [Bell?], Henry Snowden, Richard Snowden, Henry Writ Crabb, Samuel Thomas, Ann Crabb, John Thomas, Samuel Snowden, Joseph Richardson, Elizabeth Chew, Elizabeth Contee, Sarah Thomas, Elizabeth Beall, Richard Thomas, Evan Thomas, Richard Richardson.

Philip Gover, of Baltimore County, m. 11th day of 8th month called August, 1761, to **Mary Hopkins**, dau. of Gerrard, of Anne Arundel County, at the house of Gerrard Hopkins. Witnesses: Basil Brooke, Nathan Richardson, Richard Brooke, Jr., Joseph Hill Richardson, Thomas Richardson, Philip Hopkins, Richard Alexander [?] Contee, Joseph Elgar, Henry Snowden, Samuel Waters, Samuel Waters, Jr., Artridge Waters, Edward Edwards, Ann Edwards, Joseph Richardson, Rebekah Richardson, Mary Hopkins, Elizabeth Hopkins, Elizabeth Hopkins, Richard Richardson, Joseph Hopkins, Jr., Hosier Johns, Garrard Hopkins, Samuel Harris, Ezekiel Hopkins, Elizabeth Cowman, John Hopkins, Jr., Elizabeth Chew, Elizabeth Richardson, Joseph Cowman, Elizabeth Contee, Jane Contee, Philip Thomas, Jr., ---- [illegible name], Garrard Hopkins, Mary Hopkins, Garrard Hopkins, Jr., Margret Thomas, Sarah Cowman, Elizabeth Hopkins, Rachel Hopkins, Joanna Hopkins, Joseph Hopkins, Richard Hopkins, Johns Hopkins, Anna Hopkins, Elisha ----, John ----, Elizabeth ----, John C---- [all illegible].

Cornelius Garretson, of City of Annapolis, m. 1st day of 10th month called October, 1761, to **Prisiler Ruley**, at the house of Joseph Hill. Witnesses: Job [?] Richardson, ---- Richardson, [an illegible name], ---- Hopkins, ---- Richardson, Elizabeth Ruley, John Ruley, Michael Ruley, Joseph Hill, ---- Wilkinson [?], Mary Ruley, Richard Richardson, Joseph Cowman, Richard Sprigg, Joseph Hill Richardson, Jonas Green, Nathan Richardson, Mary Gillis, Milkey Gillis, Prissiler Gillis, Margret Gillis, John Cowman, John Gillis, William Paca, John Thompson, Joshua Francis, John Davige, Nathan Waters, J--- Hopkins, John Brice, Jr., Joshua Yates, [an illegible name], John Hepburn, Thomas Johnson, Jr., Robert Alexander, Charles Wallace, John Dividson, Beal Nicholas, Richard Hopkins, Joseph Johnson, Ann Catharine Green, Mary Cummings.

Moses Harris, of Virginia, m. 3rd day of 12th month called December, 1761, to **Elizabeth Plummer**, of Maryland, at the meeting house near West River. Witnesses: John Ward, Thomas Richardson, Joseph Richardson, Sarah Ward, Mary Gover, Rebekah Harris, Mary Wilkinson, Mary Moore, Charles Moore, Prisciler Lyles, Hannah Moore, Garrard Hopkins, Samuel Robertson, Philip Thomas, Jr., Sarah Gover, Jr., Robert Ward, Thomas Harris, Joseph Cowman, Lewis Griffith, Thomas Moore, Elizabeth Cowman, Ann Thomas, Ann Thomas, Jr., John Thomas, Jr., Robert Harris, Ursula Plummer, Abraham Plummer, Anna Plummer, Ann Plummer, Thomas Plummer, Mary Plummer, Joseph Richardson, Rebekah Richardson.

QUAKER MARRIAGES OF SOUTHERN MARYLAND

Thomas Richardson, m. 11th day of 2nd month called February, 1762, to **Milcah Gillis**, of Anne Arundel County, at the house of Mary Gillis. Witnesses: John Ruley, John Davige, Edward Dorsey, Elizabeth Sprigg, Mary Wilkinson, Prisciler Garrison, Elizabeth Richardson, Elizabeth Ruley, Cornelous Garrison, Joseph Cowman, William Paca, Richard Richardson, Thomas R----, Richard Sprigg, Nat. Waters, Robert Norris, Charles W----, Mary Gillis, John Gillis, Betty Dorsey, Prissilah Gillis, Margaret Gillis, Rebekah [?] Young, Joseph Richardson, Jr., Thomas Sprigg, Joseph Richardson.

Basil Brooke, of Frederick County, Maryland, m. on 1st day of 5th month called May, 1764, to **Elizabeth Hopkins**, dau. of Garrard, of Anne Arundel County, Maryland, at the house of Garrard Hopkins. Witnesses: Benjamin Gaither, John Thomas, Elizabeth Cowman, ---- [illegible name], Elizabeth Hopkins, Joseph Richardson, Rebekah Richardson, Elizabeth ----, Richard Richardson, Thomas Brooke, ---- [illegible name], Joseph Hopkins, ---- Hopkins, ----Hopkins, Richard Hopkins, Elisha Hopkins, Johns Hopkins, Garrard Hopkins, Mary Hopkins, Richard Brooke, Margret ----, Garrard Hopkins, Jr., Samuel Thomas, Philip Thomas, Ann Thomas, Jr., Ann Galloway, Allthea Smith, Philip Thomas (son of Henry?), Joseph Cowman, Samuel Snowden, Evan Thomas, John Thomas, Jr., Johns Hopkins, Jr., John Snowden, John Wilson, George Robertson, Philip Thomas, Jr., Joseph Elger, Philip Hopkins.

Evan Thomas, son of Samuel, of Frederick County, m. 26th day of 12th month called December, 1766, to **Rachel Hopkins**, dau. of Garrard, of Anne Arundel County, at Indian Spring. Witnesses: John Snowden, Philip Thomas, Samuel Harris, Jr., Mary Harris, Samuel Hopkins, Joseph Cowman, Ann Thomas, Jr., Mary Brooke, Johns Hopkins, Elisha Hopkins, John Thomas, Anna Hopkins, Bazel Brooke, Samuel Snowden, Thomas Snowden, John Thomas, Jr., Samuel Thomas, Garrard Hopkins, Mary Hopkins, Garrard Hopkins, Jr., Joseph Hopkins, Richard Hopkins, Joseph Pemberton, Richard Brooke, George Robertson, William Robertson, Samuel Buchanan, Samuel Robertson, Samuel Hopkins, Thomas Brooke, Philip Thomas, Richard Snowden, Jr., Resin Hammond, Mary Plummer, Ann Galloway, Sarah Rigbie, James Brooke, Jr., Margret Harris, John Plummer.

Joseph Pemberton, son of Israel, of City of Philadelphia, m. 2nd day of 6th month commonly called June, 1767, to **Ann Galloway**, dau. of Joseph, late of West River, Anne Arundel County, Maryland, deceased, at West River. Witnesses: Jacob Franklin, Jr., Benjamin Johns, Jr., Stephen Steward, Joseph Allien, John Steward, Jr., Nicholas Gassaway, Ann Thomas Pleasants, Mary Johns, Elizabeth Steward, Philip William Thomas, Samuel C. Morris, Benjamin Harrison, Kensey Johns, George Anthony Morris, Richard Thomas, Samuel Buchanan, Samuel Chew, Jr., John Hepburn, Jr., John Snowden, William Steuart, Sarah Norris, Rebecca Richardson, George Mason, Thomas Norris, Stephen Steward (Carpenter), Sarah Sanders, Elizabeth Sanders, Jr., Mary Robertson, John Plummer, John Thomas, Elizabeth Johns, Henrietta Hill, Elizabeth Sprigg, Dorothy Jordan, Susanna

QUAKER RECORDS OF SOUTHERN MARYLAND

Stewart, Thomas Sprigg, John Morton Jordan, Thomas Ringgold, Jr., Samuel Hepburn, John Galloway, Andrew Allen, Anthony Maxwell, Reuben Merewether, Robert Norris, John Nainby, Samuel Robertson, Jr., Samuel Meredith, Samuel Snowden, Elizabeth Cowman, Richard Cowman, Sarah Steward, Rachel Franklin, Mary Hepburn, Ann Hepburn, Artridge Allen, Gerrard Hopkins, Mary Franklin, Richard Hopkins, Jacob Franklin, William Norris, Jos: Pemberton, Philip Thomas, Ann Thomas, Jr., Ann Thomas, Sarah Rhoads, Charles Pemberton, Samuel Pleasants, Samuel Rhoads, Jr., Philip Thomas, Jr., William Harris, Rebekah Harris, Samuel Robertson, Joseph Galloway, Jos: Cowman, John Cowman, Joseph Smith, Susanna Johns, Abigail Smith, Ann Gill, Anna Steward, Mary Gassaway, Samuel Harris, Jr., William Thomas, Mary Ringgold, Mary Thomas, Ann Galloway, Mary Harris, Mary Ann Thomas, Anna Robertson.

Yate Plummer, of Anne Arundel County, m. 23rd day of 12th month called December, 1768, to **Artridge Waters**, dau. of Samuel, at Indian Spring. Witnesses: Thomas Snowden, Elizabeth Hopkins, Samuel Snowden, Johannah Hopkins, John Cowman, Richard Hopkins, John Snowden, George Robertson, William Robertson, Richard Crabb, Richard Snowden, Jr., Artridge Waters, Samuel Waters, Susanna Plummer, Robert Waters, Abraham Plummer, John Plummer, Ann Waters, Arnold Waters, Margret Mulikin, Jacob Waters, Samuel Waters, Joseph Richardson, Rebekah Richardson, Garrard Hopkins.

Richard Roberts, of City of Philadelphia, son of Richard, late of Calvert County, Maryland, m. 29th day of 5th month commonly called May, 1770, to **Mary Harris**, dau. of William, of Calvert County, at the Clifts Meeting House. Witnesses: John Talbott, Jr., Mary Talbott, Susannah Johns, Edward Clare [?], Gideon Dare, Alexander Christie, Gideon Dare, Joseph Talbott (of Joseph), John Lavile, Benjamin Talbott, Thomas Tounge [Tongue], Daniel Talbott, John Thomas, William Harris, George Harris, Rachel Robertson, Joseph Harris, Benjamin Harris, Richard Paran, Bitty Harris, Ann Johns, Stephen Steward, Joseph Pemberton, Elizabeth Johns, Moses Paran, Elizabeth Talbott, Jane Paran, Sarah Mackall, Benjamin Hance, Margaret Hance, Elizabeth Hance, Rebecca Harris, Francis Ransold [?], William Harris, Elizabeth Morgan, Samuel Harris, Jr., Allen Robert, Margret Harris, Elizabeth Harris, Elizabeth Tongue, Philip Thomas, John Plummer, Rebekah Harris, Sarah Steward.

Henry Wilson, Jr., son of Henry, of Baltimore County, m. 3rd day of 1st month commonly called January, 1771, to **Margrett Harris**, dau. of William, of Calvert County, at the Clifts Meeting House. Witnesses: Elizabeth Talbott, Sarah Allen, Joseph Talbott, Daniel Talbott, Jos: Talbott (of Jos.), Elizabeth Gantt, Benjamin Talbott, Mary Parker, Mary Beckett, Prissila Gantt, John Howard, Kensey Johns, Robert Brown, Ann Robertson, Elizabeth Harris, John Plummer, William Harris, Jr., Samuel Parran, Samuel Robertson, Mary Robertson, Sarah Howard, William Robertson, Rachel Robertson, Philip Thomas, Jr., Richard Cowman, Benjamin

QUAKER MARRIAGES OF SOUTHERN MARYLAND

Hance, William Harris [the 3rd?], Betty Harris, Elizabeth Johns, Richard Hopkins, John Talbott (of Jos.), Mary Talbott, Elizabeth Hance, Susanah Johns, William Harris, Samuel Harris, Rachel Wilson, Elizabeth Wilson, John Worthington, Philip Thomas, Ann Thomas, John Thomas, William Wilson, Samuel Wilson, Prissilla Gover.

William Robertson, son of Samuel, of Calvert County, deceased, m. 29th day of 3rd month called March, 1771, to **Elizabeth Crabb**, dau. of Henry Crabb, at Indian Spring Meeting House. Witnesses: Rachel Hopkins, Johns Hopkins, Richard Hopkins, Samuel Thomas ([of S.?], Joseph Cowman, Jr., Mary Harris [?], John Cowman, Joseph Baley, Elisha Hopkins, Margrett Waters, Samuel Hopkins, Ann Waters, Sarah Norris [?], Susanah Waters, John Crabb, Joseph Cowman, Samuel Thomas, Elizabeth Thomas, Elizabeth Snowden, John Plummer, Ann Snowden, Basel Brooke, Sarah Steward, Margrett Thomas, Mary Hopkins, John Thomas, Garrard Hopkins, Annamary Hopkins, Joseph Richardson, Rebekah Richardson, Margrett Contee, Elizabeth Cowman, Anna Robertson, George Robertson, Mary Robertson, Rachel Robertson, Richard Crabb, Ralph Crabb, Samuel Snowden, Johh Snowden, Jane Contee, Thomas Snowden.

Joseph Talbott ye 3rd of Calvert County, m. 3rd day of 3rd month commonly called March, 1772, to **Anna Plummer**, of Prince George's County, at the house of Sarah Plummer. Witnesses: Robert Ward, Robert Ward, Jr., Joseph Richardson, Rebekah Richardson, Susanna Williams, Elmer Lewen [?], Samuel Plummer, Jr., Susanna Plummer, Mary Talbott, Sarah Plummer, Anna Plummer, Benjamin Talbott, Abener [?] Plummer, Joseph Plummer, John Plummer, Sarah Plummer, Abraham Plummer, John Talbott, David Talbott, Ursula Plummer, Sarah Harris, Sarah Gardener, Ruth Allen, John Plummer, Jr.

John Plummer, of Anne Arundel County, m. 25th day of 12th month called December, 1772, to **Johannah Hopkins**, dau. of Garrard, at Indian Spring. Witnesses: Rezin Hammond, Nicholas Hopkins, Thomas Henry Hall, Samuel Hopkins, Arnold Walker, Elizabeth Hopkins, Elizabeth Hopkins, Sarah Steward, Betsey Steward, Mary Cowman, Elizabeth Thomas, Ann Snowden, Abraham Plummer, George Robertson, Ursula Plummer, Samuel Robertson, Elizabeth Robertson, Jr., Samuel Harris, Jr., Susanna Plummer, Joseph Cowman, Samuel Snowden, Joseph Cowman, Richard Richardson, Richard Snowden, Susanna Waters, Richard Crabb, Mary Plummer, Gerrard Hopkins, Richard Hopkins, Elisha Hopkins, William Harris, Philip Thomas, Ann Thomas, Jr., John Hopkins, John Thomas, Margret Thomas, Basel Brook, Joseph Hopkins, John Cowman, Rachel Thomas, Joseph Richardson, Rebekah Richardson, Evan Thomas.

George Robertson, of Frederick County, m. 2nd day of 2nd month called February, 1773, to **Susannah Waters**, of Prince George's County, at Indian Spring. Witnesses: Garrard Hopkins, Samuel Snowden, John Cowman, Richard Crabb, Richard Hopkins (of Gerrard), John Snowden, John Crabb, Richard Snowden, Thomas Snowden, Elisha Hall Hopkins, Jacob Holland, Joshua [?] Lelaland [?], John

QUAKER RECORDS OF SOUTHERN MARYLAND

Plummer, Mary Waters, Charity Waters, Josephas Waters, Margret Mulliken, Thomas Norris, Jr., Mary Norris, Ann Snowden, James Lyon, William Robertson, Anna Robertson, Samuel Waters, Thomas Waters, Arnold Waters, Elizabeth Robertson, William Norris.

Samuel Robertson, of Calvert County, m. 10th day of 2nd month called February, 1773, **Eleanor Lewing**, of Anne Arundel County, at the house of Robert Ward. Witnesses: William Robertson, Mary Robertson, Robert Ward, Elizabeth Ward, Samuel Robertson, Elenor Robertson, Thomas Belson [Balson?], James Lyon, James Stone, Nehemiah Birkhead, Mathew Birkhead, Frances Burkhead, John Balson [Belson?], Elizabeth Balson [Belson?], Ann Balson [Belson?], Sarah [?] Jones, Prisler Jones, Sarah Birkhead, William Ward, Joseph Richardson, Sarah Steward, John Steward, Elizabeth Ward, Mary Ward, Abraham Plummer, Daniel Talbott, Morgan Jones, Elizabeth Birkhead, Ralph Crabb, Sarah Plummer, Elizabeth Talbott, Robert Ward, Jr., Rachel Lyon, Mary Ward, Sarah Coale, Ann Ward, James Ward.

Richard Hopkins, son of Garrard, of Anne Arundel County, m. 23rd day of 12th month called December, 1774, to **Ann Snowden**, dau. of Samuel, of Prince George's County, at Indian Spring. Witnesses: Joseph Richardson, Samuel Hopkins, Elizabeth Hopkins, Joseph Cowman, Philip Hopkins, Jane Contee, John Thomas, John Cowman, Evan Thomas, John Plummer, Mary Cowman, Margret Hopkins, Susanna Hopkins, Mary Ann Thomas, Elizabeth Thomas, Philip Thomas, Samuel Thomas, Garrard Hopkins, Samuel Snowden, Margret Thomas, Garrard Hopkins, Jr., Elizabeth Snowden, Joseph Hopkins, Richard Snowden, Elisha Hopkins, John Snowden, Johns Hopkins, John Thomas, Thomas Snowden.

Johns Hopkins, Jr., son of Johns, of Anne Arundel County, m. 30th day of 5th month commonly called May, 1775, to **Elizabeth Harris**, dau. of William, of Calvert County, at the Clifts Meeting House. Witnesses: Rebekah Richardson, Margret Wilson, William Harris, Joseph Richardson, Henry Wilson, Jr., William Harris, Jr., Samuel Hopkins, Elisha Hopkins, Benjamin Harris, William Harris (of Chas.?), Betsey Harris, Richard Harris, Benjamin Harris, Jr., Arthur Harris, William Wilson, Jr., Elener Harris, Mary Talbott, John Talbott (of Jos.), Elizabeth Talbott, Susanna Ogg, Allesander [?] Ogg, Benjamin Johns (son of C--?), Richard Hance, David [?] Talbott, Johns Wells, Benjamin Talbott, Thomas Morgan, John Lavish [?], T--mr. [?] Fedlaine [?], Robert Brown, Arthur Skinner, Fredick [?] Skinner, Thomas Greenfield, Joseph Talbott, Elizabeth Talbott, Mary Johns, Margrett Hance, Allen Roberts, Kinsey Johns, Jane Levish [Livirb?], Betsey Johns, Rachell Harris.

Thomas Pearson, mariner, formerly of Kingdom of England, but now of Anne Arundel County, Maryland, m. 10th day of 8th month called August, 1775, to **Mary Gassaway**, widow, of Anne Arundel County, at West River Meeting House. Witnesses: Philip Thomas, Elisha Hopkins, Sarah Harrison, Richard Richardson,

QUAKER MARRIAGES OF SOUTHERN MARYLAND

Johnathan Selman, Elizabeth Selman, Thomas Sprigg, Ann Selman, Margret Selman, Benjamin Hanson, William Selman, Jr., William Murry, Samuel Hopkins, Thomas Gant, Jr., Jont. Selman, Jr., Ann Thomas Richardson, Salley Cowman, Joseph Cowman, John Cowman, John Cowman, Elizabeth Cowman, Sarah Cowman, Mary Cowman, Hannah Cowman, Gerrard Cowman, Joseph Galloway, Susanna Johns, Mary Johns, Philip Thomas, Jr., Ann Thomas, Jr., Elizabeth Sprigg, Mary Richardson, Joseph Richardson, Rebekah Richardson.

Samuel Thomas, son of Richard, of Frederick County, m. 31st day of 10th month called October, 1775, to **Mary Cowman**, dau. of John, of Anne Arundel County, at the house of John Cowman. Witnesses: Barbary Hall, Margery Hall, Sarah Odell, Philip Hopkins, Priscilla Harwood, Ann Hall, William Hall, 3rd, Thomas Henry Hall, Henry Hall, Richard Brooks, Samuel Cowman, Joseph Hopkins, Richard Hopkins, 2nd, Richard Richardson, Mary Richardson, Joseph Cowman, 2nd, Elisha Hopkins, Thomas Pearson, Elizabeth Hopkins [Jr.?], Mary Hopkins, Samuel Snowden, Samuel Hopkins, Gerrard Cowman, Sarah Cowman, Sarah Cowman, Margret Hopkins, Margret Hall, John Cowman, Sarah Cowman, Elizabeth Thomas, Gerrard Hopkins, Richard Thomas, Jr., Margret Thomas, Mary Pearson, Joseph Cowman, 3rd, John Thomas, John Cowman, Joseph Cowman, Gerrard Hopkins, Rachel Hopkins, Margaret Hopkins.

Elisha Hopkins, son of Garrard, of Anne Arundel County, m. 27th day of 6th month called June, 1777, to **Hannah Howell**, dau. of Isaac and Patience, of Philadelphia, at Indian Spring Meeting House. Witnesses: Joseph Hopkins, Richard Hopkins, Jacob Howell, Rachel Hopkins, Mary Gray, Isaac Howell, Patience Howell, Garrard Hopkins, Jr., Elizabeth Brooke, Rachel Thomas, Margrett Hopkins, Elizabeth Hopkins, Catharina Howell, Ann Fentham [?], Hannah Humphrey, Johns Hopkins, Jr., John Thomas, Evan Thomas, John Cowman, John Plummer, Nicholas Hopkins, Joseph Richardson, Joseph Cowman, Johns Hopkins, Rachel Hopkins, Mary Hopkins, Samuel Howell, Jr., Samuel Hopkins, Joseph Cowman, John Thomas, Philip Thomas, Ann Thomas, Mary Richardson, Samuel Eliott, John Richardson, Thomas Russell.

Gerard Hopkins, of Baltimore Town, joyner, son of Samuel, deceased, and Sarah, m. 19th day of 12th month, 1778, to **Rachel Harris**, widow, and dau. of Henry and Priscilla Wilson, of Harford County, at his house in Baltimore Town. Witnesses: Benkid Wilson, Nicholas Hopkins, Richard Hopkins, Richard Hopkins (of Gerrard), Gerrard Hopkins (of Richard), Benjamin Wilson, Samuel Snowden, Henry Wilson, Job Hunt, David Evans, John Brown, David Brown, Jane Humphry, Samuel Matthews, Sarah Hopkins, Jno. Hopkins, Philip Hopkins, Margt. Hunt, Elizabeth Hopkins, Cassandra Hopkins, Samuel Hopkins, Cathrine Hopkins, Joseph Hopkins, Henry Wilson, Jr., Margt. Wilson, Cassandra Wilson, Elizabeth Hopkins, Rebecah Hopkins, Rachel Hopkins, Sarah Hopkins, Rachel Hopkins.

Benjamin Hughes, son of Edward Hughes of Berks County, Pennsylvania, m. 26th day of 12th month, 1781, to **Elizabeth Boone**, dau. of Isaiah Boone of Maryland, at

QUAKER RECORDS OF SOUTHERN MARYLAND

Sandy Spring. Witnesses: Isaiah Boone, John Pancoast, Adin Pancoast, Mary Boone, William Pancoast, Mary Boone, Abigail Pancoast, Sarah Pancoast, Mary Pancoast, Margt. Thomas, Elizabeth Brooke, Sidney Hayward, Betsey Brooke, Mary Thomas, Mary Burnside, Ann Thomas, Evan Thomas, Basil Brooke, Joseph Gamble, Elizabeth Gamble, William Boone, Caleb Pancoast, Robert Pancoast, James Burnsides, Phillip Hopkins,, James Brooke, Gerrard Brooke, Samuel Thomas, 3rd, Richard Thomas, Jr., William Hayward, John Ford.

Isaac Williams, Jr., of Elk Ridge, Anne Arundel County, son of Isaac, of Baltimore Town, m. 31st day of 12th month, 1783, to **Mary Hayward**, dau. of William, of Elk Ridge, at a meeting in Elk Ridge. Witnesses: Nicholas Gassaway, Elias Ellicott, Benjamin Ellicott, Henry Reach, William Scott, William Hayward, Jr., John Peirpoint, Ann Peirpoint, Joseph Tayler, Jonus Dever, Benjamin Scott, Bazil Dever, Robert Cornthwait, James Shipley, Grace Cornthwait, Richard Scott, Deborah Peirpoint, Hannah Ellicott, Susana Shipley, Elizabeth Cornthwait, Phebe Stedman, Elizabeth Merrick, James Gillingham, Joshua Davis, William Hayward, Sidney Hayward, Elizabeth Hayward, Rachel Hayward, Rebecah Hayward, Lyda Williams, Faithfull Pierpoint, Ann Scott, Rachel Tayler, Elizabeth Ellicott, Ennion Williams, John Hayward, Martha Ellicott, William Hayward, Joseph Taylor, Henry Pierpoint, Joseph Pierpoint.

Joseph Cowman, son of John and Sarah, of Anne Arundel County, m. 23rd day of 2nd month called February, 1786, to **Mary Snowden**, dau. of Samuel and Elizabeth, of Prince George's County, at Indian Spring. Witnesses: Sarah Cowman, Jr., Henneritta Snowden, Gerrard Cowman, John Cowman, Samuel Snowden, Elizabeth Snowden, Philip Snowden, Samuel Snowden, Jr., John Cowman, Jr., Joseph Hopkins, Richard Hopkins (of Gerrard), Elisha Hopkins, John Snowden, Thomas Snowden, Sarah Cowman, Jr., Thomas Cowman, Margt. Hopkins, Elizabeth Hopkins, Hannah Hopkins, Jane Contee, Elizabeth Hopkins, Mary Snowden, Anna Warfield, Samuel Hopkins, Phillip Hopkins, Benjamin Wilson, Richard Hopkins, Edward Waters, Stephen Waters.

Elias Ellicott, of Baltimore County, m. 26th day of 4th month, 1786, to **Mary Thomas**, dau. of Evan, of Montgomery County, at Sandy Spring. Witnesses: John Ellicott, John Russell, Thomas Russell, John Belt, James Brooke, Gerard Brooke, Basil Brooke, George Chandlee, Samuel Peach, Elizabeth Brooke, Cassandra Ellicott, Sarah Ellicott, John Thomas, Basil Brooke, Mary Thomas, Deborah Brooke, Margaret Cowman, Mary Elliot, Deborah Chandlee, Sarah Russell, Mary Russell, Evan Thomas, Ann Thomas, George Ellicott, Benjamin Ellicott, Margaret Thomas.

James Gillingham, son of John, of Bucks County, Pennsylvania, m. 24th day of 5th month, 1786, to **Elizabeth Hayward**, dau. of William, of Anne Arundel County, at Elk Ridge. Witnesses: George Mathews, Joseph Evans, Deborah Pierpoint, Samuel Pierpoint, Mary Stewart, Hannah Ellicott, Mary Balderston, Benjamin Stedman,

QUAKER MARRIAGES OF SOUTHERN MARYLAND

William Hayward, Sidney Hayward, Rachel Hayward, William Hayward, Henry Pierpoint, Joseph Pierpoint, Bershaby Pierpoint, Rachel Schofield, George Ellicott, Ann Owings, Harry Dowey [Dorney?], William Dillwork, John Pierpoint, Ennion Williams, Benedict Pierpoint, Cassandra Ellicott, John Pierpoint, Phebe Stedman, John Ellicott, Martha Ellicott, Hannah Williams, Elizabeth Alibone [Allibone].

James Carey, of Baltimore Town, son of John, deceased, of Baltimore County, m. 6th day of 9th month, 1786, to **Martha Ellicott**, dau. of John, of Baltimore County, at Indian Spring in Anne Arundel County. Witnesses: John Ellicott, Casander Ellicott, Margaret Ellicott, Ellizabeth Ellicott, John Ellicott, Jr., George Ellicott, Benjamin Ellicott, Jenr. Ellicott, Sarah Ellicott, Nathl. Ellicott, Mary Ellicott, Samuel Godfrey, Rachel Ellicott, James Gillingham, William Hayward, Barsheba Pierpoint, Joseph Evans, Joseph Pierpoint, George Mathews, Daniel Lake, Elizabeth Gillingham, Mary Williams, Deborah Pierpoint, Elizabeth Allibone, Abraham Walker, Jr., John Haward, William Haward, William Waterhouse, Jacob Read, Henry Pierpoint, Nicholas Pierpoint, Ennion Williams, William Allibone.

William Gover, son of Robert, deceased, of Prince George's County, m. 28th day of 12th month, 1786, to **Sarah Cowman**, dau. of John Cowman, of Anne Arundel County, at Indian Spring. Witnesses: John Cowman, Elizabeth Gover, Joseph Cowman, Gerrard Cowman, John Cowman, Jr., Joseph Hopkins, Elisha Hopkins, Elizabeth Hopkins, Jr., Elizabeth Hopkins, Thomas Cowman, Patience Hopkins, Margaret Hopkins, Samuel Hopkins, Philip Hopkins, Richard Hopkins, Samuel Snowden, Philip Snowden, Samuel Snowden, Jr., Edward Waters, John Snowden, James Anderson.

Benjamin Allibone, of Elk Ridge, Anne Arundel County, m. 14th day of 2nd month, 1787, to **Phebe Stedman**, of same place, at Elk Ridge. Witnesses: Elizabeth Cornthwait, Robert Cornthwait, William Allibone, Amos Allibone, Benjamin Stedman, Benjamin Allibone, William Hayward, Larkin Read, Joshua Davis, Ruth Davis, Sarah Rogers, Rachel Hayward, Elizabeth Ellicott, Rebeckah Hayward, Ann Teall [?], Deborah Pierpoint, Anne Pierpoint, Hannah Williams, Lydia Williams, Mary Williams, Agness Williams, George Mathews, William Evans, Lewis Evans, William Hayward, Ennion Williams, John Hayward, Sidney Hayward, John Pierpoint, Elisha Gordon, Micajah Greenfield.

Philip Hopkins, of Anne Arundel County, m. 21st day of 3rd month, 1787, to **Mary Boone**, dau. of Isaiah, of Montgomery County, at Sandy Spring. Witnesses: Mordecai Boone, Evan Thomas, Elizabeth Brooke, Samuel Hopkins, Hesther Boone, Benjamin Hughes, Isaiah Boone, Margaret Hopkins, John Thomas, Basil Brooke, Elizabeth Brooke, Jr., Deborah Chandlee, James Brooke, Samuel Peach, Polly Brooke, Mary Thomas, Sally Brooke, Deborah Brooke, Ann Thomas, Margaret Brooke, Hannah Brooke, Sarah Thomas, Sarah Elliot, John Russell, John Elliot, Philip Thomas, Garrard Brooke, John Thomas (of Samuel), George F. Warfield, Joel Elliot, Samuel Thomnas (of Samuel).

QUAKER RECORDS OF SOUTHERN MARYLAND

George Mathiot, of Anne Arundel County, son of John, of Lancaster County, Pennsylvania, deceased, m. 31st day of 10th month, 1787, to **Ruth Davis,** dau. of Joshua, of Anne Arundel County, at Elk Ridge. Witnesses: Joshua Davis, Jane [Jone?] Davis, Hannah Underwood, Hannah Williams, Elizabeth Webill, Rachel Hayward, Rebeckah Hayward, Deborah Pierpoint, Sidney Hayward, Lydia Williams, Ennion Williams, Mary Williams, Phebe Allibone, Daniel Lake, John Hayward, James Hood, Thomas Fenton, Benjamin Allibone, James Gillingham, George Elliott, Robert Moore, John Elliott (of John), William Hayward, Jr., William Dillworth, Joseph Pierpoint, Henry Pierpoint, William Hayward, John Pierpoint.

Edward Waters (Watters), son of Samuel, of Prince George's County, m. 25th day of 12th month called December, 1788, to **Hannah Moore Snowden,** dau. of William Hopkins of Harford County, at Indian Spring. Witnesses: Gerrad Cowman, Geraad Hopkins, Gerard Hopkins, Philip Thomas (of John?), Jos. Cowman, P. H. Hopkins, Stephen Watters, Henry Watters, Sam Snowden, Rachel Husband, Susan Husbands, Elizabeth Hopkins, Samuel Snowden, Jr., Philip Snowden, Joseph Hopkins, Richard Hopkins, Elisha Hopkins, Margaret Hopkins, Jr., Margt. Hopkins, Henrietta Snowden, Elizabeth Hopkins, Elizabeth Snowden, Elizabeth Hopkins, Patience Hopkins, Elizabeth Hopkins, John Snowden, John Cowman, Thomas Snowden.

Gerrard Brooke, son of Bassel, m. 22nd day of 4th month, 1789, to **Margaret Thomas,** dau. of Richard, of Montgomery County, at Sandy Spring. Witnesses: Basil Brooke, Richard Thomas, Elizabeth Brooke, Samuel Thomas, Richard Thomas, Sarah Thomas, Deborah Brooke, James Brooke, William Thomas, Basil Brooke, William Robertson, John Thomas, Rachel Thomas, Thomas Pleasants, Eliza Brooke, James B. Pleasants, George Chandlee, Samuel Peach, Deborah Chandlee, Hannah Russel, John Elliot, Ann [?] Knott, Hannah Elliot, Thomas Brown, Thomas Knott, Jr., Jane Carl [?].

Jesse Tyson, of Baltimore County, son of Isaac, deceased, and Esther, of same place, m. 1st day of 4th month, 1790, to **Margaret Hopkins,** dau. of John, deceased, and Elizabeth, of Anne Arundel County, at Indian Spring. Witnesses: John Mason, John Tagart, Mary Ellicott, James Amoss, Phil H. Hopkins, William Amos, Polly Sappington, Patience Hopkins, Philip Snowden, John Cowman, Samuel Snowden, Gerrard Hopkins, Samuel Thomas, Gerrard Hopkins, Sarah Snowden, Richard Richardson, Elizabeth Hopkins, Sam Hopkins, Joseph Cowman, Margaret Cowman, Elizabeth Snowden, Ann Cowman, Elizabeth Hopkins, Elisha Tyson, Jacob Tyson, Nathan Tyson, Samuel Hopkins, Philip Hopkins, Elizabeth Hopkins, Gerard Hopkins, John Mitchel, Joseph Hopkins, Richard Hopkins, Elisha Hopkins, Sam Snowden, Margret Hopkins, John Cowman.

Thomas Poultney, son of Thomas and Elizabeth of Philadelphia, m. 21st day of 4th month called April, 1790, to **Ann Thomas,** dau. of Evan and Rachel of Montgomery

QUAKER MARRIAGES OF SOUTHERN MARYLAND

County, Maryland, at Sandy Spring. Witnesses: Evan Thomas, Mary Ellicott, John Thomas, Margt. Thomas, Elizabeth Brooke, Deborah Brooke, Deborah Thomas, Basil Brooke, Philip Thomas, Elias Ellicott, Rachel Schofield, Hannah Brooke, Dorothy Brooke, George Ellicott, Bassil Brooke, Jr., Samuel Peach, John Russel, Sarah Brooke, Richard Thomas, Jr., John Thomas, Deborah Chandlee, Sarah Elliot, Sarah Russell, Mary Russell, Joel Elliott, Eli Elliott.

George Ellicott, of Baltimore County, son of Andrew, of Berks County, Pennsylvania, m. 22nd day of 12th month, 1790, to **Elizabeth Brooke,** dau. of James, Jr., deceased, of Montgomery County, Maryland, at Sandy Spring Meeting House. Witnesses: Sarah Thomas, Gerard Brooke, Samuel Godfrey, Basil Brooke, Samuel Thomas, 3rd, Richard Thomas, Jr., Roger Brooke, Samuel Robertson, Ann Coates, Sarah Elliott, Deborah Thomas, Hannah Brooke, Margaret Brooke, Richard Thomas, John Thomas, Dorothy Brooke, Sarah Pleasants, James Brooke, Margaret Brooke, Mary Brooke, Cassandra Ellicott, Basil Brooke, John Ellicott, Benjamin Ellicott, Sarah Ellicott, Sarah Brooke, Mary Elliot, Hannah Russell, Hannah Elliot, Mary Russell, Sarah Robertson, Samuel Peach, Philip Thomas, John Elliot, John Russell, William Richardson, Joseph Jackson, Thomas Brown, James Driver [?].

Caleb Bentley, of Loudon County, Virginia, son of Joseph and Mary, of Chester County, Pennsylvania, m. 20th day of 4th month, 1791, to **Sarah Brooke,** dau. of Roger and Mary, of Montgomery County, Maryland, having announced their intentions to marry at Indian Spring in Anne Arundel County, were married at Sandy Spring in Montgomery County, Maryland. Witnesses: Thomas Moore, Jr., Hannah Russel, John Thomas, Evan Thomas, Samuel Peach, George Chandlee, John Russell, Hester Williams, William Thomas, Samuel Thomas, 3rd, Isaiah Boon, Joseph Jackson, John Elliot, Sarah Thomas, Henry Thomas, Mary Brooke, Jr., Samuel Brooke, Mary Brooke, Deborah Thomas, Hannah Brooke, Dorothy Brooke, Roger Brooke, Basil Brooke, Margt. Elgar, Sarah Farquhar, Ann Dorsey, Sarah Thomas, Elizabeth Brooke, Richard Thomas, Jr., James Brooke, Garrard Brooke, Ann Knott, Asa [Ann?] Moore, William H. Dorsey, Sarah Elliott, Basil Brooke, Jr., Margt. Thomas, Hannah Boon, Mary Sullivin.

Thomas Moore, Jr., of Loudoun County, Virginia, m. 21st day of 9th month, 1791, to **Mary Brooke, Jr.,** of Montgomery County, Maryland, having announced their intentions at Indian Spring in Anne Arundel County, were married at Sandy Spring in Montgomery County. Witnesses: Samuel Brooke, Basil Brooke, Sarah Bentley, Ann [Asa?] Moore, Elizabeth Moore, Jr., Roger Brooke, Elizabeth Brooke, Richard Thomas, Jr., Caleb Bentley, Basil Brooke, Jr., Garrard Brooke, Isaacar [Spencer?] Scholfield, John Thomas, Evan Thomas, Sarah Thomas, William Thomas, John Hough, Mahlon Janney, George Chandlee, Samuel Peach, John Thomas, Jr., John Elliot, Sarah Elliot, Mary Elliot, Mary Peach, John Russel, Hanah Boone, William Elliot, Samuel White, John Brown, John Price Gill, Mary Robertson, Sarah Robertson, Mary Russel, Sarah Thomas, Jane Smith, Thomas

QUAKER RECORDS OF SOUTHERN MARYLAND

Robertson, Ann Knott, Deborah Holland, Elizabeth Robertson, Susanah Holland, Hester Williams, Henneritta Thomas.

Philip Snowden, son of Samuel, of Prince George's County, m. 1st day of 12th month, 1791, to **Patience Hopkins,** dau. of Joseph, of Anne Arundel County, at Indian Spring. Witnesses: Samuel Snowden, Joseph Hopkins, Elizabeth Hopkins, Isaac Howell, Patience Howell, Richard Hopkins (of Gerrard), Elisha Hopkins, Samuel Snowden, Jr., Sarah Snowden, Henneritta Snowden, Gerrard Hopkins, Margt. Hopkins, Mary Gover, John Cowman, John C. Thomas, Elizabeth Hopkins, Jr., Elizabeth Hopkins, Mary Thomas, Elizabeth Cowman, Joseph Cowman, Jr., Isaac Howell Hopkins, Elizabeth Hopkins, John Cowman, Jr., Samuel Hopkins (of Johns), Philip Hopkins (of Johns), Philip H. Hopkins, Evan Hopkins, Steven Waters, July Waters.

Thomas Norris, son of Thomas, m. 22nd day of 11th month called November, 1792, to **Ann Cowman,** dau. of John and Sarah, of Anne Arundel County, at Indian Spring. Witnesses: Philip Hopkins (of Johns), Gerrard Hopkins (of Richard), William Hopkins (of Johns), Joseph Hopkins (of Johns), Samuel Hopkins, Maria Hopkins, John Cowman, Joseph Cowman, Jr., Peggy [?] Cowman, Mary Norris, John Cowman, Jr., Richard Harrison, Joseph Hopkins, Richard Hopkins (of Gerrard), Thomas Cowman, Elisha Hopkins, Maria Plummer, Jr., Elizabeth Hopkins, Edward Waters, Jerom Plummer, Samuel Snowden, Philip Snowden, Samuel Snowden, Jr., Samuel Hopkins, Gerrard Plummer, Elizabeth Hopkins, Mary Hopkins, Ann Hopkins, Sarah Snowden, Gerrard Hopkins, Susanah Boone.

Isaac McPherson, of Alexanderia, Virginia, son of Daniel, deceased, and Mary, m. 2nd day of 1st month, 1793, to **Hannah Ellicott,** of Baltimore County, dau. of John and Sarah, deceased, having announced their intentions to marry at Indian Spring, were married at Elk Ridge. Witnesses: Joseph Pierpoint, John Cod, Nicholas Gassaway, John Gary [?], Robert Heard [?], Thomas Poltney, James Gillingham, Joseph Liston, Joseoh Heston, Joseph Hough, Joseph Atkinson, Ruth Matthiott, Thomas Mendenall, Barth Balderston, William Clark, Dennis Read, Hanah Williams, Evan Hopkins, Samuel Hopkins, William Hayward, Sidney Hayward, Ennion Williams, Ann Pierpoint, Deborah Pierpoint, Elizabeth Patrick, Mart. Porie [?], Rebeckah Hayward, Robert Hough, Samuel Smith, John Pierpoint, John Ellicott, John Ellicott (of John), William McPherson, Sarah Ellicott, James Ellicott, Elias Ellicott, George Ellicott, Benjamin Ellicott, James Casey [Carey?], James Ellicott, Andrew Ellicott, Jr., Samuel Godfrey, Ann Evans, Rachel Evans, Marth [sic] Evans, Keziah Hayward, Elizabeth Hopkins, Francis Martain, Ann Liston, Rachel Hayward, Sarah Hopkins, Joshua Harvey, George Mathiat, Johns Hopkins, Henry Hopkins, Cha. Shomaker.

Bernard Gilpin, son of Gidion and Sarah, of Delaware County, Pennsylvania, m. 1st day of 8th month, 1793, to **Sarah Thomas,** dau. of Richard, of Montgomery County, Maryland, at Sandy Spring. Witnesses: Richard Thomas, Jr., Deborah

QUAKER MARRIAGES OF SOUTHERN MARYLAND

Thomas, Allen Gilpin, William Thomas, Margaret Brooke, Hannah Gilpin, Leydia Gilpin, Samuel Thomas, 3rd, Gidion Gilpin, Richard Thomas, John Thomas, Garrard Brooke, Roger Brooke, Basil Brooke, Margarit Brooke, Margt. Thomas, Deborah Stabler, Hanah Brooke, Elizabeth Brooke, Henneritta Pleasant, Samuel Brooke, John Thomas (of Samuel), Sarah Thomas, Basil Brooke, Caleb Bentley, Roger Brooke, Evan Thomas, William Stabler, George Chandlee, Edward Waters, Sarah Robertson, Hanah More Waters, Samuel Robertson, Ann Coats, Elizabeth Thomas, Joel Elliott, Sarah Russell, Samuel Lane, Evan Thomas, Thomas Brown, Thomas Robertson, Ann Knott, Margt. Elliott, Mary Russell, Heneritta Johnson.

Joseph Jackson, of Montgomery County, son of Isaac, m. 27th day of 2nd month called February, 1794, to **Gulielma Maria Waters**, dau. of Samuel, of Prince George's County, at Indian Spring. Witnesses: Edward Waters, John Waters, Samuel Waters, Jacob Waters, Samuel Snowden, Elizabeth Hepburn, Jr., John Cowman, Joseph Hopkins, Richard Hopkins (of Jno.?), Mary Hopkins, Elizabeth Cowman, Hennrietta Snowden, Elizabeth Hopkins, Margaret Hopkins, Elisha Hopkins, Philip Hopkins, Samuel Hopkins, Joseph Cowman, Philip Snowden.

Isaac Briggs, painter [printer?], of Georgetown, Maryland, son of Samuel and Mary, of Philadelphia, m. 27th day of 8th month, 1794, to **Hannah Brooke**, at Sandy Spring. Witnesses: Mary Brooke, Samuel Brooke, Sarah Bently, Dorothy Brooke, Mary Briggs, Samuel Briggs, Jr., Sarah Gilpin, Roger Brooke, Gerrard Brooke, Thomas Harris, Jr., Anthony Zinkes [Zirkes?], Caleb Bentley, James Brooke, Basil Brooke, Richard Thomas, Elizabeth Thomas, Elizabeth Patrick, Mary Rusill, William Stabler, Joel Eliott, Joseph Jackson, July Jackson, Thomas Brown, Bernard Gilpin, William Thomas, Patience Hopkins, Deborah Hopkins.

John Janney, of Alexandria, Virginia, son of Joseph, deceased, and Hannah, of Loudon County, Virginia, m. 26th day of 3rd month, 1795, to **Elizabeth Hopkins**, dau. of Johns, deceased, and Elizabeth, of Anne Arundel County, at Indian Spring. Witnesses: Joseph Cowman, Jr., Mary Cowman, Gerrard Cowman, Sarah Snowden, John Cowman, Jr., Samuel Hopkins Snowden, Phillip Snowden, Samuel Snowden, Jr., Elizabeth Hopkins, Jr., Anne Hopkins, Rebeckah Janney, Samuel Hopkins, Phillip Hopkins, Gerrard Hopkins, Joseph Hopkins, Richard Hopkins (of Gerrard), Elisha Hopkins, Evan Hopkins, Hester Boone, Elizabeth Hopkins, Elizabeth Hopkins, Ann Hopkins, Mary Cowman, Elizabeth Cowman, Margaret Hopkins.

Gerard Hopkins, son of Johns and Elizabeth, of Anne Arundel County, m. 6th day of 4th month, 1796, to **Dorothy Brooke**, dau. of Roger and Mary, of Montgomery County, at Sandy Spring. Witnesses: Anne Ayton, Esther Williams, Elizabeth Thomas (of Samuel), Mary Thomas, Henrietta Thomas, Elizabeth Loudon, Hannah Davis, Mary Sullivan, Sarah Milles [Miller?], Elleanor Butler, Roger Brooke, Evan Hopkins, Richard Thomas, Jr., Thomas Moore, Jr., Caleb Bentley, J. Briggs, James Brooks, Gerard Brooks, Basil Brooke, John Thomas, William Thomas, Mary Brooke, Mary Moore, Margaret Brooke, Sary Bentley, Elizabeth Thomas, Samuel

QUAKER RECORDS OF SOUTHERN MARYLAND

Brooke, Ann Hopkins, Deborah Stabler, Rachel Hopkins, Mary Hopkins, Sarah Gilpin, Margarett Brooke, Elizabeth Brown, Margarett Thomas, Mary Briggs, Elizabeth Thomas, Susanna Robertson, Sarah Robertson, Sarah Gassigues [?], Mary Kinsey, Elizabeth Robertson, Susanna Boon, Mary Bye [Byl?], George Ray, Enoch Frances, Henry Saders [Suders?], John Sullivan, Benjamin Lyon, Isaac Kinsey, Elijah Turner, William Stabler, Evan Thomas, Bernard Gilpin, Andrew Ellicott, Benjamin Ellicott, Thomas Thomas, 3rd, Ignatius Waters, Samuel Robertson, 3rd, John Waters.

Elisha Hopkins, son of Gerrard, of Anne Arundel County, deceased, m. 24th day of 11th month called November, 1796, to **Sarah Snowden**, dau. of Samuel, of Prince George's County, at Indian Spring. Witnesses: Margaret Hopkins, Rachel Hopkins, Ann Hopkins, Jery Plummer, Garrard Hopkins (of Richard), Hannah Hopkins, Samuel Hopkins, Mary Hopkins, John Cowman, Jr., Philip Hopkins, Samuel Snowden, Jr., Isaac Hopkins, Mary Hopkins, Elizabeth Hopkins, John Cowman, Elizabeth Snowden, Elizabeth Hopkins, Hanah Moor Waters, Margt. Cowman, Sally Thomas, Samuel Snowden, Jr., Ann Hopkins, Henneritta Snowden, Joseph Hopkins (of Gerrard), Phillip Snowden, Hester Boon, Gerrard Hopkins, Martha Hall Mullikin, Elizabeth Duckett, Mary Waters, Samuel Waters.

Samuel Snowden, of Prince George's County, son of Samuel, m. 1st day of 12 month, 1796, to **Elizabeth Cowman**, dau. of John, of Anne Arundel County, at Indian Spring. Witnesses: Sam: Hopkins, Isaac Hopkins, Samuel Hopkins, Elizabeth Snowden, Gerd. Plummer, Rachel Hopkins, Hanah Hopkins, Robert Baden, Garrard Hopkins, Mary Hopkins, Hetty Boone, Mary Hopkins, Phillr: Hopkins, Ann Hopkins, Samuel Waters, Susan Janney, Jacob Waters, Samuel Snowden, John Cowman, Ann Hopkins, Margt. Cowman, Sarah Hopkins, Henneritta Snowden, Phillip Snowden, Joseph Cowman, Mary Cowman, John Cowman, Joseph Hopkins, Elizabeth Hopkins, Elisha Hopkins, Sarah Thomas, Thomas Harris (of T.), Maria Hopkins, Elizabeth Hopkins, Mary Peach, William Gover, Garrard Hopkins, Margt. Hopkins, James Brooke.

James Brooke, son of Basil, m. 21st day of 6th month, 1797, to **Hester Boone**, dau. of Isaiah and Hannah, at their meeting house in Montgomery County. Witnesses: Mary Brooke, Margt. Thomas, Rachel Thomas, Deborah Thomas, Margt. Brooke, Susanah Boone, Hannah Hughes, Basil Brooke, Benjamin Hughes, Mordica Boone, Isaiah Boone, Hanah Boone, Gerrard Brooke, Sarah Bentley, Hannah Briggs, Sally Thomas, Maria Thomas, Henney Thomas, Elizabeth Thomas, Elizabeth Thomas, Jr., Richard Thomas, Jr., Caleb Bentley, Richard Thomas, John Thomas, Evan Thomas, Roger Brooke, William Thomas, Thomas Moore, J. Briggs, Samuel Thomas, Bernard Gilpin, Mary Thomas, Susanah Robertson, Sarah Robertson, Sarah Robertson, Jr., Benjamin Lyon, Thomas Wright, Ann Robertson, John Howard, Elizabeth Lowden, William Stabler.

QUAKER MARRIAGES OF SOUTHERN MARYLAND

Isaac Tyson (Tison), of City of Baltimore, son of Elisha and Mary, m. 8th day of 11th month, 1797, to **Elizabeth Thomas**, dau. of Evan and Rachel, of Montgomery County, at their meeting house at Sandy Spring. Witnesses: Mary Hopkins, Basil Brooke, Gerrard Hopkins, Gerrard Brooke, Mary Brooke, Mary Tyson, Phill. Thomas, Lucretia Tyson, John Thomas, Margt. Drian [?], Elisha Tyson, Evan Thomas, Rachel Thomas, Hannah Briggs, Sarah Bentley, Margaret Brooke, Salley Thomas, Sarah Gilpin, Sarah Robinson, Henritta Thomas, Elizabeth Robertson, Sarah Kinsey, July Jackson, Richard Thomas, Jr., William Stabler, Samuel Brooke, Evan Hopkins, Bernard Gilpin, Isaac Briggs, Roger Brooke, Caleb Bentley, Thomas Wright, John Thomas, 3rd, Isaac Kinsey, William Robertson, James Kinsey, Thomas Moore, Jr.

Joseph Thornburgh, of City of Baltimore, m. 21st day of 11th month, 1798, to **Cassandra Ellicott**, of Baltimore County, at their meeting house at Elk Ridge near Ellicott's Lower Mills in Anne Arundel County. Witnesses: John Ellicott, Thomas Thornburgh, Phebe Thornburgh, Andrew Ellicott, John McKim, Mary McKim, Garrard Hopkins, Rachel Hopkins, Martha Cary [Casy?], Ester Ellicott, Judith Ellicott, Rachel Evans, Joseph Evans, Ann Evans, James Ellicott, William Hayward, Deborah Peripoint, Ann Peripoint, Walter Peripoint, Jacob Read, Joseph Peripbint, John Hopkins, Elizabeth Hopkins, Elias Ellicott, Mary Ellicott, Jonathan Ellicott, Sarah Ellicott, Sarah Ellicott, Ennion Williams, Sarah Hopkins, Deborah Thornburgh, Elizabeth Thornburgh, Margarett Thornburgh, Sally Thornburgh, Sarah Morthland, Sarah Rich, Joseph Brown, Benjamin Rich, George Ellicott, Hannah Williams, Robert Miller, Robert Lyon, Edward Davison [?], Andrew Ellicott, Rachel Hayward.

CLIFTS MONTHLY MEETING REGISTER, 1662-1782
BIRTHS:
Rebecka Billingsley, dau. of Francis and Susanna, b. 23rd day of 3rd month, 1677.
Benjamin Lawrence, son of Benjamin, b. 13th day of 3rd month, 1677.
Elizabeth Lawrence, dau. of Benjamin, b. 25th day of 12th month, 1678.
John Astin, son of John and Hannah, b. 15th day of 1st month, 1701/2.
Abell Royston, son of George and Rebeckah, b. 5th day of 11th month, 1686/7.
Rebeckah Royston, dau. of George and Rebeckah, b. 9th day of 2nd month, 1689.
George Royston, son of George and Rebeckah, b. 14th day of 5th month, 1691.
John Royston, son of George and Rebeckah, b. 1st day of 3rd month, 1694.
Sarah Meares, dau. of William, b. 27th day of 12th month, 1680/1.
Hannah Meares, 2nd dau. of William, b. 21st day of 11th month, 1682/3.

QUAKER RECORDS OF SOUTHERN MARYLAND

BURIALLS:
Francis Billingsley, d. 10th day of 6th month, 1695 and was bur. in Friends burying place at ye Clifts.
Hannah Astin, wife of John, was bur. in Friends burying place at ye Clifts ye 19th day of 2nd month, 1702.
George Royston, father of this family, was bur. in ye Friends burying ground at the Clifts ye -- day of ----.
George Royston, son of the above George, was bur. by his father ye -- day of ----.
Thomas Simons, Sr., d. 11th day of 1st month, 1697/98.
BIRTHS:
Susanah Pardo, dau. of John and Sarah, b. 24th day of 1st month, 1662/3.
John Pardo, son of John and Sarah, b. 22nd day of 10th month, 1664.
Rebecka Pardo, dau. of John and Sarah, b. 6th day of 9th month, 1667/8.
Sarah Pardo, dau. of John and Sarah, b. 3rd day of 1st month, 1670.
Hester Pardo, dau. of John and Sarah, b. 1st day of 3rd month, 1673.
Joseph Pardo, son of John and Sarah, b. 20th day of 11th month, 1678.
John Pardo, son of John Pardo, Jr. and Mary his wife, b. 27th day of 7th month, 1690.
Peter Pardo, son of John Pardo by Louse [Lucy] his 2nd wife, b. 25th day of 11th month, 1701/2.
Joseph Pardo, son of John and Lucy, b. 27th day of 11th month, 1703/4.
Sarah Pardo, dau. of John and Lucy, b. 13th of 7th month, 1706.
BURYALLS:
John Pardo, father of this family, was bur. in Friends burying ground at the Clifts the -- day of ----.
Joseph Pardo, son of John, was bur. by his father the -- day of ----.
Sarah Pardo, wife of the above John and mother of this family, was bur. by her husband the 22nd day of 8th month, 1697.
BIRTHS:
Berenton Pardo, son of John and Lucy, b. 30th day of 9th month, 1709.
Mary Pardo, dau. of John and Lucy, b. 21st day of 6th month, 1712.
Lucy Pardoe, mother of this family, d. 26th day of 11th month, 1744/5 and lies bur. at the old grave yard at Royston's.
Darrington Pardoe, d. 1747.
William Harris, son of William and Elizabeth, b. 4th day of 10th month, 1671.
Christian Harris, dau. of William and Elizabeth, b. 30th day of 10th month, 1674.
Richard Harris, son of William and Elizabeth, b. 28th day of 8th month, 1677.
George Harris, son of William and Elizabeth, b. 27th day of 12th month, 1679.
Joseph Harris, son of William and Elizabeth, b. 16th day of 10th month, 1682.

CLIFTS MONTHLY MEETING REGISTER, 1662 - 1782

Benjamin Harris, son of William and Elizabeth, b. 18th day of 8th month, 1685.
William Harris, son of William and Elizabeth, b. 10th day of 12th month, 1688.
Ellinore Harris, dau. of William and Elizabeth, b. 15th day of 2nd month, 1691.
Mary Harris, only dau. of above Richard, b. last day of 3rd month, 1702, 4 months and 33 days after the burying of her father.
BURYALLS:
William Harris, son of William, d. 21st day of 1st month, 1694, bur. at Clifts.
William Harris, father of this family, bur. in Friends burying ground in ---- London, 21st day of 9th month, 1697.
Elizabeth, wife of said William and mother of this family, bur. in Friends burying ground at the Clifts, 1st day of 11th month, 1701/2.
Richard Harris, son of William, bur. at Clifts, 18th day of 11th month, 1701/2.
BIRTHS:
Richard Johns, b. 29th day of 1st month, 1649, being the 5th day of the week.
Abraham Johns, eldest son of Richard and Elizabeth, b. 24th day of 5th month, 1677.
Aquilla Johns, second son of Richard and Elizabeth, b. 30th day of 7th month, 1679.
Priscilla Johns, eldest dau. of Richard and Elizabeth, b. 21st day of 1st month, 1681/2.
Margrett Johns, second dau. of Richard and Elizabeth, b. 11th day of 8th month, 1683.
Aquilla Johns, 3rd son of Richard and Elizabeth, b. 5th day of 12th month, 1684/5.
Richard Johns, 4th son of Richard and Elizabeth, b. 4th day of 2nd month, 1687.
Kensey Johns, 5th son of Richard and Elizabeth, b. 12th day of 5th month, 1689.
Isaac Johns, 6th son of Richard and Elizabeth, b. 10th day of 3rd month, 1692.
Elizabeth Johns, 3rd dau. of Richard and Elizabeth, b. 26th day of 3rd month, 1694.
BURYALLS:
Aquilla Johns, second son of Richard, bur. in the Clifts grave yard, 11th day of 3rd month, 1682.
Abraham Johns, first son of Richard, d. 9th day of 10th month, 1707, and bur. in ye new grave yard at Clifts.
Aquilla Johns, 3rd son of Richard, d. 16th day of 11th month, 1709, and bur. by his brother Abraham in Clifts grave yard.
Elizabeth Johns, the dear and well beloved virtuous wife of Richard and mother of this family, d. 1st day of 12th month, 1715/6 at a quarter past 8 in the morning.
Richard Johns, father of this family, d. 16th day of 10th month, 1717, about 4 o'clock in the afternoon.
Richard Johns, 4th son, d. 16th day of 6th month, 1719.
Priscilla Johns, eldest dau., d. 1st day of 2nd month, 1725.
Kensey Johns, 5th son, d. 2nd day of 2nd month, 1729.

QUAKER RECORDS OF SOUTHERN MARYLAND

Anne Johns, wife of Isaac, d. 29th day of 9th month, 1728.
Isaac Johns, 6th son, d. 17th day of 12th month, 1733/4.
BIRTHS:
Arthur Harris, first born son of George and Anna, b. 6th day of 11th month, 1704/5.
Elizabeth Harris, dau. of George and Anna, b. 18th day of 1st month, 1706/7.
Anne Harris, dau. of George and Anna, b. 21st day of 5th month, 1709.
Mary Harris, dau. of George and Anna, b. 13th day of 9th month, 1711.
Sarah Harris, dau. of George and Anna, b. 25th day of 7th month, 1714.
William Harris, son of George and Anna, b. 29th day of 11th month, 1716.
Ann Harris, ye 2nd dau. of that name of George and Anna, b. 25th day of 11th month, 2nd week, 1719.
Samuel Harris, 3rd son of George and Anna, b. 14th day of 12th month, 1720/1.
Rachel Harris, dau. of George and Anna, b. 31st day of 1st month, 1723.
George Harris, 4th son of George and Anna, b. 19th day of 5th month, 1725.
Rebekah Harris, dau. of George and Anna, b. 7th day of 5th month, 1727.
Anna Harris, dau. of Arthur and Elizabeth, and granddaughter of George and Anna Harris, b. 22nd day of 6th month, 1728.
BURYALLS:
Anne Harris, 2nd dau. of George and Anna, d. 2nd day of 9th month, 1715, and bur. 4th day of same month.
Arthur Harris, first born of George and Anna, d. 13th day of 1st month, 1728/9, and bur. the 16th at Clifts.
Anna Harris, ye beloved wife of George Harris and mother of this family, d. 11th day of 11th month, 1737/8, and bur. the 16th near the Clifts, about 52nd year of her age.
George Harris, father of this family, d. 29th day of 7th month, 6th day of week, and bur. at the Clifts Meeting House the 3rd day of 8th month, 1738.
Sarah Duhadway, dau. of George and Anna Harris, and wife of Jacob Duhadway, d. 5th day of 4th month, 1742, and bur. in Friends burying ground at their meeting house in Kent County on Delaware on 6th day of said month.
Rachel Johns, dau. of George and Anna Harris, and wife of Benjamin Johns, d. 29th day of 9th month, and bur. in Friends burying ground near the Clifts, 2nd day of 10th month, 1748.
BIRTHS:
Frances Young, eldest dau. of Arthur and Ann, of Patuxent, b. 3rd day of 10th month, 1683, about 2 in the morning.
Anna Young, 2nd dau. of Arthur and Ann, b. 22nd day of 9th month, 1685, about morning.
Peter Young, eldest son of Arthur and Ann, b. 12th day of 11th month, 1687/8.

CLIFTS MONTHLY MEETING REGISTER, 1662 - 1782

Mary Young, 3rd dau. of Arthur and Ann, b. 2nd day of 5th month, 1689, about morning.
Arthur Young, 2nd son of Arthur and Ann, b. 3rd day of 1st month, 1690/1.
Constant Young, 4th dau. of Arthur and Ann, b. 20th day of 5th month, 1693.
Ann Young, 5th dau. of Arthur and Ann, b. 23rd day of 9th month, 1695.
Elizabeth Young, 6th dau. of Arthur and Ann, b. 2nd day of 11th month, 1697/8.
Sarah and Elizabeth Young, twin 7th and 8th daus. of Arthur and Ann, b. 2nd day of 11th month, 1698/9.
BURIALLS:
Elizabeth Young, 6th dau. of this family, d. 5th day of 11th month, and bur. at Patuxent in Friends burying ground, 6th day of 11th month, 1697/8.
Arthur Young, father of this family, d. 30th day of 3rd month, and bur. at Patuxent, 2nd day of 4th month, 1711. He had a dau. by his wife Mary, the youngest of all his children, named Rachel Young, who d. 29th day of 8th month, 1711.
Frances Bondfield, eldest dau. of Arthur Young, d. -- day of 9th month, 1763, in 80th year, and bur. at Deer Creek in Baltimore County.
BIRTHS:
Thomas Wilson, son of Joseph and Frances, b. 8th day of 7th month, 1691.
Margaret Wilson, dau. of Joseph and Frances, b. 18th day of 4th month, 1694.
Frances Wilson, 2nd dau. of Joseph and Frances, b. 2nd day of 2nd month, 1697.
Mary Wilson, 3rd dau. of Joseph and Frances, b. 9th day of 5th month, 1699.
Joseph Wilson, 2nd son of Joseph and Frances, b. last day of 12th month, 1701/2.
Elizabeth and Sophia Wilson, twin 4th and 5th daus. of Joseph and Frances, b. 10th day of 12th month, 1704/5.
Josiah Wilson, son of Joseph and Frances, b. 17th day of 3rd month, 1707.
James Wilson, son of Joseph and Frances, b. 17th day of 6th month, 1710.
John Wilson, son of Joseph and Frances, b. 11th day of 7th month, 1713.
Robert Day, son of Robert and Sarah, b. 21st day of 12th month, 1699, and d. 6th day of 2nd month, 1700.
BURIALLS:
Robert Day, father of this family, d. 8th day of 10th month, 1697.
Elizabeth Day, wife of said Robert and mother of this family, d. 12th day of 10th month, 1697.
BIRTHS:
Isaac Rawlings, son of Daniel and Anne, b. 27th day of 2nd month, 1701.
Mary Rawlings, dau. of Daniel and Anne, b. 3rd day of 7th month, 1703.
Elizabeth Rawlings, 2nd dau. of Daniel and Anne, b. 18th day of 8th month, 1705.
Anne Rawlings, 3rd dau. of Daniel and Anne, b. 29th day of 8th month, 1707.
Daniel Rawlings, son of Daniel and Anne, b. 7th day of 5th month, 1711.

QUAKER RECORDS OF SOUTHERN MARYLAND

BURIALLS:
Mary Rawlings, sister of Daniel Rawlings, of Patuxent, d. 24th day of 8th month, 1699.
Ann Rawlings, wife of Daniel, d. 18th day of 4th month, 1713.
BIRTHS:
Elizabeth Roberts, dau. of Robert and Priscilla, b. 26th day of 4th month, 1705.
Richard Roberts, eldest son of Robert and Priscilla, b. 21st day of 11th month, 1706/7.
Priscilla Roberts, 2nd dau. of Robert and Priscilla, b. 11th day of 12th month, 1708/9.
Isaac Roberts, 2nd son of Robert and Priscilla, b. 4th day of 2nd month, 1711.
Robert Roberts, 3rd son of Robert and Priscilla, b. 12th day of 10th month, 1712.
Kensey Roberts, 4th son of Robert and Priscilla, b. 28th day of 7th month, 1714.
Margaret Roberts, 3rd dau. of Robert and Priscilla, b. 23rd day of 5th month, 1716.
Jane Roberts, 4th dau. of Robert and Priscilla, b. 19th day of 5th month, 1718.
Robert Roberts, 5th son of Robert and Priscilla, b. 21st day of 12th month, 1720/1.
BURIALLS:
Robert Roberts, 3rd son of Robert and Priscilla, d. ----.
Robert Roberts, 1st son of Robert and Priscilla, d. 20th day of 5th month, 1722.
Priscilla Roberts, wife of Robert, d. 1st day of 2nd month, 1725, and same day, some few hours before her death, their dau. Patience Roberts was born.
Robert Roberts, Sr., d. 11th day of 11th month ----.
BIRTHS:
Elizabeth Giles, dau. of Nathaniel and Elizabeth, b. 24th day of 8th month, 1704.
Mary Giles, dau. of Nathaniel and Elizabeth, b. 31st day of 11th month, 1705/6.
John Astin, son of John and Hannah, b. 15th day of 1st month, 1701.
BURIALLS:
Sarah Astin, wife of John Astin, and once the widow of John Pardoe, Sr., d. 22nd day of 8th month, 1697.
Hannah Astin, wife of John Astin, d. 16th day of 2nd month, 1702.
BIRTHS:
Sarah Meares, dau. of John and Sarah, b. 4th day of 6th month, 1673, and is the mother of this family.
Elizabeth Talbott, dau. of John and Sarah, b. 5th day of 1st month, 1690/1.
Thomas Talbott, eldest son of John and Sarah, b. 29th day of 9th month, 1695.
Richard Talbott, 2nd son of John and Sarah, b. 12th day of 5th month, 1696.
Daniel Talbott, 3rd son of John and Sarah, b. 24th day of 2nd month, 1699.
John Talbott, 4th son of John and Sarah, b. 19th day of 12th month, 1701/2.
Sophia Talbott, 2nd dau. of John and Sarah, b. 7th day of 7th month, 1704.

CLIFTS MONTHLY MEETING REGISTER, 1662 - 1782

Mary Talbott, great gr. dau. of ye above families and the 1st dau. of Daniel and Elizabeth Talbott, b. 3rd day of 6th month, 1765.
Abraham Talbott, 1st son of Daniel and Elizabeth, b. 31st day of 12th month, 1768.
George Talbott, 2nd son of Daniel and Elizabeth, b. 18th day of 3rd month, 1771.
Sarah Talbott, 2nd dau. of Daniel and Elizabeth, b. 27th day of 10th month, 1774.
BURIALLS:
John Talbott, father of this family, d. 4th day of 4th month, 1707, and bur. in new grave yard at the Clifts, 9th day of said month.
BIRTHS:
Samuel Gover, son of Samuel and Elizabeth, b. 30th day of 3rd month, 1707.
Robert Gover, son of Samuel and Elizabeth, b. 19th day of 10th month, 1708.
Elizabeth Gover, dau. of Samuel and Elizabeth, b. 13th day of 6th month, 1710.
Cassandra Gover, dau. of Samuel and Elizabeth, b. 30th day of 3rd month, 1712.
Priscilla Gover, dau. of Samuel and Elizabeth, b. 11th day of 4th month, 1714.
Benjamin Gover, son of Samuel and Elizabeth, b. 17th day of 6th month, 1716.
Ephraim Gover, son of Samuel and Elizabeth, b. 18th day of 7th month, 1718.
Richard Gover, son of Samuel and Elizabeth, b. 20th day of 9th month, 1720.
Rachell Gover, dau. of Samuel and Elizabeth, b. 28th day of 9th month, 1722.
Phillip Gover, son of Samuel and Elizabeth, b. 7th day of 8th month, 1726.
BURIALLS:
Robert Gover (sic), father of this family, d. 4th day of 2nd month, 1700.
BIRTHS:
Elizabeth Davis, dau. of Thomas and Mary, b. 11th day of 10th month, 1703.
Thomas Davis, son of Thomas and Mary, b. 16th day of 1st month, 1706.
Jacob Davis, son of Thomas and Mary, b. 27th day of 1st month, 1715.
Robert Davis, son of Thomas and Mary, b. 18th day of 10th month, 1708, about 3 in the afternoon.
William Davis, son of Thomas and Mary, b. 17th day of 9th month, 1711.
Mary Wilkinson, dau. of John and Elizabeth, b. 18th day of 11th month, 1701.
Priscilla Wilkinson, 2nd dau. of John and Elizabeth, b. 22nd day of 1st month, 1703/4.
John Wilkinson, son of John and Elizabeth, b. 2nd day of 2nd month, 1706.
Elizabeth Wilkinson, dau. of John and Elizabeth, b. 5th day of 2nd month, 1708.
Mary Wilkinson, dau. of John and Elizabeth, b. 2nd day of 12th month, 1711.
Orton Wilkinson, son of John and Elizabeth, b. 12th day of 2nd month, 1715.
William Wilkinson, son of John and Elizabeth, b. 31st day of 5th month, 1717.
Phillip Wilkinson, son of John and Elizabeth, b. 31st day of 5th month, 1722.
Henry Wilkinson, son of John and Elizabeth, b. 26th day of 8th month, 1724.
BURIALLS:
John Wilkinson, father of this family, d. 29th day of 10th month, 1728.

QUAKER RECORDS OF SOUTHERN MARYLAND

Orton Wilkinson, son of John, d. 14th day of 2nd month, 1734.
BIRTHS:
John Wright, son of Joseph and Elizabeth, b. 23rd day of 8th month, 1691.
Joseph Wright, son of Joseph and Elizabeth, b. 23rd day of 4th month, 1694.
Sarah Wright, dau. of Joseph and Elizabeth, b. 26th day of 10th month, 1696.
Charles Wright, son of Joseph and Elizabeth, b. 18th day of 3rd month, 1699.
Samuel Wright, son of Joseph and Elizabeth, b. 1st day of 1st month, 1701/2.
Mary Wright, dau. of Joseph and Elizabeth, b. 8th day of 9th month, 1704.
Thomas Wright, son of Joseph and Elizabeth, b. last day of 1st month, 1707.
BURIALLS:
Joseph Wright, son of Joseph and Elizabeth, bur. 17th day of 6th month, 1696.
BIRTHS:
Richard Johns, son of Abraham and Margaret, b. 11th day of 10th month, 1703, about midnight.
Abraham Johns, son of Abraham and Margaret, b. 7th day of 12th month, 1704/5, about 2 in the afternoon.
Elizabeth Johns, dau. of Abraham and Margaret, b. 2nd day of 10th month, 1706, about 7 at night.
Aquilla Johns, 3rd son of Richard, m. Mary Hozier, 2nd dau. of Henry, 16th day of 9th month, 1704.
Rebecka Johns, dau. of Richard and Mary, b. 4th day of 12th month, 1705/6.
Richard Johns, son of Richard and Mary, b. 2nd day of 10th month, 1707.
Aquilla Johns, son of Richard and Mary, b. 14th day of 11th month, 1709/10.
BURIALLS:
Abraham Johns, father of this family, d. 9th day of 10th month, 1707, and bur. in new meeting house burying ground at the Clifts.
Elizabeth Johns, dau. of Abraham, d. ----, 17--.
Margaret England, formerly wife of Abraham Johns, and mother of this family, d. 10th day of 4th month, 1733, at White Clay Creek, Pa., and was bur. at Joppa, Baltimore County.
Richard Johns, son of Abraham and Margaret, d. 24th day of 9th month, 1748, and bur. at meeting house near the Clifts.
Aquilla Johns, father of this family, d. 16th day of 11th month, 1709/10, and was bur. in the Clifts burying ground by his brother Abraham.
Mary Hall, formerly wife of Aquilla Johns, d. 14th day of 5th month, 1762, and bur. by her late husband in the burying ground where that family mostly lie.
BIRTHS: Elizabeth Orton, dau. of Henry and Mary, b. 8th day of 3rd month, 1683.
Henry Orton, son of Henry and Mary, b. 4th day of 11th month, 1689.
Elizabeth Johns, dau. of Richard Johns, Jr., b. 31st day of 6th month, 1708.

CLIFTS MONTHLY MEETING REGISTER, 1662 - 1782

Richard Johns, son of Richard and Priscilla, b. 4th day of 11th month, 1709/10.
Abraham Johns, 2nd son of Richard and Priscilla, b. 31st day of 6th month, 1711.
Priscilla Johns, 2nd dau. of Richard and Priscilla, b. 21st day of 6th month, 1713.
Margaret Johns, 3rd dau. of Richard and Priscilla, b. 22nd day of 5th month, 1715.
Sarah Johns, 4th dau. of Richard and Priscilla, b. 14th day of 11th month, 1716.
Mary Johns, 5th dau. of Richard and Priscilla, b. 29th day of 1st month, 1719.
Priscilla Johns, dau. of Francis Hitchins, and mother of this family, b. 12th day of 6th month, 1690.
Priscilla Johns, dau. of Richard and Sarah, b. 23rd day of 6th month, 1731.
Richard Johns, 1st son of Richard and Sarah, b. 2nd day of 5th month, 1734.
Elizabeth Johns, 2nd dau. of Richard and Sarah, b. 5th day of 1st month, 1737.
Richard Johns, 2nd son of Richard and Sarah, b. in 6th month, 1739.
Joseph Johns, b. in 11th month, 1742/3.
BURIALLS:
Abraham Johns, d. 11th day of 3rd month, 1720.
Priscilla Johns, d. 20th day of 8th month, 1724.
Sarah Jones, d. 29th day of 1st month, 1731.
Elizabeth Johns, 1st dau. of Richard and Priscilla, d. 13th day of 10th month, and was bur. in Friends burying ground on 21st day of 1st month, 1742.
Richard Johns, 1st son of Richard and Priscilla, d. in 12th month, 1745/6, being unfortunately drowned, his body was taken up and buried at Lowes Island on the Eastern Shore.
Priscilla Beckit, formerly Priscilla Johns, and mother of ye above family, d. 24th day of 3rd month [March], 1766, being in the 76th year of her age.
BIRTHS:
Ursilla Sawell, dau. of Peter and Mary, b. 20th day of 10th month, 1703.
Mary Sawell, dau. of Peter and Mary, b. 11th day of 2nd month, 1706.
Ellinor Sawell, dau. of Peter and Mary, b. 21st day of 2nd month, 1709.
Peter Sawell, son of Peter and Mary, b. 14th day of 12th month, 1711/2.
Elizabeth Littell, dau. of Thomas and Elizabeth, b. 19th day of 6th month, 1713, 4th day of the week, about 3 in the morning.
Christopher Birkhead, son of Sollomon and Ann, b. 17th day of 11th month, 1705, being 5th day of the week, about 6 in the morning.
Ann Birkhead, dau. of Sollomon and Ann, b. 18th day of 10th month, 1707.
Anna Maria Bourne, dau. of Jesse and Hannah, b. 2nd day of 8th month, 1715.
Benjamin Bourne, son of Jesse and Hannah, b. 15th day of 4th month, 1717.
Jesse of Wellist Bourne, son of Jesse and Hannah, b. 16th day of 5th month, 1719.
Jacob Bourne, son of Jesse Jacob Bourne and Ailse, his 2nd wife, b. 14th day of 3rd month, 1724.

QUAKER RECORDS OF SOUTHERN MARYLAND

Thomas Bourne, son of Jesse Jacob Bourne and Ailse, b. 14th day of 11th month, 1725/6.
Anna Maria Bourne, dau. of Jesse Jacob Bourne and Ailse, b. 23rd day of 1st month, 1728/9.
Susanna Bourne, dau. of Jesse Jacob Bourne and Ailse, b. 25th day of 11th month 1730/1.
George Bourne, son of Jesse Jacob Bourne and Ailse, b. 14th day of 4th month, 1733.
BURIALLS:
Anna Birkhead, dau. of Sollomon and Ann, d. 27th day of 6th month, 1708.
Hannah Bourne, wife of Jesse, d. 25th day of 11th month, 1719.
Benjamin Bourne, son of Jesse and Hannah, d. 16th day of 9th month, 1722.
Anna Maria Bourne, dau. of Jesse and Hannah, d. 4th day of 4th month, 1728.
Jesse Bourne, father of this family, d. 3rd day of 6th month, 1736, and bur. on the 5th.
BIRTHS:
Joseph Harris, son of Joseph and Anne, b. 31st day of 6th month, 1715.
Benjamin Harris, son of Joseph and Anne, b. 28th day of 11th month, 1716/7.
Benjamin Harris, 3rd son of Joseph and Anne, b. 20th day of 8th month, about 2nd hour in the morning and 2nd day of ye week in year 1718.
Richard Harris, 4th son of Joseph and Anne, b. 29th day of 6th month, 1720.
Ann Harris, eldest dau. of Joseph and Anne, b. 25th day of 8th month, 1722.
Christian Harris, 2nd dau. of Joseph and Anne, b. 2nd[?] day of 2nd month, 1725.
BURIALLS:
Joseph Harris, Sr., d. at Philadelphia in 7th month, 1725, and was buried there in Friends burying ground.
Benjamin Harris, son of above Joseph, d. 26th day of 6th month, 1717.
Benjamin Harris, 2nd son of that name of ye said Joseph, d. 15th day of 6th month, 1719.
Richard Harris, 4th son of ye said Joseph, d. 25th day of 6th month, 1723.
Joseph Harris, son of Joseph and Ann, d. 31st day of 5th month, 1742, and was bur. at the Clifts.
BIRTHS:
Richard Johns, 1st son of Isaac and Anne, b. 11th day of 9th month, 1714.
Samuel Johns, 2nd son of Isaac and Anne, b. 31st day of 5th month, 1716.
Abraham Johns, 3rd son of Isaac and Anne, b. 5th day of 6th month, 1718.
Isaac Johns, 4th son of Isaac and Anne, b. 18th day of 11th month, 1719.
Anne Johns, eldest dau. of Isaac and Anne, b. 28th day of 12th month, 1721/2.
Jacob Johns, 5th son of Isaac and Anne, b. 4th day of 12th month, 1723/4.

CLIFTS MONTHLY MEETING REGISTER, 1662 - 1782

Elizabeth Johns, 2nd dau. of Isaac and Anne, b. 21st day of 7th month, 1728.
Aquilla Johns, 1st son of Isaac and Eliza, b. 11th day of 9th month, 1731.
BURIALLS:
Anne Johns, beloved wife of Isaac, d. 29th day of 9th month, 1728, and bur. at Clifts.
Elizabeth Johns, 2nd dau. of Isaac and Anne, d. 15th day of 7th month, 1729, and bur. at Clifts.
Isaac Johns, father of this family, d. 17th day of 12th month, 1733/4, and bur. at Clifts.
Aquilla Johns, youngest son of Isaac and his last wife, d. 20th day of 7th month, 1737.
BIRTHS:
Richard Bond, son of Richard and Elizabeth, b. 6th day of 6th month, 1707.
Sarah Bond, dau. of Richard and Elizabeth, b. 6th day of 8th month, 1708.
Benson Bond, son of Richard and Elizabeth, b. 25th day of 6th month, 1710.
Thomas Bond, son of Richard and Elizabeth, b. 2nd day of 8th month, 1713.
John Bond, son of Richard and Elizabeth, b. 7th day of 3rd month, 1715.
Phinebas Bond, son of Richard and Elizabeth, b. 13th day of 7th month, 1717.
Ann Wallis, dau. of Samuel and Frances, b. 2nd day of 12th month, 1702.
Samuel Wallis, son of Samuel and Frances, b. 8th day of 3rd month, 1705.
Mary Wallis, dau. of Samuel and Frances, b. 23rd day of 9th month, 1707.
Arthur Wallis, son of Samauel and Frances, b. 28th day of 11th month, 1709.
Frances Wallis, dau. of Samuel and Frances, b. 24th day of 3rd month, 1712.
Mary Wallis, dau. of Samuel and Frances, b. 19th day of 3rd month, 1714.
Abraham Wallis, son of Samuel and Frances, b. 26th day of 10th month, 1716.
Constant Wallis, dau. of Samuel and Frances, b. 10th day of 3rd month, 1719, lived 11 days, and was bur. at Patuxent.
BURIALLS:
Mary Wallis, d. 6th day of 8th month, 17--.
Arthur Wallis, d. in ----, 1710.
Samuel Wallis, father of this family, d. 14th day of 12th month, 1718.
BIRTHS:
Job Hunt, son of Job and Sarah, b. 16th day of 7th month, 1718.
Elizabeth Hunt, dau. of Job and Sarah, b. 17th day of 4th month, 1722.
Mary Hunt, dau. of Job and Sarah, b. 28th day of 11th month, 1724.
Sarah Hunt, dau. of Job and Sarah, b. 8th day of 10th month, 1726.
Richard Johns, 1st son of Kensey and Elizabeth, b. 26th day of 2nd month, 1712, the last day of the week.
Benjamin Johns, 2nd son of Kensey and Elizabeth, b. 22nd day of 11th month, 1713/4, the 6th day of the week.

QUAKER RECORDS OF SOUTHERN MARYLAND

Elizabeth Johns, 1st dau. of Kensey and Elizabeth, b. 16th day of 11th month, 1715/6, the 2nd day of the week.
Samuel Johns, 3rd son of Kensey and Elizabeth, b. 3rd day of 1st month, 1717/8, the 2nd day of the week.
Ann Johns, 2nd dau. of Kensey and Elizabeth, b. 27th day of 12th month, 1719/20, the 7th day of the week.
Kensey Johns, 4th son of Kensey and Elizabeth, b. 11th day of 3rd month, 1722, the 6th day of the week, at three quarter past 4 in the morning.
Rachel Johns, 3rd dau. of Kensey and Elizabeth, b. 18th day of 2nd month, 1724, the 6th day of the week.
Mary Johns, 4th dau. of Kensey and Elizabeth, b. ---- 1725/6.
BURIALLS:
Ann Johns, 2nd dau. of Kensey and Elizabeth, d. 30th day of 5th month, 1720, and bur. at the Clifts.
Elizabeth Johns, the dear and well beloved wife of Kensey Johns and tender mother of this family, d. 9th day of 12th month, 1726/7, and bur. at Clifts.
Kensey Johns, father of this family, d. 2nd day of 2nd month, 1729.
Richard Johns, son of Kensey and Elizabeth, died in 1st month of 1730/1, being unfortunately drowned, and was bur. at Joppa in Baltimore County.
Elizabeth Hance, dau. of Kensey and Elizabeth Johns, and wife of Benjamin Hance, Jr., d. 27th day of 6th month, 1744, and bur. at Clifts.
Benjamin Johns, son of Kensey and Elizabeth, d. 9th day of 3rd month, 1750, and bur. at Clifts.
BIRTHS:
Ann Walker, dau. of William and Jane, b. ----, 17--.
John Walker, son of William and Sarah, b. 9th day of 8th month, 1716.
Sarah Walker, dau. of William and Sarah, b. 19th day of 6th month, 1719.
BURIALLS:
Jane Walker, wife of William, d. 11th day of 7th month, 17-- and bur. at Patuxent.
Ann Walker, dau. of William and Jane, d. 24th day of 11th month, 1715.
John Walker, son of William and Sarah, his second wife, d. 8th day of 8th month, 1717.
George Walker, son of William and Jane, d. 24th day of 10th month, 1719.
Francis Hutchins, son of Francis and Elizabeth, b. 21st day of April, 1724.
BIRTHS:
Richard Hutchins, son of Francis and Elizabeth, b. ----.
Margrett Bondfield, dau. of Christopher and Frances, b. 16th day of 11th month, 1725/6.
Ann Bonfield, dau. of Christopher and Frances, b. 10th day of 3rd month, 1727.

CLIFTS MONTHLY MEETING REGISTER, 1662 - 1782

James Bonfield, son of Christopher and Frances, b. 17th day of 7th month, 1729.
Samuel Robertson and Elizabeth Harris took each other in marriage, 22nd day of 8th month, 1720.
Sarah Robertson, first born of above Samuel and Elizabeth, b. 15th day of 6th month, 1731.
Daniell Robertson, son of Samuel and Elizabeth, b. 26th day of 12th month, 1732/3.
Daniell Robertson, son of Samuel and Elizabeth, b. 29th day of 5th month, 1734.
George Robertson, 3rd son of Samuel and Elizabeth, b. 30th day of 8th month, 17--.
Ann Robertson, 2nd dau. of Samuel and Elizabeth, b. 26th day of 11th month, 17--.
Samuel Robertson, 4th son of Samuel and Elizabeth, b. 2nd day of 2nd month, 1741.
Mary Robertson, 3rd dau. of Samuel and Elizabeth, b. 11th day of 8th month, 1743.
William Robertson, 5th son of Samuel and Elizabeth, b. 10th day of 3rd month, 1746.
Rachel Robertson, 4th dau. of Samuel and Elizabeth, b. 11th day of 3rd month, 1751.
John Plummer, 1st son of Jerrom and Mary, b. 5th day of 10th month, 1750.
BURIALLS:
Daniel Robertson, eldest son of Samuel and Elizabeth, d. 29th day of 1st month, 1733.
Elizabeth Harris, eldest dau. of Daniel and Sarah Robertson, was first ye lawful wife of Arthur Harris, secondly wife of Isaac Johns, and lastly wife of Joseph Harris. She d. 9th day of 4th month, 1758, and bur. at Herring Creek.
Sarah Coale, eldest dau. of Samuel and Elizabeth Robertson, d. 28th day of 1st month, 1766, and bur. on plantation of her husband William Coale, of Baltimore County, being in the 35th year of her age.
Samuel Robertson, beloved father of this family, d. 8th day of 8th month, 1767, in the 63rd year of his age, and bur. at Herring Creek Meeting House.
Elizabeth Robertson, beloved wife of above Samuel, d. 15th day of 11th month, 17--, about 10 o'clock, in the 77th year of her age, and bur. at Herring Creek.
Samuel Robertson, beloved husband of this family, d. 22nd day of 10th month, 1784, in 43rd year, and bur. at Herring Creek Meeting House.
BIRTHS:
Frances Harris, dau. of William and Elizabeth, b. 6th day of 3rd month, 1719.
Mary Harris, dau. of William and Elizabeth, b. 5th day of 12th month, 1721/2.
William Harris, son of William and Elizabeth, b. 26th day of 12th month, 1723/4.
Joseph Harris, son of William and Elizabeth, b. 21st day of 10th month, 1725.
Benjamin Harris, son of William and Elizabeth, b. 29th day of 11th month, 1727/8.
Elizabeth Harris, dau. of William and Elizabeth, b. 7th day of 2nd month, 1731.
BURIALLS:
William Harris, father of this family, d. ----, and bur. at Clifts.

QUAKER RECORDS OF SOUTHERN MARYLAND

BIRTHS:
Elizabeth Wilkinson, dau. of John and Ann, b. 29th day of 10th month, 1728.
Mary Wilkinson, 2nd dau. of John and Ann, b. 5th day of 12th month, 1731/2.
Anna Wilkinson, 3rd dau. of John and Ann, b. 30th day of 6th month, 1734.
John Benjamin Wilkinson, son of John and Ann, b. 4th day of 8th month, 1737.
Richard Johns, b. 11th day of 9th month, 1714.
Margaret Johns, b. 22nd day of 1st month, 1715/6.
Philip Johns, 1st son of Richard and Margaret, b. 30th day of 9th month, 1735.
William Johns, 2nd son of Richard and Margaret, b. in 1st month, 1737/8.
Ann Thomas Johns, 1st dau. of Richard and Margaret, b. 29th day of 2nd month, 1740.
Margaret Johns, 2nd dau. of Richard and Margaret, b. 22nd day of 8th month, 1741.
Mary Johns, 3rd dau. of Richard and Margaret, b. 6th day of 12th month, 1743/4.
Elizabeth Johns, 4th dau. of Richard and Margaret, b. 28th day of 4th month, 1746.
BURIALLS:
Philip Johns, dear and well beloved 1st son of Richard and Margaret, d. 14th day of 12th month, 1746/7, and bur. at the Clifts.
Margaret Johns, mother of ye above deceased, d. 1750.
BIRTHS:
Ann Harris, dau. of Joseph and Elizabeth, b. 10th day of 10th month, 1738.
Sarah Harris, 2nd dau. of Joseph and Elizabeth, b. 27th day of 8th month, 1741.
Joseph Hance, son of Benjamin, b. 10th day of 9th month, 1716.
Ann Hance, wife of Joseph Hance and dau. of Isaac Johns, b. 28th day of 12th month, 1721/2.
Mary Hance, 1st dau. of Joseph and Ann, b. 5th day of 9th month, 1738.
Ann Hance, 2nd dau. of Joseph and Ann, b. 1st day of 1st month, 1739/40.
Elizabeth Hance, 3rd dau. of Joseph Hance, b. in 17th month, 1741.
Benjamin Hance, 1st son of Joseph and Ann, b. 19th day of 3rd month, 1744.
Richard Roberts, son of Richard and Elizabeth, b. 13th day of 4th month, 1735.
Allen Roberts, 2nd son of Richard and Elizabeth, b. 17th day of 9th month, 1737.
Isaac Roberts, 3rd son of Richard and Elizabeth, b. 7th day of 7th month, 1739.
Robert Roberts, 4th son of Richard and Elizabeth, b. 22nd day of 1st month, 1741/2.
Hugh Roberts, 5th son of Richard and Elizabeth, b. 26th day of 1st month, 1745.
Elizabeth Roberts, 1st dau. of Richard and Elizabeth, b. 5th day of 8th month, 1747.
["The parents of these children are not looked upon to be members of our society at present."]
John Hunt, son of Thomas and Elizabeth, b. 3rd day of 1st month, 1727.
Elizabeth Hunt, dau. of Thomas and Elizabeth, b. 7th day of 7th month, 1729.
Thomas Hunt, Jr., son of Thomas and Elizabeth, b. 3rd day of 3rd month, 1731.

CLIFTS MONTHLY MEETING REGISTER, 1662 - 1782

Job Hunt, Jr., son of Thomas and Elizabeth, b. 28th day of 12th month, 1732/3.
William Hunt, son of Thomas and Elizabeth, b. 31st day of 1st month, 1735.
Orton Hunt, son of Thomas and Elizabeth, b. 29th day of 6th month, 1737.
Philip Hunt, son of Thomas and Elizabeth, b. 10th day of 12th month, 1739/40.
Mary Hunt, dau. of Thomas and Elizabeth, b. 23rd day of 1st month, 1742.
Priscilla Hunt, dau. of Thomas and Elizabeth, b. 15th day of 2nd month, 1744.
BURIALS:
John Hunt, son of Thomas and Elizabeth, d. 24th day of 1st month, 1743/4.
BIRTHS:
Mary Harris, dau. of William and Margaret, b. 31st day of 3rd month, 1741.
William Harris, son of William and Margaret, b. 31st day of 5th month, 1744.
Samuel Harris, 2nd son of William and Margaret, b. 24th day of 12th month, 1746.
Margaret Harris, 2nd dau. of William and Margaret, b. 27th day of 4th month, 1749.
Elizabeth Harris, 3rd dau. of William and Margaret, b. 25th day of 3rd month, 1752.
BURIALS:
William Harris, son of William and Margaret, d. 7th day of 11th month, 1746/7.
Margaret Harris, the dear and well beloved wife of William Harris and mother of this family, d. 23rd day of 4th month, 1766, and bur. at Friends burying ground near the Clifts.
William Harris, father of this family, d. 16th day of 7th month [July], 1782, in the 66th year of his age, and bur. near the Clifts.
BIRTHS:
Abraham Johns, 1st son of Richard and Margaret, b. 16th day of 8th month, 1733, between hours of 6 and 7 in the morning.
Thomas Johns, 2nd son of Richard and Margaret, b. 20th day of 6th month, 1735.
Elizabeth Johns, 1st dau. of Richard and Margaret, b. 12th day of 3rd month, 1738[?].
Margaret Johns, 2nd dau. of Richard and Margaret, b. 30th day of 3rd month, 1740.
Joseph Johns, 3rd son of Richard and Margaret, b. 20th day of 12th month, 1741.
Jane Johns, 3rd dau. of Richard and Margaret, b. 3rd day of 12th month, 1743.
Priscilla and Aquilla Johns, 4th dau. and 4th son of Richard and Margaret, born at one birth, 12th day of 12th month, 1745.
John Plummer, first born of Jerrom and Mary, the daughter of George and Anna Harris, b. 5th day of 10th month, 1750.
Sarah Stewart, dau. of Steven and Anna, b. 5th day of 3rd month, 1751.
John Stewart, son of Steven and Anna, b. 8th day of 12th month, 1753.
Stephen and Elizabeth Stewart, son and dau. of Stephen and Anna, b. 25th day of 2nd month, 1756.

QUAKER RECORDS OF SOUTHERN MARYLAND

BURIALLS:
Jerrom Plummer, d. 12th day of 3rd month, 1751, and was bur. at West River burying ground.
BIRTHS:
Kinsey Johns, first born of Benjamin and Rachel, b. in 11th month, 1744.
Benjamin Johns, 2nd son of Benjamin and Rachel, b. in 8th month, 1746.
Richard Johns, 3rd son of Benjamin and Rachel, b. 14th day of 9th month, 1748.
BURIALS:
Rachel Johns, mother of this family, d. 2nd day of 10th month, 1748.
Benjamin Johns, father of this family, d. 9th day of 3rd month, 1750.
BIRTHS:
Sarah Cole, dau. of William and Sarah Cole, of Baltimore County, b. 21st day of 3rd month, 1759.
Samuel Robertson Coale, 1st son of William and Sarah Coale, of Baltimore County, b. 10th day of 1st month, 1761.
Elizabeth Coale, dau. of William and Sarah Coale, b. 5th day of 6th month, 1763.
John Talbott, son of Joseph, m. Mary Johns, dau. of Abraham and Elizabeth, 22nd day of 2nd month, 1760.
Benjamin Talbott, son of John and Mary, b. 11th day of 5th month, 1762.
Joseph Talbott, son of John and Mary, b. 26th day of 6th month, 1764.
John Talbott, son of John and Mary, b. 3rd day of 1st month, 1766.
Elizabeth Talbott, dau. of John and Mary, b. 29th day of 9th month, 1767.
Susanna Talbott, dau. of John and Mary, b. 15th day of 7th month, 1769.
Ann Talbott, dau. of John and Mary, b. 8th day of 5th month, 1771.
Samuel Talbott, son of John and Mary, b. 18th day of 12th month, 1772.
Rachel Talbott, dau. of John and Mary, b. 21st day of 11th month, 1774.
Peggy Talbott, dau. of John and Mary, b. 9th day of 11th month, 1776.
George Robertson and Susanna Waters m. 2nd day of 2nd month, 1773.
Elizabeth Robertson, 1st dau. of George and Susanna, b. 4th day of 10th month, 1774.
Sarah Robertson, 2nd dau. of George and Susanna, b. 9th day of 3rd month, 1776.
Samuel Robertson, 1st son of George and Susanna, b. 23rd day of 3rd month, 1778.
Elizabeth Robertson, eldest dau. of George and Susanna, d. 3rd day of 7th month, 1775.
Daniel Robertson and Elizabeth Webster m. 13th day of 8th month, 1768.
Elizabeth Robertson, 1st dau. of Daniel and Elizabeth, b. 20th day of 1st month, 1771.
Margarett Robertson, 2nd dau. of Daniel and Elizaebth, b. 11th day of 2nd month, 1773.

CLIFTS MONTHLY MEETING REGISTER, 1662 - 1782

Mary Robertson, 3rd dau. of Daniel and Elizabeth, b. 5th day of 9th month, 1774.
Hannah Robertson, 4th dau. of Daniel and Elizabeth, b. 20th day of 6th month, 1776.
Samuel Robertson, 1st son of Daniel and Elizabeth, b. 24th day of 7th month, 1778.
Isaac Robertson, 2nd son of Daniel and Elizabeth, b. 20th day of 10th month, 1780.

MONTHLY MEETING MINUTES, 1677 - 1771

The following was abstracted from two sets of the minutes of the Monthly Meetings held alternately at West River and the Clifts, and at Patuxent and later at Herring Creek.

Meeting held at house of John Gary - 29th day of 9th month, 1677.
John Gary gives land for burying ground of Cliffs Meeting - 29th day of 9th month, 1677.
Meeting held at house of Benjamin Laurence - 21st day of 4th month, 1678.
Quarterly Meeting established at house of Anne Chew - 23rd day of 3rd month, 1679.
Yearly Meeting held at house of Thomas Hooker - 23rd day of 3rd month, 1679.
Thomas Bink makes truth clear regarding his conduct - 18th day of 5th month, 1679.
John Thomson [Thompson], formerly a servant who ran away from these parts, is at Boston, under the pretense of a Quaker preacher - reported 3rd day of 10th month, 1680 - disowned.
John Gary reported as deceased - meeting moved from his house - William Mears assists in holding Patuxent Meeting - 30th day of 10th month, 1681.
Daniell Rawlings - certificate to visit England - 30th day of 10th month, 1681.
Henry Orton and Mary Davis - intentions to marry - 21st day of 2nd month, 1682 [1st time] and 16th day of 5th month, 1682 [2nd time].
Meeting held at house of Richard Johns - 21st day of 2nd month, 1682.
William Berry furnished land for Patuxent Meeting House - 11th day of 6th month, 1682.
Benjamin Laurence has removed from Patuxent and carried records and books that belonged to that meeting - reported 6th day of 8th month, 1682, and 1st day of 10th month, 1682.
William Sharp gives title to Patuxent burying ground - 1st day of 10th month, 1682.
Nehemiah Birkhead and Elizabeth Sloper - intentions to marry - 1st day of 10th month, 1682.
Meeting held at house of John Pardo - 28th day of 10th month, 1683.
William Sharp gives 5 acres to build Cliffs Meeting House - 28th day of 10th month, 1683.

QUAKER RECORDS OF SOUTHERN MARYLAND

George Royston and Rebecka Cullin - intentions to marry - 28th day of 10th month, 1683.
Ann Chew intends a voyage to England - reported 28th day of 10th month, 1683.
Certificate of removal from Tread Haven Monthly Meeting for Samuel Preston - 22nd day of 12th month, 1683.
Anne Chew - certificate to visit England - 22nd day of 12th month, 1683.
William Dixon gives 5 acres of land to build Cliffs Meeting House - 22nd day of 12th month, 1683.
Margaret Holland guilty of unchastity with Hugh Gill - 18th day of 2nd month, 1684.
Joseph Chew and Mary Smith - intentions to marry - 4th day of 7th month, 1685.
Witnessed by John Astin, the verbal will of John Pardoe was sustained - 10th day of 5th month, 1685.
John Pardoe, son of John Pardoe, deceased, informs that he, having attained to his full age of 21 years, is willing to make over the land that his father did verbally bequeath to his younger brother, Joseph Pardoe - 30th day of 8th month, 1685. [Land was conveyed - 25th day of 10th month, 1685].
Margaret Holland, alias Gill, brought her paper of condemnation - 30th day of 8th month, 1685.
Meeting held at house of George Royston - 26th day of 9th month, 1686.
John Astin and Sarah Pardoe - intentions to marry - 26th day of 9th month, 1686. [Meeting to determine what is done for orphans of John Pardoe].
Meeting held at house of John Astin - 28th day of 8th month, 1687.
Samuel Thomas and Mary Hutchins - intentions to marry - 13rd day of 2nd month, 1688.
John Pardoe and Mary Webb - intentions to marry - 30th day of 6th month, 1689.
Mary Webb found to be under a former engagement to another person - 25th day of 8th month, 1689.
Mary Webb produces a discharge from whom she was formerly engaged - 20th day of 10th month, 1689.
William Coale procures title to burying ground from William Sharp - 25th day of 6th month, 1691.
Abraham Birckhead and Rebecca Billingsley - intentions to marry, with her parents consent - 18th day of 10th month, 1691 [2nd time].
Thomas Evernden to visit Friends in Pennsylvania - 18th day of 9th month, 1692.
William Berry gives 2 acres for Patuxent burying ground - 25th day of 6th month, 1693.
James Berry gives title to burying ground - 25th day of 6th month, 1693.

MONTHLY MEETING MINUTES, 1677 - 1771

Robert Day and Sarah Meares - intentions to marry - 3rd day of 5th month, 1698/9.

----sting[?] and Hannah Ferrest[?] - intentions to marry - 31st day of 9th month, 1698.

Samuel Harrison and Elizabeth Parrott - intentions to marry - 28th day of 2nd month, 1699.

Robert Gover and Susanna Billingsley - intentions to marry - inquiry to be made into care of her children - 8th day of 10th month, 1699.

Richard Webb intends to remove to Choptank to dwell - desires certificate concerning his clearness for marriage - 2th day of 12th month, 1699.

John Pardoe and Levicey [Lucey?] Webb - intentions to marry - 13th day of 7th month, 1700 [2nd time].

Gerrard Hopkins and Margaret Johns - intentions to marry - 6th day of 10th month, 1700.

John Webb and Hannah Parker [Parkes?] - intentions to marry - 6th day of 10th month, 1700.

John Parrish and Sarah Horne - intentions to marry - she has child by former husband - 3rd day of 11th month, 1700/1.

Samuell Wallis and Frances Young - intentions to marry - 28th day of 1st month, 1701.

Orphan children of Mathews [Mathers?] Feris delivered to Friends - 20th day of 4th month, 1701.

Richard Harris and Elizabeth Webb - intentions to marry - 20th day of 4th month, 1701 [2nd time] - with consent of their mothers at meeting on 15th day of 6th month, 1701.

Elizabeth Keys, a travelling Friend - certificate from Philadelphia - 30th day of 11th month, 1701.

Benjamin Laurence and Rachell Mariartee - intentions to marry - 5th day of 10th month, 1701 [1st time], and 2nd day of 11th month, 1701 [2nd time].

Jacob Giles and Elizabeth Arnold - intentions to marry - 5th day of 10th month [1st time], and 2nd day of 11th month, 1701 [2nd time].

Thomas Davis and Mary Day - intentions to marry - 5th day of 10th month, 1701 [1st time], and 2nd day of 11th month, 1701 [2nd time].

John Belt and Lucey Laurence - intentions to marry - with consent of parents - 2nd day of 11th month, 1701 [1st time], and 30th day of 11th month, 1701/2 [2nd time].

Sampson Warring and Hanna Meares - intentions to marry - 27th day of 1st month, 1702.

Richard Bond and Elizabeth Chew, widow of Benjamin Chew - intentions to marry [she has children] - 17th day of 5th month, 1702. At the meeting on 11th day of 7th month, 1702, he produced papers from his neighbors in Virginia, his former abode.

QUAKER RECORDS OF SOUTHERN MARYLAND

Letter from John Pickett, who formerly belonged to Clifts Meeting and now Philadelphia, who now desires certificate to signify his clearness for marriage - 1st day of 11th month, 1702.
Henry Child, lately from England with divers of his children, produces certificate showing unity with Friends and clearness from engagement of marriage - 1st day of 11th month, 1702.
John Pickett - certificate to Philadelphia - 2nd day of 11th month, 1702.
Samuel Chew, Jr. and Mary Harrison - intentions to marry - 16th day of 5th month, 1703 [1st time], and 13th day of 6th month, 1703 [2nd time].
Robert Roberts and Priscilla Johns - intentions to marry - 3rd day of 10th month, 1703 [1st time], and 31st day of 10th month, 1703 [2nd time].
Nathaniel Giles and Elizabeth Harris - intentions to marry - 3rd day of 10th month, 1703 [1st time], and 31st day of 10th month, 1703 [2nd time].
Daniel Robison [Robinson?] and Sarah Hewes [Neves?] - intentions to marry - 3rd day of 10th month, 1703 [1st time], and 31st day of 10th month, 1703 [2nd time].
Thomas Turner - certificate from England - 28th day of 11th month, 1703.
Certificate of removal from Friends in London for Mary Bannister and Mary Elerton - 28th day of 11th month, 1703/4.
George Harris and Anna Young - intentions to marry - 25th day of 12th month, 1703 [1st time], and 24th day of 1st month, 1703 [2nd time].
Solomon Birckhead and Anne Child - intentions to marry - 24th day of 1st month, 1703/4 [1st time], and 21st day of 2nd month, 1704 [2nd time].
Thomas Miles and Ruth Jones - intentions to marry - 21st day of 2nd month, 1704 [1st time], and 19th day of 3rd month, 1704 [2nd time].
Samuel Chew and Elizabeth Coale, widow - intentions to marry [she has children] - 19th day of 3rd month, 1704 [1st time], and 16th day of 4th month, 1704 [2nd time].
Meeting to protect children of Elizabeth Coale in right to property [she is a widow marrying] - 16th day of 4th month, 1704.
Thomas Hawkins and Elizabeth Giles - intentions to marry - 25th date of 12th month, 1703/4 [1st time], and 24th day of 1st month, 1703/4 [2nd time].
Mordecai Moore desires a certificate to signify unity and clearness for marriage - 14th day of 5th month, 1704.
Arthur Young and Mary Ball [Bell?] - intentions to marry [the young woman producing a certificate from Friends in London] - 8th day of 7th month, 1704 [1st time], and 6th day of 8th month, 1704 [2nd time].
William Harrison, intending to inhabit Pennsylvania, desires certificate of removal - 8th day of 7th month, 1704.
John Hutchins and Elizabeth Talbott, Jr. - intentions to marry - 8th day of 7th month, 1704 [1st time], and 6th day of 8th month, 1704 [2nd time].

MONTHLY MEETING MINUTES, 1677 - 1771

Thomas Barklett [Bartlett?] Jr. and Margaret Willson [has children] - intentions to marry - 3th day of 9th month, 1704 [1st time], and 1st day of 10th month, 1704 [2nd time].
Richard Giest [Guest?] and Zeporah Murry - intentions to marry - 3rd day of 9th month, 1704 [1st time], and 1st day of 10th month, 1704 [2nd time].
Samuel Galloway - certificate to....29th day of 10th month, 1704.
Thomas Day and Hannah Harris - intentions to marry - 15th day of 4th month, 1705 [1st time], and 3rd day of 5th month, 1705 [2nd time].
Ephraim Gover and Mary Harper - intentions to marry - 15th day of 4th month, 1705 [1st time], and 3rd day of 5th month, 1705 [2nd time].
John Talbot and Elizabeth Galloway - intentions to marry - 3rd day of 5th month, 1705.
John Tydings and Mary Ellis - intentions to marry - 3rd day of 5th month, 1705.
Joseph Richardson and Sarah Thomas - intentions to marry, with consent of parents - 7th day of 7th month, 1705 [1st time], and 5th day of 8th month, 1705 [2nd time].
Thomas Cromwell and Jemima Murry, widow - intentions to marry - 5th day of 8th month, 1705 [1st time], and 2nd day of 9th month, 1705 [2nd time]. Meeting will inquire into care of children of James Murry.
Thomas Carr and Elizabeth Price - intentions to marry - 5th day of 8th month, 1705 [1st time], and 2nd day of 9th month, 1705 [2nd time].
Richard Lewen and Mary Child, with consent of Henry Child - intentions to marry - 30th day of 9th month, 1705 [1st time], and 28th day of 10th month, 1705 [2nd time].
William Harrison - certificate to go to England - 25th day of 11th month, 1705/6.
John Preston - certificate to go to England - 22nd day of 1st month, 1705/6.
Henry Child - certificate to western Virginia - 22nd day of 1st month, 1705/6.
Samuel Gover and Elizabeth Roberts - intentions to marry, with consent of parents - 14th day of 4th month, 1706 [1st time], and 12th day of 5th month, 1706 [2nd time].
Anne Galloway to visit Pennsylvania and to be accompanied by her husband Samuel Galloway, and Eliza Chew - 12th day of 5th month, 1706.
John Giles - certificate to England - 12th day of 5th month, 1706.
Nehemiah Birckhead, Jr. and Sarah Hutchins - intentions to marry - 1st day of 9th month, 1706 [1st time], and 29th day of 9th month, 1706 [2nd time].
Jonathan Hanson and Keziah Murry - intentions to marry - 1st day of 9th month, 1706 [1st time], and 29th day of 9th month, 1706 [2nd time].
Richard Harrison, Jr. and Elizabeth Hall, dau. of Elisha Hall - intentions to marry, with parents consent - 21st day of 11th month, 1706 [1st time], and 21st day of 12th month, 1706 [2nd time].
Robert Roberts - certificate to visit Eastern Shore - 21st day of 12th month, 1706.
John Talbot and Mary Waters - intentions to marry - 11th day of 5th month, 1707.
Quarterly Meeting held at house of Ann Chew - 23rd day of 5th month, 1707.

QUAKER RECORDS OF SOUTHERN MARYLAND

Richard Johns [Jr.] and Priscilla Huctchins - intentions to marry - 4th day of 7th month, 1707 [1st time], and 3rd day of 8th month, 1707 [2nd time].
John Chew and Elizabeth Harrison - intentions to marry - 19th day of 1st month, 1707/8 [1st time], and 20th day of 6th month, 1707 [2nd time].
Reference to death of Abraham Johns - reference made on 28th day of 11th month, 1707.
Anthony Conwell and Elizabeth Talbott - intentions to marry - 9th day of 5th month, 1708.
Thomas Norris and Sarah Parrish - intentions to marry - 26th day of 9th month, 1708 [1st time], and 24th day of 10th month, 1708 [2nd time].
Richard Moore, son of Mordecai Moore, having made some orderly proceedings upon account of marriage with a young woman of Pennsylvania, desires certificate for behavior and clearness for marriage - 15th day of 2nd month, 1709.
Richard Snowden the youngest, and Elizabeth Coale, Jr. - intentions to marry - 13th day of 3rd month, 1709.
Henry Child, Jr. presents a paper condemning himself for seeking a wife not educated in the way of the truth - 23rd day of 10th month, 1709.
Henry Child, Jr. and Margaret Preston, both of Herring Creek Meeting - intentions to marry - 23rd day of 11th month, 1709/10 [1st time], and 17th day of 12th month, 1709/10 [2nd time].
Reference to death of Acquilla Johns - reference made on 23rd day of 11th month, 1709/10.
Joseph Smith and Laurana Richardson - intentions to marry - 17th day of 12th month, 1709.
William Foard and Hannah Galloway, dau. of Samuel Galloway - married without consent of the Meeting - disowned - 7th day of 5th month, 1710.
Thomas Little and Elizabeth Day - intentions to marry - 7th day of 5th month, 1710 [1st time], and 2nd day of 7th month, 1710 [2nd time].
John Harper desires certificate for clearness for marriage - 7th day of 5th month, 1710.
Kensey Johns, son of Richard, and Elizabeth Chew, dau. of Benjamin Chew, deceased - intentions to marry - 24th day of 9th month, 1710 [1st time], and 22nd day of 10th month, 1710 [2nd time].
Eleanor Harris, dau. of William Harris, deceased, disowned for marrying contrary to the Society of Friends - 22nd day of 10th month, 1710.
Mary Young, dau. of Arthur Young, of Patuxent Meeting, disowned for marrying contrary to the Society of Friends - 16th day of 12th month, 1710/11.
William Preston has taken a wife contrary to the Society of Friends and offers acknowledgement - 16th day of 12th month, 1710/11 [from Herring Creek Meeting].

MONTHLY MEETING MINUTES, 1677 - 1771

Reference to death of Arthur Young - reference made on 5th day of 2nd month, 1711.
Samuel Galloway to go to England with his wife to see her relations and friends - 8th day of 4th month, 1711.
Samuel Harrison, son of Richard Harrison, and Sarah Hall, dau. of Elisha Hall - intentions to marry - 8th day of 4th month, 1711 [1st time], and 6th day of 5th month, 1711 [2nd time].
Henry Troth, son of William Troth of Talbot County, and Elizabeth Johns, Jr., dau. of Richard Johns - intentions to marry [young man having a certificate from Treadhaven Monthly Meeting] - 6th day of 5th month, 1711 [1st time], and 3rd day of 6th month, 1711 [2nd time].
Joseph Pennington, of Swarthmore Meeting in Great Britain, produces a certificate of removal - 3rd day of 6th month, 1711.
Reference to death of Joseph Pennington and assistance to his widow and children - reference made on 28th day of 7th month, 1711.
Benjamin Hance and Mary Hutchins - intentions to marry - 3rd day of 6th month, 1711 [1st time], and last day of 6th month, 1711 [2nd time].
Meeting to assist orphans of Joseph Pennington, and a letter from his brother Isaac Pennington, of Swarthmore, England - 26th day of 8th month, 1711.
Francis Wallis, wife of Samuel Wallis, to keep orphan children of Joseph Pennington - 18th day of 11th month, 1711.
William Walker and wife Jane produce a certificate of removal from the Monthly Meeting at Raby, County of Durham, Great Britain - 18th day of 11th month, 1711. They have settled at Patuxent.
Thomas Holland and Margaret Watters - intentions to marry - 15th day of 12th month, 1711 [1st time], and 14th day of 1st month, 1711 [2nd time].
Robert Roberts to visit Friends in Pennsylvania and New England - 14th day of 1st month, 1711/12.
John Farmer - certificate from Colester, Great Britain - 14th day of 1st month, 1712.
Robert Stork and wife Tabitha - certificate from Hounslow [?] Down in London, England - 11th day of 2nd month, 1712.
Nehemiah Birkhead and Margaret Johns - intentions to marry - 4th day of 5th month, 1712 [1st time], and 5th day of 6th month, 1712 [2nd time].
Ralph Somerfield and wife Hannah - certificate from Kettesing [?], Great Britain - 5th day of 6th month, 1712.
Richard Hall and Mary Johns - intentions to marry - 5th day of 6th month, 1712 [1st time], and 29th day of 6th month, 1712 [2nd time].
Joseph Coleman and Mary Thomas - intentions to marry - 5th day of 6th month, 1712 [1st time], and 29th day of 6th month, 1712 [2nd time].
Jacob Duhadaway and Elizabeth Parrish - intentions to marry - 26th day of 7th month, 1712 [1st time], and 24th day of 8th month, 1712 [2nd time].

QUAKER RECORDS OF SOUTHERN MARYLAND

Isaac Johns and Ann Galloway, Jr. - intentions to marry - 25th day of 9th month, 1712 [1st time], and 19th day of 10th month, 1712 [2nd time].
John Astin - married and disowned - 20th day of 11th month, 1712.
Mary Cousins - married and disowned - 22nd day of 8th month, 1713.
Jesse Jacob Bourne and Hannah Nellis, both of Patuxent Meeting - intentions to marry - 12th day of 1st month, 1713/14 [1st time], and 9th day of 2nd month, 1713/14 [2nd time]. He produces a certificate from meeting in London for clearness for marriage.
Robert Stork and wife - certificate to....on 12th day of 1st month, 1714.
William Lovell - certificate to....in 1714.
John Saul - certificate from Dublin, England - 9th day of 2nd month, 1714.
Benjamin Ball, of Kent Island, and Elizabeth Richardson, dau. of William Richardson, of Anne Arundel County - intentions to marry - 4th day of 4th month, 1714 [1st time], and 2nd day of 5th month, 1714 [2nd time].
Isaac Pennington requests this meeting to draw an indenture for an orphan of Joseph Pennington, or refer to the monthly meeting in Pennsylvania to which William Baldwin belongs - 2nd day of 5th month, 1714.
Letter of condemnation for William Walker's outgoing in taking a wife contrary to the practice of Friends - 2nd day of 5th month, 1714.
Joseph Harris and Ann Young - intentions to marry - 27th day of 6th month, 1714 [1st time], and 22nd day of 8th month, 1714 [2nd time].
Thomas Miles and Elizabeth White - intentions to marry - 19th day of 9th month, 1714 [1st time], and 17th day of 10th month, 1714 [2nd time].
John Wilson and Elizabeth White - intentions to marry - 11th day of 12th month, 1714/15 [1st time], and 11th day of 1st month, 1714/15 [2nd time].
Representatives to visit Nicholas Fitsimons and examine the truth of his having a bastard child - 8th day of 2nd month, 1715.
William Wilson and Rachel Child - intentions to marry - 8th day of 2nd month, 1715 [1st time].
Richard Galloway, Jr. and Sophia Richardson, dau. of William Richardson - intentions to marry - 1st day of 5th month, 1715 [1st time]. On 29th day of 5th month, 1715, his father's illness and his own indisposition hinders his coming to this meeting, so he requests matter be referred to next quarterly meeting. On 23th day of 7th month, 1715, Richard and Sophia delayed by sickness.
Samuell Chew, of Maidstone, son of Benjamin Chew, and Mary, dau. of Samuel Galloway - intentions to marry, with consent of parents - 23rd day of 7th month, 1715 [1st time], and 21st day of 8th month, 1715 [2nd time].
John Hawkins, Jr. and Sarah Norris - intentions to marry - 21st day of 8th month, 1715 [1st time], and 18th day of 9th month, 1715 [2nd time].

MONTHLY MEETING MINUTES, 1677 - 1771

Peter Galloway and Elizabeth Rigbie - intentions to marry - 16th day of 10th month, 1715 [1st time], and 13th day of 11th month, 1715 [2nd time].
Joseph Bedlow who hath resided in these parts for some time past, signifies his design of returning to England, the place of his nativity, and requests a certificate - 9th day of 1st month, 1715/16.
John Crockett and Mary Coale - intentions to marry - 1st day of 4th month, 1716 [1st time], and 29th day of 4th month, 1716 [2nd time].
Kensey Johns - certificate to London - 1st day of 4th month, 1716.
William Coale and Sarah White - intentions to marry - 29th day of 4th month, 1716 [1st time], and 27th day of 5th month, 1716 [2nd time].
Steven Price and Constant Horne - intentions to marry - 29th day of 4th month, 1716 [1st time], and 27th day of 5th month, 1716 [2nd time].
Nathaniel Chew - disowned - 27th day of 5th month, 1716.
William Harris and Elizabeth Young - intentions to marry - 24th day of 6th month, 1716 [1st time], and 21st day of 7th month, 1716 [2nd time].
Difference exists between John Chew and his brother Samuel, and their brother-in-law Samuel Harrison, relating to their father, Richard Harrison's, estate - 31st day of 3rd month, 1717.
James Dickinson and Hannah Coale - intentions to marry - 20th day of 7th month, 1717 [1st time], and 15th day of 9th month, 1717 [2nd time]. He produces a certificate from Friends of the Eastern Shore for clearness for marriage, with consent of his parents.
Nathan Rigbie and Cassandra Coale, Jr. - intentions to marry - 20th day of 7th month, 1717 [1st time], and 15th day of 9th month, 1717 [2nd time].
Richard Snowden and Elizabeth Thomas - intentions to marry, with consent of parents - 15th day of 9th month, 1717 [1st time], and 13th day of 10th month, 1717 [2nd time].
Jobe Hunt and Sarah Day - intentions to marry - 15th day of 9th month, 1717 [1st time], and 13th day of 10th month, 1717 [2nd time].
Samuel Harrison to make a voyage to England - 10th day of 11th month, 1717/18.
John Galloway and Mary Thomas, Jr. - intentions to marry, parents consenting - 27th day of 4th month, 1718 [1st time], and 25th day of 5th month, 1718 [2nd time].
Jonathan Hanson and Mary Price - intentions to marry - 27th day of 4th month, 1718 [1st time], and 25th day of 5th month, 1718 [2nd time].
Richard Galloway, Sr. and Sarah Sparrow - intentions to marry - 26th day of 1st month, 1719 [1st time], and 24th day of 5th month, 1719 [2nd time].
Robert Roberts to visit old England - 29th day of 3rd month, 1719.
Benjamin Small, of Nancemond, Virginia, and Elizabeth Coale, of West River, Maryland - intentions to marry - 22th day of 6th month, 1719 [1st time], and 13th day of 9th month, 1719 [2nd time].

Reference to death of Richard Johns - reference made on 18th day of 7th month, 1719.

Elizabeth Small, formerly Elizabeth Coale, about to remove to Virginia - 11th day of 10th month, 1719 [see above].

Elihu Hall and Elizabeth Coale - intentions to marry - 27th day of 3rd month, 1720 [1st time], and 24th day of 4th month, 1720 [2nd time].

Richard Hill and Deborah Moore, Jr. - intentions to marry - 6th day of 10th month, 1720 [1st time], and 3rd day of 12th month, 1720/21 [2nd time].

Richard Franklin [Frankling] and Elliner Ward - intentions to marry - 6th day of 10th month, 1720 [1st time], and 3rd day of 12th month, 1720/21 [2nd time].

Henry Troth, on behalf of Priscilla Coale, requests certificate signifying clearness for marriage - 3rd day of 12th month, 1720/21.

Henry Hill, Jr. and Sarah Galloway, Jr. - intentions to marry - 3rd day of 12th month, 1720/21 [1st time], and 3rd day of 1st month, 1720/21 [2nd time].

Phillip Thomas and Francis Holland - intentions to marry - 3rd day of 12th month, 1720/21 [1st time], and 3rd day of 1st month, 1720/21 [2nd time].

Caleb Clark, having resided on this side of the Bay and now removed to the Eastern Shore, desires a certificate of clearness for marriage - 12th day of 3rd month, 1721.

Priscilla Coale - certificate to....12th day of 3rd month, 1721.

Jesse Jacob Bourne - certificate to go to Pennsylvania in 1721.

Deborah Moore, member of West River Meeting, to remove to Philadelphia for some time, requests a certificate - 2nd day of 1st month, 1721/22.

Daniel Rawlings - too old to represent Patuxent Meeting - 24th day of 2nd month, 1722.

Elihu Hall and Elizabeth Chew - intentions to marry - 14th day of 7th month, 1722.

John Appleton - certificate to go to Philadelphia in 1722.

Elizabeth Giles desires a certificate to New Garden Monthly Meeting, Pennsylvania, regarding her clearness for marriage - 7th day of 10th month, 1722.

Application on behalf of Margaret Bartlett, for many years resident of this side of the Bay - lately removed among Friends of Treadhaven Monthly Meeting - 7th day of 10th month, 1722.

Levin Hill and Elizabeth Hopkins - intentions to marry - 7th day of 10th month, 1722 [1st time], and 4th day of 11th month, 1722 [2nd time].

Assistance to widow of Ralph Somerfield - 4th day of 11th month, 1722.

John Giles, Jr. and Cassandra Smith - intentions to marry - 7th day of 10th month, 1722 [1st time], and 4th day of 11th month, 1722/23 [2nd time].

John Parrish and Elizabeth Roberts - intentions to marry - 4th day of 10th month, 1722/23 [1st time], and 1st day of 11th month, 1722/23 [2nd time].

Joseph Richardson, Jr. and Rebeckah Johns - intentions to marry - 1st day of 11th month, 1722/23 [1st time], and 1st day of 1st month, 1722/23 [2nd time].

MONTHLY MEETING MINUTES, 1677 - 1771

Richard Lewen [Lewes?] and Betey Giles - intentions to marry - 26th day of 2nd month, 1723.

Melchizadick Murry and Sophia Giles - intentions to marry - 13th day of 7th month, 1723 [1st time].

Joseph Cowman, of Great Britain, mariner, and Sarah Hill, widow, of Anne Arundel County, Maryland - intentions to marry - 13th day of 11th month, 1723 [1st time], and 28th day of 12th month, 1723/24 [2nd time]. He produces a certificate from the Monthly Meeting of Parslow Cragg in Cumberland, within the compass of which he dwelt when at home. His mother is living.

John Steward and Sarah Franklin - intentions to marry - 13th day of 11th month, 1723 [1st time], and 28th day of 12th month, 1723 [2nd time].

Samuell Plummer and Sarah Miles - intentions to marry - 13th day of 11th month, 1723 [1st time], and 28th day of 12th month, 1723 [2nd time].

Mordicai Price and Elizabeth White - intentions to marry - 27th day of 1st month, 1724 [1st time], and 24th day of 2nd month, 1724 [2nd time].

Philip Thomas and Ann Chew - intentions to marry - 17th day of 5th month, 1724.

Joseph Johns - certificate to New Garden, Pennsylvania - 14th day of 6th month, 1724.

Joseph Hill and Sarah Richardson - intentions to marry - 4th day of 7th month, 1724.

Aquilla Massy and Sarah Coale - intentions to marry - 1st day of 11th month, 1724.

Richard Simmons - certificate to Long Island [?] - 3rd day of 11th month, 1724.

Susanna Morris - certificate to Abington - 13th day of 11th month, 1724.

Ann Roberts - certificate to Abington - 13th day of 11th month, 1724.

James Brooks and Deborah Snowden - intentions to marry - 23rd day of -- month, 1725.

Thomas Taylor and Sarah Price - intentions to marry - 3rd day of 10th month, 1725.

Richard Harrison - certificate to Pennsylvania - 2nd day of 10th month, 1726.

Benjamin Chase and Sarah Bond - intentions to marry - 30th day of 10th month, 1726.

Gilbert Crockett and Mary Chew - intentions to marry - 24th day of 12th month, 1726/27.

Thomas Little and Usila Sewell - intentions to marry - 24th day of 12th month, 1726/27.

John Thomas and Elizabeth Snowden - intentions to marry - 24th day of 12th month, 1726/27.

Thomas Hunt and Elizabeth Wilkinson - intentions to marry - 21st day of 2nd month, 1727.

John England and Margaret Birckhead - intentions to marry - 21st day of 2nd month, 1727.

QUAKER RECORDS OF SOUTHERN MARYLAND

Arthur Harris and Elizabeth Robertson - intentions to marry - 21st day of 2nd month, 1727.
John Wilkinson, Jr. and Ann Harris - intentions to marry - 16th day of 4th month, 1727.
Sarah Marssey, formerly Sarah Coale, being removed near the territories of Pennsylvania - 11th day of 6th month, 1727.
Joseph Hopkins and Ann Chew - intentions to marry - 11th day of 6th month, 1727.
Richard Johns and Ann Coale - intentions to marry - 11th day of 6th month, 1727.
Aquila Johns and Ann Chew - intentions to marry - 11th day of 6th month, 1727.
Ruth Jones, a travelling Friend - certificate to Pennsylvania - 6th day of 7th month, 1727.
Nathaniel Giles and Elizabeth Welch - intentions to marry - 21st day of 12th month, 1728/9.
Agnes Goslin - certificate from Sedsberg, County York, England - 19th day of 2nd month, 1728.
Mary Hanson [of Patapsco] - married and disowned - 27th day of 10th month, 1728.
Sarah Giles - certificate to New Garden, Pennsylvania - 26th day of 12th month, 1728.
Ann Wallis - married and disowned - 21st day of 12th month, 1728.
Richard Johns, of Fuller[?], and Sarah Robertson, Jr. - intentions to marry, 23rd day of 11th month, 1729/30.
Samuell Wallis and Cassandra Talbott - intentions to marry - 20th day of 1st month, 1729/30.
Hannah Jenkinson - certificate to Pennsylvania - 12th day of 4th month, 1730.
Samuell Thomas and Mary Snowden, Jr. - intentions to marry - 20th day of 5th month, 1730.
Abraham Johns married out of the unity of Friends - 5th month, 1730.
Samuell Robertson and Elizabeth Harris - intentions to marry - 4th day of 7th month, 1730.
Edward Fell and Ann Thomas - intentions to marry - 4th day of 7th month, 1730.
Elishell [Eliphell?] Harper, a travelling Friend - reported 2nd day of 8th month, 1730.
Thomas Coale, of Nottingham, and Mary Richardson - intentions to marry - 2nd day of 8th month, 1730.
Isaac Johns and Elizabeth Harris - intentions to marry - 25th day of 10th month, 1730.
Littleton Waters and Elizabeth Birckhead - intentions to marry - 16th day of 2nd month, 1731.
Constance Young - disowned - 3rd day of 7th month, 1731.

MONTHLY MEETING MINUTES, 1677 - 1771

Jacob Giles - certificate to Nottingham - 29th day of 8th month, 1731.
Sarah Webster - certificate to Nottingham - 29th day of 8th month, 1731.
Samuell Waters, Jr. and Artridge Franklin [Frankling], Jr. - intentions to marry - 17th day of 1st month, 1731/2.
Gerard Hopkins, Samuel Harrison, Richard Hall, George Harris, Isaac Johns, Richard Richardson, Philip Thomas, and Benjamin Hance welcome Lord Baltimore - 14th day of 2nd month, 1732.
Dr. Samuel Chew and wife - certificate to Philadelphia - 14th day of 2nd month, 1732.
Robert Gover and Elizabeth Johns - intentions to marry - 13th day of 2nd month, 1733.
Hannah Dent - certificate to Eastern Shore - 23rd day of 9th month, 1733.
Cassandra Coale - certificate to Nottingham - 31st day of 10th month, 1733.
John Webster and Mary Talbott, from Nottingham Meeting - intentions to marry - 30th day of 6th month, 1734.
Nathan Smith and Cassandra Child - 11th day of 2nd month, 1735.
Mary Webster's visit regarding the marriage of her daughter, Lucey Talbott, was not satisfactory - 3rd day of 6th month, 1735.
Last meeting held at house of Richard Johns - 29th day of 6th month, 1735.
Reference to death of Isaac Johns and meeting held at his house - reference made on 29th day of 6th month, 1735.
John Hance and Sarah Hall - intentions to marry - 26th day of 7th month, 1735.
Nathan Richardson and Elizabeth Crockett - intentions to marry - 26th day of 7th month, 1735.
Samuel Wallis and family - certificate to Deer Creek - 6th day of 8th month, 1735.
Mary Webster has removed to within verge of Nottingham Monthly Meeting [see above] - 21st day of 9th month, 1735.
Benjamin Hance, Jr. and Elizabeth Johns, Jr. - intentions to marry in 1735.
Lucy Webster, now Lucy Talbott - married and disowned in 1735.
Samuell Chew and Mary Galloway - intentions to marry - 27th day of 6th month, 1736.
Philip Hopkins and Elizabeth Hall - intentions to marry - 27th day of 6th month, 1736.
John Pearpoint and Ann Gassoway - intentions to marry - 29th day of 5th month, 1737.
William Foard and wife separates - 29th day of 5th month, 1737.
Nehemiah Birckhead, Jr. and Sarah Coale - intentions to marry - 21st day of 8th month, 1737.
Joseph Hance and Ann Johns - intentions to marry - 13th day of 11th month, 1737/38.

QUAKER RECORDS OF SOUTHERN MARYLAND

Francis Pairpoint and Sarah Richardson - intentions to marry - 13th day of 11th month, 1737/38.
Isaac Roberts - certificate to....7th day of 2nd month, 1738.
Joseph Coleman - certificate to New England - 2nd day of 4th month, 1738.
Henry Hill and Sarah Galloway - intentions to marry - 22nd day of 7th month, 1738.
Phineas Bond - certificate to Philadelphia - 10th day of 12th month, 1738.
Dr. Samuel Chew and family - certificate to Kent on Delaware - 6th day of 2nd month, 1739.
Mordica More and Elizabeth Coleman - intentions to marry - 24th day of 6th month, 1739.
Peter Galloway and family - certificate to Kent on Delaware - 21st day of 7th month, 1739.
Robert Freeland and Elizabeth Gover - intentions to marry - 11th day of 11th month, 1739.
Jacob Duhadaway - certificate to Kent on Delaware - 2nd day of 3rd month, 1740.
William Harris and Margaret Thomas - intentions to marry - 2nd day of 3rd month, 1740.
Abraham Johns and Elizabeth Hance - intentions to marry - 25th day of 5th month, 1740.
Samuel Johns - certificate to....25th day of 5th month, 1740.
William Wilson, Jr. and Cassandra Gover - intentions to marry - 22nd day of 6th month, 1740.
Francis Bonfield - certificate to Baltimore County - 6th day of 1st month, 1741.
Jacob Duhadway and Sarah Harris - intentions to marry - 24th day of 5th month, 1741.
Jerrom Plummer [Plumber] and Mary Harris - intentions to marry - 8th day of 11th month, 1741/42.
Robert Gover and Sarah Walker - intentions to marry - 8th day of 11th month, 1741/42.
Henry Wilson and Priscilla Gover - intentions to marry - 11th day of 10th month, 1742.
Isaac Walker - certificate to....24th day of 2nd month, 1743.
William Walker - certificate to....20th day of 5th month, 1744.
Thomas Bourne - certificate to....20th day of 5th month, 1743.
Richard Holland and Ruth Plummer [Plumber] - intentions to marry - 11th day of 9th month, 1743.
William Richardson, Jr. and Ann Harris - intentions to marry - 6th day of 11th month, 1743.
Johns Hopkins and Mary Giles - intentions to marry - 27th day of -- month, 1744.

MONTHLY MEETING MINUTES, 1677 - 1771

Nehemiah Birckhead and Elizabeth Richardson - intentions to marry - 14th day of 7th month, 1744.
John Birckhead and Christian Harris - intentions to marry - in 11th month, 1745.
Charles Pierpont - married his first cousin - disowned - 29th day of 1st month, 1745.
Letter from Thomas and Sarah Harris condemning their taking each other in marriage from outside the Society of Friends - 24th day of 12th month, 1745/46.
Elizabeth Gover and son Philip Gover - certificate to Nottingham - 28th day of 1st month, 1746.
John Crockett and Mary Richardson - intentions to marry - 12th day of 3rd month, 1747.
Ephraim Gover and family - certificate to Nottingham - 19th day of 4th month, 1747.
William Wilson and family - certificate to Nottingham - 19th day of 4th month, 1747.
Samuel Preston Moore, and wife Hannah, reinstated - certificate to Philadelphia - 11th day of 7th month, 1747.
Henry Hill and Mary Thomas - intentions to marry - 29th day of 2nd month, 1748.
Samuel Harrison - certificate to Nottingham - 25th day of 9th month, 1748.
Joseph and Thomas Plumber [Plummer] - certificate to Monoquecy - 26th day of 3rd month, 1749.
William Smith and Hannah Walker - intentions to marry - 23rd day of 4th month, 1749.
Joseph Galloway and Ann Harris - intentions to marry - 23rd day of 4th month, 1749.
Johns Hopkins and Mary Crockett - intentions to marry - 28th day of 5th month, 1749.
John Cromwell - certificate to Fairfax - 28th day of 5th month, 1749.
Stephen Stewart and Ann Harris - intentions to marry - 25th day of 3rd month, 1750.
Joseph White - certificate to....23rd day of 7th month, 1750.
Sarah Chew's daughter married and certificate to Nottingham - 23rd day of 9th month, 1750.
Thomas Ross - certificate to....23rd day of 9th month, 1750.
William Coale - certificate to Gunpowder - 25th day of 11th month, 1750.
James Brook and son James Brook - certificate to travel to western Virginia - 27th day of 5th month, 1751.
Aquilla Massey - certificate from Fairfax - 9th day of 3rd month, 1754.
Richard Johns - certificate from Wilmington - 20th day of 10th month, 1754.
Thomas Moore - certificate to Philadelphia - 29th day of 11th month, 1754.
Margaret Smith - certificate to Pennsylvania - 29th day of 11th month, 1754.
Israel Thompson and Ann Richardson - intentions to marry - 28th day of 12th month, 1754.

QUAKER RECORDS OF SOUTHERN MARYLAND

Joseph Cowman and Elizabeth Snowden - intentions to marry - 28th day of 12th month, 1754.
Philip Thomas and Ann Galloway - intentions to marry - 28th day of 12th month, 1754.
Daniel Richardson and Margaret Hopkins - intentions to marry - 25th day of 10th month, 1754.
John Talbott and wife Margaret - certificate to Baltimore - 25th day of 4th month, 1755.
Benkid Willson and Elizabeth Gover - intentions to marry - 26th day of 12th month, 1755.
George Robertson - certificate to Nottingham - 24th day of 11th month, 1756.
William Coale, Jr. and Sarah Robertson - intentions to marry - 24th day of 11th month, 1756.
Priscilla Gover - certificate to Nottingham - 28th day of 1st month, 1757.
Sarah Robertson - certificate to Gunpowder - 28th day of 1st month, 1757.
Samuel Waters to be visited in regard to his daughter's marriage from outside the Society of Friends - 25th day of 2nd month, 1757.
Gerrard Hopkins, son of Philip Hopkins, has taken a wife from outside the Society of Friends - 29th day of 4th month, 1757.
Sarah Plummer [Plumber] - certificate to Monoquecy - 25th day of 5th month, 1757.
John Cowman and Sarah Hopkins - intentions to marry - 26th day of 8th month, 1757.
John Giles admitted as a member - 25th day of 11th month, 1757.
Daniel Robertson - certificate to Gunpowder - 27th day of 1st month, 1758.
Roger Brook - certificate to....27th day of 1st month, 1758.
Johns Hopkins and Elizabeth Thomas - intentions to marry - 27th day of 1st month, 1758.
Elizabeth Wilson - certificate to Gunpowder - 26th day of 5th month, 1758.
John Thomas and Margaret Richardson - intentions to marry - 29th day of 9th month, 1758.
Samuel Thomas and wife Mary - certificate to Nottingham - 23rd day of 2nd month, 1759.
James Brook - certificate to Fairfax - 27th day of 7th month, 1759.
Robert Pleasants, of Virginia, and Mary Hill - intentions to marry - 23rd day of 11th month, 1759.
John Harris, of Virginia, and Rachel Plummer [Plumber] - marriage accomplished - 23rd day of 11th month, 1759.
Letter from Rebeckah Grayhorn condemning her marriage contrary to the rules of Friends - 23rd day of 11th month, 1759.

MONTHLY MEETING MINUTES, 1677 - 1771

Rachel Harris - certificate to Cedar Creek, Virginia - 25th day of 3rd month, 1760.
Mary Hepburn reinstated as a member - 26th day of 9th month, 1760.
Joseph Gill and Anne Cowman - intentions to marry - 26th day of 9th month, 1760.
Isaac Webster, son of Margaret Webster, and Sarah Richardson - marriage accomplished - 28th day of 11th month, 1760.
Richard Johns - certificate to Philadelphia - 28th day of 11th month, 1760.
Margaret Matthews - certificate from Fairfax - 26th day of 11th month, 1760.
Rebecca Trayhorn - certificate to Fairfax - 28th day of 11th month, 1760.
William Cox - certificate from Nottingham in 1761.
Mary Pleasants - certificate to Henrico County, Virginia - 23rd day of 1st month, 1761.
Herman Husband - certificate from Cane Creek, North Carolina - 27th day of 2nd month, 1761.
Thomas Pleasants [from Black Water Monthly Meeting, Virginia], son of Mary Pleasants, and Elizabeth Brooke - marriage accomplished - 24th day of 4th month, 1761.
Hannah Brook - certificate from Fairfax - 24th day of 4th month, 1761.
Samuel Hopkins - certificate to Deer Creek - 26th day of 6th month, 1761.
Elizabeth Pleasants - certificate to Cedar Creek, Virginia - 26th day of 6th month, 1761.
Herman Husband - certificate to Cane Creek, North Carolina - 24th day of 7th month, 1761.
Philip Gover and Mary Hopkins - intentions to marry - 24th day of 7th month, 1761.
Cornelius Garrison and Priscilla Ruly - intentions to marry - 28th day of 8th month, 1761.
Mary Gover - certificate to Deer Creek - 28th day of 8th month, 1761.
James Rigbie - certificate from Nottingham - 28th day of 8th month, 1761.
Moses Harris, of Virginia, and Elizabeth Plummer [Plumber] - intentions to marry - 27th day of 11th month, 1761.
David Brown - certificate to Philadelphia - 27th day of 11th month, 1761.
Elizabeth Harris - certificate to Cedar Creek, Virginia - 26th day of 12th month, 1761.
Dr. Richard Johns and daughters Anne, Margaret, Mary, and Elizabeth - certificate to Philadelphia - 26th day of 12th month, 1761.
Abraham Plummer [Plumber] and Sarah Ward - intentions to marry - 29th day of 1st month, 1762.
George Robertson - certificate from Deer Creek - 29th day of 1st month, 1762.
Priscilla Fantham [Fentham?], formerly Johns - reinstated, and certificate to Philadelphia - 23rd day of 4th month, 1762.

QUAKER RECORDS OF SOUTHERN MARYLAND

Richard Richardson and children Milcah, William, and Lucretia - certificate from Fairfax - 23rd day of 4th month, 1762.
Rebecca Tucker - certificate from Tread Haven - 23rd day of 4th month, 1762.
Letter from Frances Dallam, formerly Frances Wallis - acknowledges her marriage contrary to the good order of Friends, and requests a certificate to Deer Creek - 26th day of 8th month, 1762.
Joseph Jones, a travelling Friend - certificate from Philadelphia - 26th day of 8th month, 1762.
Ezekiel Hopkins - certificate to Philadelphia - 24th day of 12th month, 1762.
Reference to scandalous practice of Henry Sanders - disowned - 24th day of 6th month, 1763.
William Hanks - certificate to Virginia - 29th day of 7th month, 1763.
Sarah Webster - certificate to Deer Creek - 29th day of 7th month, 1763.
Reference to scandalous practice of Richard Hopkins - disowned - 23rd day of 9th month, 1763.
Mary Sprigg, formerly Mary Wilkinson - married outside the Society of Friends - disowned - 25th day of 11th month, 1763.
Ann Magruder, formerly Ann Harris - married outside the Society of Friends - disowned - 25th day of 11th month, 1763.
Daniel Talbott admitted as member - 25th day of 11th month, 1763.
Daniel Talbott and Elizabeth Ward - intentions to marry - 27th day of 1st month, 1764.
Bazel Brooke and Elizabeth Hopkins - intentions to marry - 23rd day of 3rd month, 1764.
Mordecai Smith - married and disowned - 25th day of 5th month, 1764.
John Ward and Rachel Talbot - intentions to marry - 27th day of 7th month, 1764.
William Norris - certificate to London - 24th day of 8th month, 1764.
Thomas Norris, Jr. - certificate to Tread Haven - 25th day of 1st month, 1765.
John Ward [Warde] and wife - certificate to Gunpowder - 25th day of 1st month, 1765.
Benjamin Feris [Fearis], a travelling Friend from ----, 29th day of 3rd month, 1765.
Rachel Gover, now Rachel Allen - married and disowned - 29th day of 3rd month, 1765.
Benjamin Hance, son of Joseph Hance - married and disowned - 26th day of 4th month, 1765.
Reference to Ann Hance and Elizabeth Hance acting disorderly - disowned - and Joseph Hance "treated with" on account of children - 26th day of 4th month, 1765.
Philip Hopkins - certificate to Philadelphia - 26th day of 4th month, 1765.

MONTHLY MEETING MINUTES, 1677 - 1771

Joseph Smith, wife Rachel, and children Isaac, Jacob, Abraham, Nathan, Seth, and Levy - certificate from Warrington, Pennsylvania - 20th day of 6th month, 1765.
Reference to conduct of Robert Norris - disowned - 25th day of 6th month, 1765.
Elizaebth Richardson has illegitimate child - disowned - 28th day of 6th month, 1765.
Mary Norris - certificate from....23rd day of 8th month, 1765.
Sarah Pancoast - certificate to Fairfax - 27th day of 9th month, 1765.
Sarah Gover, Jr. - married and disowned - 29th day of 11th month, 1765.
Priscilla Fantham [Fentham?] and children Ann, Mary, and William - certificate from Philadelphia - 23rd day of 7th month, 1766.
Richard Brooke - disowned - 27th day of 12th month, 1765.
Samuel Snowden, wife Elizabeth, and children - reinstated - 25th day of 12th month, 1766.
Margaret Hance and Rebecca Hance - both married and disowned - 27th day of 2nd month, 1767.
Margaret Matthews - certificate to York, Pennsylvania - 27th day of 3rd month, 1767.
Daniel Smith debauches a young woman - disowned - 25th day of 9th month, 1767.
Isaac Andrew, a travelling friend from Haddonfield, New Jersey - reported 25th day of 3rd month, 1768.
Hannah Brooke - certificate to Fairfax - 24th day of 6th month, 1768.
Ann Johns - married and disowned - 26th day of 8th month, 1768.
John Hopkins - certificate to Philadelphia - 27th day of 1st month, 1769.
Elizabeth Yarnall - certificate from Fairfax - 24th day of 3rd month, 1769.
Elizabeth Hopkins - certificate from Philadelphia - 26th day of 1st month, 1770.
Hannah Smith - married and disowned - 26th day of 1st month, 1770.
Lewis Griffin - married and disowned - 26th day of 1st month, 1770.
Hannah Gover - married and disowned - 26th day of 1st month, 1770.
Henry Hill and Margaret, formerly Ogle - married and disowned - 25th day of 11th month, 1770.
Richard and Mary Roberts - certificate to Philadelphia - 25th day of 11th month, 1770.
Samuel Harris - certificate to Gunpowder - 25th day of 1st month, 1771.
Margaret Wilson - certificate to Gunpowder - 25th day of 1st month, 1771.
Joseph Oxley, a travelling Friend - certificate from Old England - 28th day of 3rd month, 1771.
John Talbott and wife admitted as members - 28th day of 8th month, 1771.
Children of Samuel and Ann Galloway:
Richard Galloway, b. 5th day of 11th month, 1689, in London, England.
Peter Galloway, b. 12th day of 5th month, 1690, in West River, Maryland.

John Galloway, b. 6th day of 12th month, 1693.
Ann Galloway, b. 12th day of 2nd month, 1695.
Peter Biner[?] Galloway, b. 2nd day of 2nd month, 1696.
Mary Galloway, b. 15th day of 5th month, 1697.
---- Galloway, a child, b. in 8th month, 1698, and died ----.
Joseph Galloway, b. 8th day of 8th month, 1699.
Sarah Galloway, b. 15th day of 11th month, 1700.
Richard Galloway, b. 10th day of 11th month, 1701.
Agagts. [Augustus?] Galloway, b. 12th day of 8th month, 1702.

BIRTHS AND DEATHS OF SANDY SPRING MONTHLY MEETING

"This is the continuation of Cliffs, West River, Herring Creek, and Indian Spring Monthly Meeting. Placed in vault at Park Avenue Meeting House, 7th month, 5th day, 1897."

BIRTHS:
Children of James and Deborah Brooke, of Sandy Spring:
James Brooke, b. 28th day of 2nd month, 1730/1.
Roger Brooke, b. 9th day of 8th month, 1734.
Richard Brooke, b. 8th day of 7th month, 1736.
Basil Brooke, b. 13th day of 12th month, 1738.
Elizabeth Brooke, b. 22nd day of 3rd month, 1740/1.
Thomas Brooke, b. 8th day of 3rd month, 1743/4.
Children of Samuel and Mary Thomas:
Mary Thomas, b. 3rd day of 9th month, 1731.
Samuel Thomas, b. 23rd day of 7th month, 1733.
Philip Thomas, b. 18th day of 2nd month, 1734/5.
Elizabeth Thomas, b. 10th day of 1st month, 1736.
Evan Thomas, b. 21st day of 11th month, 1738.
Children of Evan and Rachel Thomas:
Mary Thomas, b. 14th day of 8th month, 1768.
Ann Thomas, b. 6th day of 8th month, 1771.
Philip Thomas and Samuel Thomas twins, b. 12th day of 1st month, 1774.
Philip [Philip E.?] Thomas, b. 13th day of -- month, 1776.
Elizabeth Thomas, b. 26th day of 3rd month, 1779.
Evan Thomas, Jr., b. 2nd day of 3rd month, 1781.

BIRTHS AND DEATHS OF SANDY SPRING MONTHLY MEETING

Margarett Thomas, b. 26th day of 4th month, 1783.
Children of Samuel 3d and Mary Thomas:
Samuel Thomas, b. 13th day of 11th month, 1776.
John Thomas 3d, b. 30th day of 1st month, 1778.
Sarah Thomas, b. 25th day of 1st month, 1781.
Henry Thomas, b. 9th day of 12th month, 1782.
Elizabeth Thomas, b. 28th day of 4th month, 1784.
Mary Thomas, b. 16th day of 11th month, 1785.
Children of Roger and Mary Brooke, of Sandy Spring:
Samuel Brooke, b. 9th day of 12th month, 1758.
Mary Brooke, b. 27th day of 9th month, 1760.
James Brooke, b. 13th day of 3rd month, 1762.
Deborah Brooke, b. 6th day of 2nd month, 1764.
Margaret Brooke, b. 23rd day of 11th month, 1765.
Sarah Brooke, b. 29th day of 12th month, 1767.
Hannah Brooke, b. 5th day of 6th month, 1770.
Elizabeth Brooke, b. 25th day of 8th month, 1772.
Roger Brooke, b. 24th day of 11th month, 1774.
Dorothy Brooke, b. 24th day of 12th month, 1776.
Children of Richard and Sarah Thomas, of Sandy Spring:
Samuel Thomas, 3d, b. 2nd day of 12th month, 1753.
Elizabeth Thomas, b. 28th day of 10th month, 1755.
Richard Thomas, Jr., b. 21st day of 2nd month, 1758.
John Thomas, b. 27th day of 9th month, 1760.
Mary Thomas, b. 12th day of 3rd month, 1762.
Sarah Thomas, b. 26th day of 11th month, 1764.
Henrietta Thomas, b. 17th day of 2nd month, 1767.
Margaret Thomas, b. 11th day of 6th month, 1769.
William Thomas, b. 11th day of 12th month, 1771.
Ann Thomas, b. 25th day of 5th month, 1774.
Henrietta Thomas, 2d, b. 7th day of 3rd month, 1777.
Children of Basil and Elizabeth Brooke, of Sandy Spring:
James Brooke, b. 5th day of 5th month, 1766.
Gerrard Brooke, b. 12th day of 8th month, 1768.
Deborah Brooke, b. 4th day of 9th month, 1770.
Basil Brooke, b. 28th day of 4th month, 1772.
Children of John and Sarah Cowman, of South River:
Joseph Cowman, b. 8th day of 9th month, 1758.
Mary Cowman, b. 18th day of 4th month, 1760.

QUAKER RECORDS OF SOUTHERN MARYLAND

Gerard Cowman, b. 6th day of 5th month, 1762.
John Cowman, b. 10th day of 4th month, 1764.
Sarah Cowman, b. 9th day of 2nd month, 1766.
Margaret Cowman, b. 22nd day of 5th month, 1769.
Ann Cowman, b. 24th day of 7th month, 1771.
Elizabeth Cowman, b. 12th day of 3rd month, 1774.
Richard Cowman, b. 13th day of 9th month, 1777.
Children of Joseph and Elizabeth Hopkins, of South River:
Isaac Howel Hopkins, b. 19th day of 12th month, 1770.
Patience Hopkins, b. 5th day of 11th month, 1771.
Gerard Hopkins, b. 22nd day of 1st month, 1775.
Hannah and Mary Hopkins, twins, b. 12th day of 4th month, 1777.
Margaret Hopkins, b. 2nd day of 3rd month, 1779.
Joseph and Elizabeth Hopkins, twins, b. 10th day of 3rd month, 1781.
Isaac Gray Hopkins, b. 16th day of 6th month, 1783.
Prisillah Hopkins, b. 24th day of 10th month, 1785.
Mary Hopkins, b. 9th day of 4th month, 1788.
Samuel Hopkins, b. 9th day of 4th month, 1790.
Sarah Hopkins, b. 3rd day of 8th month, 1792.
Children of John and Johannah Plummer, of West River:
Jerom Plummer, b. 3rd day of 1st month, 1774.
Gerrard Plummer, b. 7th day of 9th month, 1775.
Mary Plummer, b. 13th day of 3rd month, 1777.
Ann Thomas Plummer, b. 12th day of 1st month, 1779.
John Plummer, b. 20th day of 4th month, 1781.
Joseph P. Plummer, b. 4th day of 10th month, 1783.
Children of Richard and Deborah Thomas, of Sandy Spring:
Elizabeth Thomas, b. 1st day of 8th month, 1784.
Frederick Augustus Thomas, b. 27th day of 9th month, 1788.
Mary Thomas, b. 18th day of 10th month, 1791.
Sarah B. Thomas, b. 26th day of 4th month, 1794.
Deborah Thomas, b. 2nd day of 3rd month, 1796.
Margarett E. Thomas, b. 3rd day of 3rd month, 1798.
Roger Brooke Thomas, b. 9th day of 4th month, 1803.
Children of Bernard and Sarah Gilpin, of Sandy Spring:
Sarah Gilpin, b. 30th day of 5th month, 1794.
Elizabeth Gilpin, b. 21st day of 11th month, 1795.
Ann Robinson Gilpin, b. 1st day of 7th month, 1797.

BIRTHS AND DEATHS OF SANDY SPRING MONTHLY MEETING

Thomas Gilpin, b. 10th day of 2nd month, 1799.
Samuel Gilpin, b. 28th day of 3rd month, 1801.
Hannah Gilpin, b. 20th day of 5th month, 1803.
Lydia Gilpin, b. 16th day of 4th month, 1805.
Children of Basil and Mary Brooke, of Sandy Spring:
Elizabeth Cummins Brooke, b. 26th day of 9th month, 1798.
James Harvey Brooke, b. 15th day of 5th month, 1801.
Thomas Brooke, b. 18th day of 8th month, 1805.
Deborah Brooke, b. 24th day of 7th month, 1807.
Jane Brooke, b. 12th day of 6th month, 1812.
Children of William and Deborah Stabler, of Sandy Spring:
Thomas Pleasants Stabler, b. 5th day of 11th month, 1791.
Edward Stabler, b. 26th day of 9th month, 1794.
James Stabler, b. 14th day of 9th month, 1796.
Caleb Bentley Stabler, 24th day of 1st month, 1799.
William Henry Stabler, b. 13th day of 4th month, 1802.
Children of Samuel and Elizabeth Snowden, Indian Spring, Snow Hill:
Samuel and Elizabeth Snowden, twins, b. 27th day of 10th month, 1797.
John Snowden, b. 25th day of 1st month, 1799.
Samuel Snowden, b. 13th day of 9th month, 1800.
Richard Snowden, b. 26th day of 7th month, 1802.
Mary Snowden, b. 2nd day of 3rd month, 1804.
Sarah Snowden, b. 31st day of 12th month, 1806.
Martha Snowden, b. 28th day of 6th month, 1810.
Rebecca and Joseph Snowden, twins, b. 17th day of 12th month, 1814.
Children of Richard and Ann Hopkins:
Elizabeth Hopkins, b. 20th day of 11th month, 1775.
Gerrard R. Hopkins, b. 10th day of 8th month, 1777.
Mary Hopkins, b. 1st day of 9th month, 1779.
Samuel Snowden Hopkins, b. 15th day of 7th month, 1783.
Henrietta Hopkins, b. 20th day of 1st month, 1786.
Ann Hopkins, b. 29th day of 6th month, 1789.
Richard Hopkins, 26th day of 12th month, 1791.
Sarah Hopkins, b. 16th day of 4th month, 1793.
Margaret Hopkins, b. 6th day of 10th month, 1795.
Children of Joseph and Mary Cowman:
Elizabeth Cowman, b. 29th day of 12th month, 1786.
Sarah Cowman, b. 28th day of 5th month, 1789.
Gerard Cowman, 9th day of 11th month, 1791.

QUAKER RECORDS OF SOUTHERN MARYLAND

Samuel Snowden Cowman, b. 9th day of 2nd month, 1794.
John G. Cowman, b. 22nd day of 4th month, 1796.
Mary Cowman, b. [blank].
Joseph Cowman, b. 22nd day of 5th month, 1801.
Children of Gerard and Margaret Brooke, of Sandy Spring:
Richard Brooke, b. 6th day of 1st month, 1790.
John Thomas Brooke, b. 12th day of 11th month, 1791.
Elizabeth P. Brooke, b. 12th day of 8th month, 1794.
Children of William and Sarah Gover:
Sarah Gover, b. 2nd day of 11th month, 1787.
Mary Cowman Gover, b. 24th day of 2nd month, 1789.
William Alexander Gover, b. 16th day of 2nd month, 1791.
Augustus Frederick Gover, b. 18th day of 1st month, 1793.
Elizabeth Gover, b. 22nd day of 12th month, 1794.
Margaret Gover, b. 10th day of 9th month, 1796.
John Gover, b. 17th day of 3rd month, 1798.
Eliza Gover, b. 31st day of 5th month, 1800.
Ann Maria Gover, b. 1st day of 8th month, 1802.
Caroline Gover, b. 4th day of 9th month, 1804.
Robert Gover, b. 1st day of 1st month, 1806.
Children of Samuel and Hannah Hopkins, of Indian Spring:
Joseph Janney Hopkins, b. 28th day of 8th month, 1793.
Johns Hopkins, b. 19th day of 5th month, 1795.
Eliza Hopkins, b. 19th day of 5th month, 1797.
Sarah Hopkins, b. 27th day of 2nd month, 1799.
Hannah Hopkins, b. 19th day of 11th month, 1801.
Samuel Hopkins, b. 20th day of 11th month, 1803.
Mahlon Hopkins, b. 18th day of 6th month, 1805.
Philip Hopkins, b. 31st day of 5th month, 1807.
Margaret Hopkins, b. 13th day of 3rd month, 1808.
Gerard Hopkins, b. 26th day of 11th month, 1809.
Mary Hopkins, b. 8th day of 10th month, 1811.
Children of Philip and Patience Snowden, of Indian Spring:
Elizabeth Snowden, b. 8th day of 10th month, 1792.
Samuel Snowden, b. 13th day of 1st month, 1794.
Mary Ann Snowden, b. 28th day of 5th month, 1796.
Joseph Snowden, b. 26th day of 4th month, 1798.
Richard Snowden, 2d, b. 13th day of 5th month, 1802.

BIRTHS AND DEATHS OF SANDY SPRING MONTHLY MEETING

Philip Thomas Snowden, b. 26th day of 6th month, 1804.
Caroline Snowden, b. 4th day of 1st month, 1807.
John P. Snowden, b. 25th day of 2nd month, 1809.
James Snowden, b. 6th day of 10th month, 1811.
Isaac Snowden, b. 9th day of 9th month, 1813.
William Snowden, b. 20th day of 5th month, 1815.
Children of John Jr. and Mary Cowman, of South River:
John Cowman, b. 27th day of 3rd month, 1794.
Gerard Cowman, b. 17th day of 4th month, 1796.
Sarah Cowman, b. 12th day of 7th month, 1798.
Joanna P. Cowman, b. 12th day of 8th month, 1800.
Mary Cowman, b. 2nd day of 4th month, 1803.
Children of Isaac and Hannah Briggs, of Sandy Spring:
Anna Briggs, b. 18th day of 5th month, 1796, m. Joseph E. Beatty, 6th day of 8th month, 1812, moved to Ohio, and d. 1st day of 8th month, 1890.
Mary Brooke Briggs, b. 17th day of 2nd month, 1798, m. Richard B---k, 21st day of 4th month, 1824.
Deborah Briggs, b. 19th day of 8th month, 1799.
Sarah Bentley Briggs, b. 9th day of 8th month, 1801.
Isaac Briggs, b. 15th day of 10th month, 1803.
Elizabeth Briggs, b. 5th day of 10th month, 1807.
Margaret Briggs, b. 24th day of 9th month, 1812.
William Henry Briggs, b. 6th day of 5th month, 1815.
Children of Elisha and Hannah Hopkins, of South River:
Isaac Howel Hopkins, b. 31st day of 3rd month, 1781.
Deborah Hopkins, b. 8th day of 7th month, 1782.
Patience Hopkins, b. [blank].
Elizabeth Hopkins, b. [blank].
Hannah Hopkins, b. [blank].
Children of Elisha and Sarah Hopkins:
Samuel Snowden Hopkins, b. 6th day of 11th month, 1797.
Basil Brooke Hopkins, b. 6th day of 11th month, 1799.
Henrietta Ann Hopkins, b. 30th day of 7th month, 1801.
Thomas Snowden Hopkins, b. 18th day of 10th month, 1803.
John Snowden Hopkins, b. 16th day of 5th month, 1805.
Richard Snowden Hopkins, b. 21st day of 9th month, 1807.
Children of Thomas and Mary Moore, of Sandy Spring:
Mary Moore, Jr., b. 8th day of 7th month, 1794.
Asa Moore, b. 25th day of 4th month, 1797.

QUAKER RECORDS OF SOUTHERN MARYLAND

Ann Moore, b. 17th day of 11th month, 1799.
Caleb Moore, b. 26th day of 4th month, 1802.
Children of Philip and Mary Hopkins, of South River:
Hannah Hopkins, b. 10th day of 5th month, 1788.
Johns Hopkins, b. 28th day of 5th month, 1790.
Elizabeth Hopkins, b. 3rd day of 6th month, 1791.
Isaiah B. Hopkins, b. 25th day of 7th month, 1793.
Susannah Hopkins, b. 2nd day of 10th month, 1795.
Ezekiel Hopkins, b. 4th day of 12th month, 1797.
Hesther Hopkins, b. 4th day of 4th month, 1800.
Mary Hopkins, b. 10th day of 12th month, 1802.
Ann Hopkins, b. 10th day of 5th month, 1805.
Rachel Hopkins, b. 2nd day of 5th month, 1808.
Richard Hopkins, b. 28th day of 7th month, 1810.
Sarah Hopkins, b. 30th day of 7th month, 1812.
Children of Benjamin and Elizabeth Hughes:
Hannah Hughes, b. 23rd day of 2nd month, 1783.
Edward Hughes, b. 2nd day of 1st month, 1786.
Elizabeth Hughes, b. 6th day of 8th month, 1788.
Hesther Hughes, b. 3rd day of 7th month, 1791.
Isaiah B. Hughes, b. 23rd day of 7th month, 1796.
John Hughes, b. 30th day of 1st month, 1799.
Caroline Hughes, b. 13th day of 9th month, 1801.
Mary Hughes, b. 8th day of 6th month, 1804.
James Williams Hughes, b. 11th day of 10th month, 1807.
Mordicai B. Hughes, b. 12th day of 1st month, 1810.
Children of Isaiah and Hannah Boone:
Elizabeth Boone, b. [blank].
Mary Boone, b. 15th day of 5th month, 1769.
Mordicai Boone, b. 15th day of 2nd month, 1772.
Hesther Boone, b. 11th day of 5th month, 1774.
Susanna Boone, b. 30th day of 4th month, 1779.
Arnold Boone, b. 4th day of 1st month, 1782.
Anne Boone, b. 2nd day of 6th month, 1786.
Hannah Boone, b. 23rd day of 11th month, 1788.
Children of Gideon and Elizabeth Dare, of the Clifts:
Sarah Dare, b. 9th day of 2nd month, 1776.
Priscilla Dare, b. 17th day of 9th month, 1777.

BIRTHS AND DEATHS OF SANDY SPRING MONTHLY MEETING

Thomas C. Dare, b. 22nd[?] day of 10th month, 1779.
Henry Dare, b. 18th day of 10th month, 1781.
Elizabeth Dare, b. 6th day of 9th month, 1783.
Gideon Dare, b. 8th day of 3rd month, 1786.
William Dare, b. 18th day of 12th month, 1787.
Rachel and John Dare, b. 27th day of 5th month, 1790.
Richard Dare, b. 20th day of 5th month, 1792.
George Dare, b. 19th day of 8th month, 1795.
Children of George and Deborah Chandler:
Brooke Chandler, b. 21st day of 8th month, 1784.
Nathan Chandler, b. 6th day of 3rd month, 1786.
Hannah Chandler, b. 29th day of 3rd month, 1789.
Mahlon Chandler, b. 22nd day of 12th month, 1790.
Children of George and Gainer Chandler:
Edward Chandler, b. 17th day of 3rd month, 1799.
George Chandler, b. 26th day of 10th month, 1801.
Children of James and Hesther Brooke, of Sandy Spring:
Basil Brooke, b. 19th day of 10th month, 1798.
Isaih Boone Brooke, b. 30th day of 12th month, 1800.
Basil Brooke, 2d, b. 5th day of 2nd month, 1803.
Children of William Ward:
Yate Ward, b. 6th day of 9th month, 1800.
Elizabeth Ward, b. 3rd day of 10th month, 1804.
William Ward, b. 26th day of 1st month, 1809.
Sarah E. Ward, b. 26th day of 1st month, 1813.
DEATHS:
Elizabeth Brooke, wife of Basil Brooke, Sr., d. 17th day of 8th month, 1794, age 53 years, bur. at Sandy Spring.
Basil Brooke, son of James Brooke, d. 22nd day of 8th month, 1794, age 52 years, bur. at Sandy Spring.
Philip Thomas, son of Samuel and Mary Thomas, d. in 11th month, 1754, age 20 years, bur. at Sandy Spring.
Mary Thomas, wife of Samuel Thomas, and dau. of Richard Snowden, d. 15th day of 8th month, 1755, age 43 years, bur. at Sandy Spring.
Deborah Brooke, wife of James Brooke, Sr., d. 29th day of 4th month, 1758, bur. at Sandy Spring.
James Brooke, son of Roger and Mary Brooke, d. 9th day of 3rd month, age 2 years, bur. at Sandy Spring.
James Brooke, Jr., son of James Brooke, Sr., d. 21st day of 8th month, 1767, age 36 years., bur. at Sandy Spring.

Elizabeth Brooke, dau. of Roger and Mary Brooke, d. 21st day of 1st month, 1774, age 1 1/2 years, bur. at Sandy Spring.
Samuel Thomas, son of Samuel Thomas and father of Evan Thomas, d. 3rd day of 2nd month, bur. at Sandy Spring.
Mary Thomas, wife of Samuel Thomas 3rd, d. in 3rd month, 1787, age 27 years, bur. at Sandy Spring.
Hannah Boone, infant dau. of Isaiah Boone, d. in 12th month, 1788, bur. at Sandy Spring.
Gerard Cowman, son of John Cowman, Sr., d. 31st day of 12th month, 1789, age 26 years, bur. at Indian Spring; late residence: South River.
John Snowden, son of Samuel Snowden, Sr., d. 26th day of 1st month, 1790, age 16 years, bur. at Indian Spring; late residence: Snow Hill.
Elizabeth Snowden, wife of Samuel Snowden, Sr., d. 30th day of 1st month, 1790, bur. at Indian Spring; late residence: Snow Hill.
Deborah Chandler, dau. of James Brooke [Sr.?], d. 31st day of 12th month, 1790, bur. at Sandy Spring.
Elizabeth Snowden, dau. of Samuel Snowden, Sr., d. 25th day of 8th month, 1793, age 35 years, bur. at Indian Spring; late residence: Snow Hill.
Frederick A. Thomas, son of Richard and Deborah Thomas, d. 16th day of 8th month, 1794, age 6 years, bur. at Sandy Spring.
Mary Thomas, dau. of Richard and Deborah Thomas, d. 21st day. of 8th month, 1794, age 3 years, bur. at Sandy Spring.
Elizabeth Snowden, dau. of Philip Snowden, d. 7th day of 11th month, 1795, age 3 years, bur. at Indian Spring.
Margarett Brooke, wife of Gerard Brooke, d. 5th day of 3rd month, 1797, age 28 years, bur. at Sandy Spring.
Deborah Thomas, dau. of Richard and Deborah Thomas, d. 27th day of 5th month, 1797, age 1 year, bur. at Sandy Spring.
Brooke Chandler, son of George and Deborah Chandler, d. 24th day of 3rd month, 1798, age 13 years, bur. at Sandy Spring.
Samuel Snowden, son of Samuel Snowden, Jr., d. 29th day of 6th month, 1798/9; late residence: Snow Hill.
Elizabeth Snowden, dau. of Samuel Snowden, Jr., d. 21st day of 7th month, 1798, age 10 months; late residence: Snow Hill.

INDEX

-A-
ADAMS, Joseph, 24
ALDRIGE, Mary, 35
ALEXANDER,
  Robert, 38
ALIBONE, Elizabeth,
  45
ALLEN, Andrew, 40
  Artridge, 40
  Rachel, 84
  Ruth, 41
  Sarah, 40
ALLIBONE, Amos, 45
  Benjamin, 45, 46
  Elizabeth, 45
  Phebe, 46
  William, 45
ALLIEN, Joseph, 39
AMOS, William, 46
AMOSS, James, 46
ANDERSON, James,
  45
ANDREW, Isaac, 85
  John, 33
APPLETON, John, 76
ARME, Robart, 13
ARMITT, John, 37
ARNALD, Richard, 1
ARNALLD, Martha, 1
  Richard, 1
ARNELL, Elizabeth,
  1, 17
  Margaret, 19
  Martha, 1, 17
  Richard, 1, 17, 19
ARNOLD, Elizabeth,
  69
ASHMAN, John, 19
ASTIN, Hannah, 51,
  52, 56
  John, 21, 51, 52, 56, 68,
  74
  Sarah, 56
ATKINS, Thomas, 22
ATKINSON, Joseph,
  48
AUSTIN, John, 14
AYTON, Anne, 49

-B-
BADEN, Robert, 50

BALDERSTON,
  Barth, 48
  Mary, 44
BALDWIN, William,
  20, 74
BALE, Sarah, 19
BALES, James, 20
BALEY, Joseph, 41
BALL, Benjamin, 22,
  25, 74
  Elizabeth, 25, 28
  Gerrard, 26, 32, 33
  Mary, 70
  Robert, 38
  Thomas, 23
BALLENGER,
  Cassandra, 37
BALLY, Misleyson, 16
BALSON, Ann, 42
  Elizabeth, 42
  John, 42
  Thomas, 42
BANNISTER, Mary,
  70
BARKLETT, Thomas,
  71
BARROSS, William,
  14
BARTLETT, Margaret, 76
  Thomas, 71
BATTEE, Elizabeth,
  14, 15, 16, 17
  Fardinando, 14, 15, 16
  Millessent, 13
  Samuel, 20
BATTY, Millesson, 13
BAYTON, Henry, 17
BEALL, Elizabeth, 38
BEATTY, Anna, 91
  Joseph, 91
BECK, Anthony, 33
BECKETT, Mary, 40
BECKIT, Priscilla, 59
BECKWORTH,
  Richard, 13
  Sarah, 13
BEDLOW, Joseph, 75
BELL, Lid, 35
  Mary, 70
  Robert, 38

  Sid, 35
BELSON, Ann, 42
  Elizabeth, 42
  John, 42
  Thomas, 42
BELT, Elizabeth, 13,
  15, 16
  Jo., 19
  John, 13, 14, 16, 17, 24,
  25, 44, 69
  Lucey, 24, 25
  Lucy, 23
BENFIELD, C., 30
  Frances, 30
BENSON, Elizabeth,
  14, 15, 16
BENTLEY, Caleb, 47,
  49, 50, 51
  Joseph, 47
  Mary, 47
  Sarah, 47, 50, 51
  Sary, 49
BENTLY, Sarah, 49
BERRY, James, 68
  William, 67, 68
BERSHER, John, 34
BIGGS, Mary, 16, 17
BILINGSLY, Francis,
  14
BILLINGSLEY,
  Francis, 1, 51, 52
  Rebecca, 68
  Rebecka, 1, 51
  Susanna, 1, 51, 69
BILLINGSLY, Frances, 14
BINK, Thomas, 67
BIRCKHEAD, ---, 16
  Abraham, 18, 68
  Ann, 14, 15, 19, 33
  C---, 36
  Christian, 7
  Elizabeth, 2, 28, 29, 30,
  34, 78
  John, 7, 33, 36, 81
  Joseph, 5
  Margaret, 2, 5, 18, 23,
  28, 29, 77
  Mathew, 34
  Neh., 16, 23, 26, 29, 30,
  36

Neh:, 18, 24, 32
Nehemiah, 2, 5, 7, 18,
21, 34, 36, 71, 79, 81
Rebeckah, 19
Samuel, 34
Sarah, 29, 32, 36
Solomon, 18, 70
BIRKHEAD,
Abraham, 13, 16
Ann, 13, 59, 60
Anna, 60
Christopher, 59
Elizabeth, 29, 42
Fran., 29
Francis, 29
Joseph, 29
Margaret, 25, 29
Margarett, 29
Mary, 13
Mathew, 42
Neh., 16, 29, 31
Nehemiah, 13, 18, 29, 42, 67, 73
Rebecca, 16
Sarah, 29, 42
Sollomon, 59, 60
BLAKE, Thomas, 16
BOLDEN, Elizabeth, 14
BOLTON, Henry, 35
BOND, Benson, 29, 61
Elizabeth, 18, 21, 22, 23, 26, 28, 61
Elza:, 19
Ephraim, 37
John, 61
Joshua, 32
Phineas, 80
Phinebas, 61
Richard, 18, 20, 21, 23, 61, 69
Sarah, 26, 28, 61, 77
Thomas, 32, 61
BONDFIELD,
Christopher, 62
Frances, 55, 62
Margrett, 62
BONFIELD, Ann, 62
Christopher, 62, 63
Frances, 62, 63

Francis, 80
James, 63
BOON, Hannah, 47
Hester, 50
Isaiah, 47
Susanna, 50
BOONE, Anne, 92
Arnold, 92
Elizabeth, 43, 92
Hanah, 47, 50
Hannah, 50, 92, 94
Hester, 49, 50
Hesther, 45, 92
Hetty, 50
Isaiah, 43, 44, 45, 50, 92, 94
Mary, 44, 45, 92
Mordecai, 45
Mordica, 50
Mordicai, 92
Susanah, 48, 50
Susanna, 92
William, 44
BOSTON, Henry, 35
BOURNE, Alise, 59, 60
Anna, 59
Anna Maria, 60
Benjamin, 59, 60
George, 60
Hannah, 59, 60
Jacob, 59
Jesse, 21, 59, 60
Jesse Jacob, 59, 60, 74, 76
Susanna, 60
Thomas, 60, 80
Wellist, 59
BOYD, Mary, 22
BR--, Ann, 29
BR--E, Dorothy, 29
BREWER, William, 28
BRICE, John, 38
BRIGGS, Anna, 91
Deborah, 91
Elizabeth, 91
Hannah, 50, 51, 91
Isaac, 49, 51, 91
J., 49, 50
Margaret, 91

Mary, 49, 50
Mary Brooke, 91
Samuel, 49
Sarah Bentley, 91
William Henry, 91
BROKE, Basil, 50
BROOK, Basel, 37, 41
Basil, 34
Hannah, 83
James, 81, 82
Richard, 37
Roger, 37, 82
BROOKE, Basel, 41
Basil, 7, 10, 37, 38, 39, 44, 45, 46, 47, 49, 50, 51, 86, 87, 89, 93
Bassel, 46
Bassil, 47
Bazel, 39, 84
Betsey, 44
Deborah, 29, 35, 44, 45, 46, 47, 86, 87, 89, 93, 94
Dorothy, 47, 49, 87
Eliza, 46
Elizabeth, 7, 10, 26, 35, 37, 43, 44, 45, 46, 47, 49, 83, 86, 87, 93, 94
Elizabeth Cummins, 89
Elizabeth P., 90
Garrard, 45, 47, 49
Gerard, 44, 47, 90, 94
Gerrard, 44, 46, 49, 50, 51, 87
Hanah, 49
Hannah, 37, 45, 47, 49, 85, 87
Hesther, 93
Isaih Boone, 93
James, 10, 29, 35, 37, 39, 44, 45, 46, 47, 49, 50, 86, 87, 93, 94
James Harvey, 89
Jane, 89
John Thomas, 90
Margaret, 45, 47, 49, 50, 51, 87, 90
Margarett, 50, 94
Margarit, 49

INDEX

Mary, 37, 39, 47, 49, 50, 51, 87, 89, 93, 94
Polly, 45
Richard, 35, 37, 38, 39, 85, 86, 90
Roger, 35, 37, 47, 49, 50, 51, 86, 87, 93, 94
Sally, 45
Samuel, 47, 49, 51, 87
Sarah, 47, 87
Thomas, 35, 37, 39, 86, 89
BROOKES,
Elizabeth, 25
James, 29
Mary, 25
BROOKS, Basil, 49
Dorothy, 28
Gerard, 49
James, 25, 49, 77
Richard, 43
Thomas, 15
BROTHERS, Samuel, 16
BROWEN, William, 28
BROWN, David, 43, 83
Elizabeth, 32, 50
John, 43, 47
Joseph, 51
Joshua, 32
Margaret, 32
Robert, 40, 42
Samuel, 37
Thomas, 46, 47, 49
Vallin, 32
BUCHANAN, Samuel, 39
BURGES, Ann, 14, 17
Benjamin, 15
Elizabeth, 22
Joseph, 15
S---, 15
Ursulla, 22
BURGETT, Samuel, 33
BURKHEAD, Frances, 42
BURNSIDE, Mary, 44
BURNSIDES, James, 44
BURTON, George, 17

Joseph, 14
BUTLER, Elleanor, 49
Ffran., 19
BYE, Mary, 50
BYL, Mary, 50

-C-
CAMTON, John, 14
CAPELL, Beniamen, 20
CAREY, James, 45, 48
John, 45
CARL, Jane, 46
CARPENTER,
Elizabeth, 33
CARR, Elizabeth, 28
John, 27
Lartha, 20
Thomas, 20, 71
Walter, 20
CARROLL, Jeames, 24
CARTER, Elizabeth, 13, 16
CARY, Martha, 51
CASEY, James, 48
CASWELL, Richard, 32
CASY, Martha, 51
CATLING, John, 14
CEAR, Thomas, 27
CHALKLEY,
Thomas, 21, 22, 23
CHAMBERS, Jane, 33
Samuel, 24
CHANDELEE,
Nathan, 17
CHANDLEE,
Deborah, 45, 46, 47
George, 44, 46, 47, 49
CHANDLER,
Brooke, 93, 94
Deborah, 93, 94
Edward, 93
Gainer, 93
George, 93, 94
Hannah, 93
Mahlon, 93
Nathan, 93
CHANDLES,
Deborah, 44

CHAPMAN,
Elizabeth, 33
CHASE, Benjamin, 77
CHESTER, Richard, 16
CHEW, Ann, 2, 13, 14, 15, 16, 17, 24, 26, 27, 28, 29, 68, 71, 77, 78
Ann Thomas, 10
Anne, 16, 67
Benjamin, 13, 16, 17, 23, 29, 33, 69, 72, 74
Caleb, 13, 15, 16, 17
Eliza, 71
Elizabeth, 15, 16, 17, 18, 22, 23, 26, 29, 32, 33, 38, 69, 72, 76
Frances, 34
John, 2, 13, 15, 16, 20, 23, 24, 28, 29, 72, 75
Joseph, 13, 14, 15, 16, 17, 18, 68
Lydia, 16
Mary, 10, 23, 24, 25, 26, 28, 29, 30, 31, 32, 33, 77
Nath., 23, 28, 29
Nathaniel, 75
Nathl., 34
P---, 15
Richard, 34, 35
Samuel(l), 2, 10, 13, 15, 16, 18, 19, 21, 22, 23, 24, 25, 26, 27, 28, 29, 30, 31, 32, 35, 37, 39, 70, 74, 75, 79, 80
Sarah, 35, 81
Will, 15
William, 13, 14, 15, 16, 17
CHILD, Anne, 70
Cassandra, 79
Henery, 30
Henry, 18, 19, 20, 25, 26, 27, 28, 29, 30, 31, 32, 70, 71, 72
Margaret, 32
Mary, 19, 71
Rachel, 74
CHRISTIE,
Alexander, 40

CLARE, Edward, 40
CLARK, Caleb, 76
  Elizabeth, 29
  John, 21
  Mary, 20, 21
  Rachel, 23
  Sarah, 17
  Thomas, 29
  William, 48
COAL, Elizabeth, 13
COALE, Ann, 28, 34, 78
  Anne, 5
  Casandare, 30
  Cassandra, 18, 19, 21, 22, 23, 25, 30, 31, 75, 79
  Eliza, 20
  Elizabeth, 1, 2, 4, 12, 14, 16, 17, 18, 19, 20, 21, 22, 23, 24, 25, 30, 66, 70, 72, 75, 76
  Ester, 1
  Hanah, 20, 21, 22, 23
  Hannah, 1, 4, 12, 24, 75
  John, 36
  Margaret, 30, 34
  Mary, 4, 20, 21, 22, 23, 24, 30, 31, 32, 75
  Phil., 14
  Philip, 13, 14, 15, 16, 19, 20, 21, 23, 36
  Phillip, 12, 18
  Priscilla, 4, 25, 76
  Richard, 16
  Samuel, 1, 4, 13, 16, 20, 23, 34
  Samuel Robertson, 66
  Samuell, 13, 14, 16, 21, 22, 24
  Sarah, 5, 24, 27, 28, 29, 30, 31, 32, 42, 63, 66, 77, 78, 79
  Skipwith, 31
  Thomas, 5, 29, 31, 32, 34, 78
  William, 1, 2, 4, 12, 13, 14, 15, 16, 17, 18, 19, 20, 21, 22, 23, 24, 27, 28, 29, 30, 31, 32, 34, 36, 63, 66, 68, 75, 81, 82

COATES, Ann, 47
COATS, Ann, 49
  Elizabeth, 22
COD, John, 48
COLE, Elizabeth, 13, 15, 16, 19
  George, 14
  Humphry, 13
  Margaret, 30
  Philip, 14, 17
  Phillip, 13, 16
  Sarah, 66
  William, 13, 14, 16, 17, 66
COLEGATE,
  Thomas, 32
COLEMAN,
  Elizabeth, 33, 80
  Joseph, 22, 33, 73, 80
  Margaret, 33
CONSTABLE,
  Samuell, 14
CONTEE, Elizabeth, 38
  Jane, 38, 41, 42, 44
  John, 35
  Margaret, 35
  Margrett, 41
  Richard, 38
  Richard Alexander, 38
CONWELL, Anthony, 72
CORNTHWAIT,
  Elizabeth, 44, 45
  Grace, 44
  Robert, 44, 45
COULSTON, John, 30
COUSINS, Mary, 74
COWMAN, Ann, 6, 9, 34, 35, 36, 37, 46, 48, 88
  Anne, 83
  Elizabeth, 8, 9, 35, 36, 38, 39, 40, 41, 43, 48, 49, 50, 88, 89
  Garrard, 9
  Gerard, 88, 89, 91, 94
  Gerrad, 46
  Gerrard, 43, 44, 45, 49
  Hannah, 43
  Joanna P., 91

  John, 7, 8, 9, 34, 35, 36, 37, 38, 40, 41, 42, 43, 44, 45, 46, 48, 49, 50, 82, 87, 88, 91, 94
  John G., 90
  Joseph, 6, 7, 8, 9, 26, 27, 29, 30, 31, 32, 33, 34, 35, 36, 37, 38, 39, 40, 41, 42, 43, 44, 45, 46, 48, 49, 50, 77, 82, 87, 89, 90
  Margaret, 9, 44, 46, 50, 88
  Mary, 7, 9, 34, 41, 42, 43, 49, 50, 87, 89, 90, 91
  Peggy, 48
  Philip, 49
  Richard, 8, 9, 40, 88
  Salley, 43
  Samuel, 8, 43
  Samuel Snowden, 90
  Sarah, 6, 7, 8, 9, 31, 32, 33, 34, 36, 38, 43, 44, 45, 48, 87, 88, 89, 91
  Thomas, 44, 45, 48
COX, William, 83
COYL, Elizabeth, 32
CRABB, Ann, 35, 38
  Elizabeth, 41
  Henry, 41
  Henry Wright, 35
  Henry Writ, 38
  John, 41
  Ralph, 41, 42
  Richard, 40, 41
CRESTON, Thomas, 17
CROCKET, John, 21, 22
CROCKETT, Agnes, 32
  Elizabeth, 31, 79
  Gilbert, 29, 32, 77
  John, 5, 7, 20, 22, 23, 24, 31, 32, 75, 81
  Mary, 24, 31, 32, 34, 81
CROMWELL,
  Elizabeth, 19
  John, 27, 81

INDEX

Mary, 19
Oliver, 27
Rich, 19
Thomas, 19, 71
Will:, 19
CULLIN, Rebecka, 68
CUMMINGS, Mary, 38
CUTTING, John, 14

-D-
DALLAM, Frances, 84
 William, 32
DARE, Elizabeth, 10, 92, 93
 George, 93
 Gideon, 10, 40, 92, 93
 Henry, 10, 93
 John, 93
 Priscilla, 10, 92
 Rachel, 93
 Richard, 93
 Sarah, 10, 92
 Thomas C., 93
 Thomas Cleaverly, 10
 William, 10, 93
DARNALL, Henry, 32
 Philip, 32
DAVIDGE, Ann, 33
 Robert, 33
DAVIGE, John, 38, 39
DAVIS, Ed:, 19
 Elizabeth, 57
 Hannah, 49
 Jacob, 57
 Jane, 46
 Jone, 46
 Joshua, 44, 45, 46
 Mary, 57, 67
 Robert, 57
 Ruth, 45, 46
 Thomas, 35, 57, 69
 William, 57
DAVISON, Edward, 51
DAY, Elizabeth, 55, 72
 Mary, 69
 Robert, 55, 69
 Sarah, 55, 75
 Thomas, 71
DEAVER, Mary, 16

DELAPLAINE, Nicholas, 15
DENT, Hannah, 79
DEVER, Bazil, 44
 Jonus, 44
DICKENSON, Elizabeth, 24
 James, 24
 Samuel, 24
 William, 24
DICKINSON, James, 75
DILLWORK, William, 45
DILLWORTH, William, 46
DIVIDSON, John, 38
DIXON, William, 68
DORNEY, Harry, 45
DORRUMPLE, William, 13
DORSEY, Ann, 47
 Betty, 39
 Caleb, 32, 33
 Edward, 39
 Priscilla, 32, 33
 William H., 47
DOVELL, William, 23
DOWELL, Mary, 19
 Phillip, 19
 William, 22
DOWEY, Harry, 45
DRANE, James, 33
DRIAN, Margaret, 51
DRIVER, James, 47
DUCKETT, Elizabeth, 50
DUHADAWAY, Jacob, 73, 80
DUHADWAY, Jacob, 54, 80
 Sarah, 54
DUHATAWAY, Elizabeth, 24
 Jacob, 22
 Margaret, 22
DULANY, Henr: Mari:, 33
 Thomas, 33
DURDEN, John, 14
DURDIN, Honor, 14

DUVALL, Aquilla, 35
 Eliner, 32
 Elizabeth, 32
 Fras., 22
 Maran, 32
 Mareen, 23, 28
 Samuell, 32
 Sarah, 35
 Zeporah, 28

-E-
EASTIPP, Benjamin, 16
ECCLESTON, John, 25
EDEETAR, James, 24
EDMONDSON, William, 14, 15, 16
EDMONSON, William, 13
EDWARDS, Ann, 36, 38
 Cadde., 20
 Edward, 33, 36, 38
ELDERTON, James, 24, 25, 30
 John, 25
ELDESTON, James, 24
ELERTON, Mary, 70
ELGAR, Joseph, 38
 Margaret, 47
ELGER, Joseph, 39
ELIEY, Ann, 14
 John, 14, 15
ELIOTT, Joel, 49
 Samuel, 43
ELLICOTT, Andrew, 47, 48, 50, 51
 Benjamin, 44, 45, 47, 48, 50
 Casander, 45
 Cassandra, 44, 45, 47, 51
 Elias, 44, 47, 48, 51
 Elizabeth, 44, 45
 Ester, 51
 George, 44, 45, 47, 48, 51
 Hannah, 44, 48
 James, 48, 51

Jenr., 45
John, 44, 45, 47, 48, 51
Jonathan, 51
Judith, 51
Margaret, 45
Martha, 44, 45
Mary, 45, 46, 47, 51
Nathl., 45
Rachel, 45
Sarah, 44, 45, 47, 48, 51
ELLIOT, Hannah, 46, 47
  Joel, 45
  John, 45, 46, 47
  Mary, 44, 47
  Sarah, 45, 47
  William, 47
ELLIOTT, Eli, 47
  George, 46
  Joel, 47, 49
  John, 11, 46
  Margaret, 49
  Mary, 11
  Sarah, 47
ELLIS, James, 15, 19
  John, 23
  Mary, 19, 71
ENGLAND, John, 29, 77
  Margaret, 58
EVANS, Ann, 48, 51
  David, 43
  Elizabeth, 16
  Job, 13, 14, 15
  John, 23, 27
  Joseph, 44, 51
  Lewis, 45
  Margaret, 13
  Margreat, 14
  Marth, 48
  Martha, 28
  Rachel, 48, 51
  Thomas, 23
  William, 45
EVANSW, Joseph, 45
EVERDEN, Thomas, 16, 19
EVEREST, Hanah, 14
  Thomas, 14
  William, 20

EVERNDEN, Thomas, 13, 14, 16, 68
EVESTON, Thomas, 17

-F-
FAIRBROTHER,
  Jane, 14
  John, 14
FANTHAM, Ann, 85
  Mary, 85
  Priscilla, 83, 85
  William, 85
FARMER, John, 73
FARQUHAR, Sarah, 47
FEARIS, Benjamin, 84
FEDLAINE, T--mr., 42
FELL, Ann, 31
  Edward, 30, 31, 78
  Ellen, 31
  William, 31
FENTHAM, Ann, 43
  Priscilla, 83, 85
FENTON, Thomas, 46
FERDUE, Henry, 33
  Richard, 33
FERIS, Benjamin, 84
  Mathers, 69
  Matthews, 69
FERREST, Hannah, 69
FISHMAN, John, 27
FITSIMONS, Nicholas, 74
FLOWLAR, Mary, 29
FLUD, John, 13
FOARD, Hanah, 30, 31
  Hannah, 25, 30
  Richard, 34
  William, 25, 27, 31, 34, 72, 79
FORD, Hanah, 22
  Hannah, 30
  John, 44
  William, 20, 27
FOWLER, Mary, 29
FRANCES, Enoch, 50

FRANCIS, Joshua, 38
FRANKLIN, Artheridge, 17, 18
  Artredge, 20
  Artridge, 21, 79
  J., 31
  Jacob, 39, 40
  John, 31
  Mary, 40
  Rachel, 40
  Richard, 76
  Robard, 20
  Robert, 17, 18, 19, 21, 22, 26, 29
  Sarah, 17, 27, 77
FRANKLING,
  Artradge, 27
  Artridg, 30
  Artridge, 27, 30, 31, 79
  John, 27
  Richard, 27, 76
  Robert, 25, 27, 30, 31
  Sarah, 27
FRANKLINS, Robert, 26
  Sarah, 26
FREELAND, Robert, 80
FRINKLIN, Artridg, 31
  Isabell, 31
  Jacob, 31
  John, 31
  Richard, 31

-G-
GAILE, John, 19
GAITHER, Benjamin, 36, 39
  Cassandra, 36
  Edward, 29
  M., 36
  Mary, 36
GALE, John, 19, 20
GALLAWAY, Ann, 20
  Hana, 20
  Richard, 20
  Samuell, 20
GALLOWAY, ---, 24
  Agagts, 86

INDEX

Ann, 2, 6, 7, 14, 15, 16, 17, 18, 19, 20, 21, 22, 23, 24, 25, 26, 30, 31, 34, 35, 39, 40, 74, 82, 85, 86
Anne, 71
Augustus, 86
Elizabeth, 6, 14, 15, 16, 17, 19, 24, 25, 26, 28, 30, 31, 71
Hanah, 20
Hanna, 20
Hannah, 1, 2, 6, 72
J., 23
John, 2, 20, 21, 22, 24, 25, 26, 27, 28, 29, 30, 31, 33, 40, 75, 86
Joseph, 7, 22, 23, 24, 25, 26, 27, 29, 30, 31, 32, 33, 34, 35, 36, 37, 39, 40, 43, 81, 86
Mary, 20, 22, 23, 25, 28, 30, 31, 32, 33, 74, 79, 86
Peter, 2, 20, 24, 25, 26, 28, 29, 30, 31, 75, 80, 85
Peter Biner, 86
Petr:, 22
Rich, 19
Richard, 1, 2, 6, 13, 14, 15, 16, 17, 18, 19, 20, 21, 22, 23, 24, 25, 26, 27, 28, 29, 30, 31, 33, 74, 75, 85, 86
Sam, 18, 19
Sammuell, 21
Samuel, 1, 2, 6, 13, 14, 15, 16, 17, 18, 19, 20, 22, 23, 24, 25, 31, 33, 34, 35, 71, 72, 73, 74, 85
Sarah, 2, 24, 25, 26, 28, 29, 30, 31, 32, 33, 76, 80, 86
Sophia, 6, 9, 23, 24, 25, 26, 27, 29, 30, 31, 32, 33, 34, 35, 36, 37
Sophiah, 35
Susanna, 34
GAMBLE, Elizabeth, 44
Joseph, 44
GAMBRILL, Anne, 36
Augt., 36
Martha, 36
GANT, Thomas, 43
GANTT, Elizabeth, 40
Prissila, 40
GARDENER, Sarah, 41
GARRETSON, Cornelius, 10, 38
John Hutchinson, 10
Priscilla, 10
Thomas, 10
GARRISON, Cornelius, 83
Cornelous, 39
Cornelus, 36
Prisciler, 39
GARY, John, 48, 67
GASSAWAY, Ann, 32
Elizabeth, 32
John, 32
Mary, 35, 36, 37, 40, 42
Nicholas, 32, 39, 44, 48
Thomas, 20, 23, 36
GASSIGUES, Sarah, 50
GASSOWAY, Ann, 79
GATES, William, 34
GAUL, Richard, 19
GEIST, Richard, 19
GELLIS, Mary, 26
GIELS, Jacob, 17
John, 17
Nath., 17
GIEST, Richard, 71
GILES, Ann Magy, 27
Artheridge, 17
Artridge, 1
Betey, 77
Betty, 26, 27
Cassandra, 27, 33
Elizabeth, 12, 19, 21, 56, 70, 76
Jacob, 12, 17, 23, 26, 27, 28, 69, 79
John, 1, 12, 13, 17, 19, 20, 21, 22, 23, 24, 26, 27, 28, 29, 71, 76, 82
Mary, 1, 12, 13, 16, 17, 56, 80
Nath., 18, 27, 28
Nathaniel, 12, 17, 29, 56, 70, 78
Nathaniell, 21
Nathn., 21
Rachel, 30
Richard, 14
Sara, 17
Sarah, 17, 18, 19, 20, 21, 24, 25, 26, 27, 28, 33, 78
Sophia, 21, 27, 28, 77
GILL, Ann, 40
Hugh, 68
John Price, 47
Joseph, 83
Margaret, 68
Margret, 13
Mary, 16
GILLES, Jacob, 12
GILLINGHAM, Elizabeth, 45
James, 44, 45, 46, 48
John, 44
GILLIS, Betty, 34
Elizabeth, 33
Ezekiel, 33
Henry, 34
John, 38, 39
Margaret, 39
Margret, 38
Mary, 33, 34, 38, 39
Milcah, 39
Milkey, 38
Prissilah, 39
Prissiler, 38
GILLISS, Betty, 33, 34
Ezekiel, 33
Henry, 33, 34
Mary, 29, 33
GILPIN, Allen, 49
Ann Robinson, 11, 88
Bernard, 11, 48, 49, 50, 51, 88
Berrnard, 50
Elizabeth, 11, 88
Gidion, 48, 49
Hannah, 11, 49, 89
Leydia, 49
Lydia, 11, 89
Samuel, 11, 89

Sarah, 11, 48, 49, 50, 51, 88
Thomas, 11, 89
GIST, Zepporah, 27
GODFREY, Samuel, 45, 47, 48
GOLLEN, Jane, 16
GONG, Faith, 13
GOOT, Elizabeth, 20
GORDON, Elisha, 45
GORE, Joseph, 35
GORSUCH, Char:, 19
Charles, 15
GOSIDGE, Ann, 15
Charles, 15
John, 15
GOSLIN, Agnes, 78
GOTT, Anthony, 27
Elizabeth, 17
Richard, 17
GOTTE, Eliza, 19
GOVER, Ann Maria, 90
Augustus Frederick, 90
Benjamin, 57
Caroline, 90
Cassandra, 57, 80
Eliza, 90
Elizabeth, 9, 26, 28, 30, 45, 57, 80, 81, 82, 90
Ephraim, 9, 57, 71, 81
Hannah, 9, 85
Jean, 9
John, 90
Margaret, 90
Margarett, 9
Mary, 9, 36, 38, 48, 83
Mary Cowman, 90
Philip, 38, 81, 83
Phillip, 57
Priscilla, 57, 80, 82
Prissilla, 41
Rachel, 9, 84
Rachell, 57
Richard, 57
Robert, 9, 16, 37, 45, 57, 69, 79, 80, 90
Sam, 19
Samuel, 26, 57, 71
Samuell, 18, 30

Sarah, 9, 36, 37, 38, 85, 90
William, 9, 45, 50, 90
William Alexander, 90
GRAHAME, Charles, 33
GRAY, George, 17
John, 14
Mary, 43
GRAYHORN, Rebeckah, 82
GREEN, Ann
Catharine, 38
Jonas, 38
Sarah, 22
GREENFIELD, Micajah, 45
Thomas, 42
GRESHAM, Mary, 15
GRIFFIN, Lewis, 85
GRIFFITH, Lewis, 38
Samuel, 23
GUEST, Richard, 71

-H-
HAGUE, Isaac, 37
HALL, ---, 28
Aaron, 16, 18
Ann, 16, 36, 43
Barbary, 43
Benjamin, 16
Edward, 36
El---, 18
Elihu, 21, 29, 30, 76
Elisha, 16, 18, 19, 21, 30, 71, 73
Elizabeth, 13, 16, 26, 28, 29, 35, 36, 71, 79
Henry, 19, 43
Isaac, 36
John, 27
Joseph, 16
Levey, 13
Margery, 43
Margret, 43
Mary, 24, 26, 28, 30, 58
Rachel, 13
Richard, 13, 21, 26, 29, 30, 32, 33, 34, 36, 73, 79

Sarah, 16, 19, 21, 26, 28, 29, 30, 73, 79
Thomas Henry, 41, 43
William, 43
HALLE, Elizabeth, 19
HAMBURY, John, 27
HAMMOND, Ann, 35
Anna Mary, 36
Anne, 36
Hannah, 32
Joseph West, 37
Philip, 36
Resin, 39
Rezin, 41
HANBURY, John, 27
HANCE, Ann, 10, 64, 84
Benjamin, 10, 21, 40, 62, 64, 73, 79, 84
Elizabeth, 40, 41, 62, 64, 80, 84
John, 79
Joseph, 64, 79, 84
Margaret, 40, 85
Margrett, 42
Mary, 25, 64
Rebecca, 85
Richard, 42
Samuel, 10
Sarah, 10
Thomas Cleverly, 10
HANKS, William, 84
HANSLAP, Frances, 15
Francis, 14
Joseph, 14, 15, 16
HANSLIP, Fras., 22
HANSON, Barbara, 25
Benjamin, 43
John, 27
Jona., 24
Jonathan, 5, 25, 28, 71, 75
Kezia, 5
Margaret, 5
Mary, 5, 28, 78
Mordaca, 5
Timothy, 25
HARPE, Robert, 21
HARPER, Eliphell, 78

INDEX

Elishell, 78
John, 72
Mary, 19, 71
Robert, 14, 19, 21
HARRINGTON,
Abra., 28
HARRIS, Ann, 21, 33, 34, 36, 37, 54, 60, 64, 78, 80, 81, 84
  Anna, 34, 54, 65
  Anne, 54, 60
  Arthur, 26, 42, 54, 63, 78
  Auther, 28
  Benjamin, 20, 40, 42, 53, 60, 63
  Betsey, 42
  Betty, 41
  Bitty, 40
  Charles, 42
  Christian, 33, 52, 60, 81
  Christopher, 14
  Eleanor, 72
  Elener, 42
  Elizabeth, 33, 40, 42, 52, 53, 54, 63, 64, 65, 70, 78, 83
  Ellinore, 53
  Frances, 63
  George, 17, 21, 30, 40, 52, 54, 65, 70, 79
  Hannah, 71
  John, 16, 37, 82
  Joseph, 21, 40, 52, 60, 63, 64, 74
  Margaret, 10, 35, 65
  Margret, 39, 40
  Margrett, 40
  Mary, 33, 36, 39, 40, 41, 53, 54, 63, 65, 80
  Moses, 38, 83
  Rachel, 10, 43, 54, 83
  Rachell, 42
  Rebecca, 40
  Rebeckah, 54
  Rebekah, 35, 36, 38, 40
  Richard, 21, 42, 52, 53, 60, 69
  Robert, 36, 38
  Samuel, 10, 38, 39, 40, 41, 54, 65, 85
  Sarah, 36, 37, 41, 54, 64, 80, 81
  T., 50
  Thomas, 37, 38, 49, 50, 81
  William, 10, 20, 33, 34, 35, 37, 40, 41, 42, 52, 53, 54, 63, 65, 72, 75, 80
HARRISON,
  Benjamin, 35, 39
  Elisha, 35, 36
  Elizabeth, 2, 13, 15, 16, 17, 18, 19, 21, 72
  Josiah, 2
  Mary, 2, 16, 18, 70
  Richard, 2, 13, 14, 15, 16, 17, 18, 19, 22, 32, 48, 71, 73, 75, 77
  Sam, 16
  Samuel, 2, 14, 15, 16, 18, 19, 21, 22, 23, 25, 26, 28, 29, 32, 69, 73, 75, 79, 81
  Sarah, 2, 14, 16, 17, 21, 22, 26, 28, 29, 32, 36, 42
  Susanna, 36
  William, 17, 70, 71
HARTLAND, Robert, 15
HARVEY, Joshua, 48
HARWOOD, Mary, 18
  Priscilla, 43
  Thomas, 32
HAWARD, John, 45
  William, 45
HAWKINES, John, 19
  Mary, 19
  Thomas, 19
HAWKINGS, ---, 17
  Aaron, 5
  Elizabeth, 5
  John, 25
  Joseph, 5
  Ruth, 5
  Thomas, 5
HAWKINS, Ann, 15
  Augustin, 17
  Elizabeth, 20
  John, 15, 20, 22, 25, 74
  Mary, 15
  Thomas, 70
HAYES, Elizabeth, 19
HAYSE, John, 19
HAYWARD,
  Elizabeth, 44
  John, 44, 45, 46
  Keziah, 48
  Mary, 44
  Rachel, 44, 45, 46, 48, 51
  Rebecah, 44
  Rebeckah, 45, 46, 48
  Sidney, 44, 45, 46, 48
  William, 44, 45, 46, 48, 51
HEARD, Robert, 48
HEATH, James, 19
HEATHCOTE,
  Joseph, 14, 15
  Martha, 15
  Ruth, 19
HEIGH, James, 17
  Thomas, 17
HEPBURN, Ann, 37, 40
  Elizabeth, 49
  John, 34, 35, 36, 38, 39
  Mary, 34, 35, 37, 40, 83
  Samuel, 40
HESTON, Joseoh, 48
HEWES, Sarah, 70
HEWITT, Thomas, 29
HICKSIMONS, Ni:, 19
HIGGINSON, John, 32
HILL, ---, 6
  Deborah, 26, 29, 33
  Easter, 32
  Elizabeth, 4, 29, 33, 36
  Hannah, 33
  Henrietta, 9, 39
  Henry, 5, 9, 25, 26, 28, 29, 33, 34, 37, 76, 80, 81, 85
  Joseph, 9, 26, 28, 30, 33, 34, 36, 38, 77
  Leaven, 29
  Levin, 26, 30, 76
  Margaret, 33, 85
  Mary, 5, 9, 25, 26, 29, 33, 37, 82
  Priscilla, 5

Richard, 19, 23, 24, 26, 33, 76
Sarah, 9, 27, 30, 33, 34, 36, 77
HILLEN, Deborah, 1
Joanna, 1
Johannes, 1
John, 1
HITCHINS, Francis, 59
Priscilla, 59
HODGES,
Humphrey, 14, 16
Mathers, 14
HOLAND, Thomas, 20
HOLLAND, Ann, 35
Anthony, 21
Arnold, 37
Cassandri, 33
Deborah, 48
Elizabeth, 28
Frances, 76
Francis, 13
Isabell, 21
Jacob, 21, 41
Margaret, 17, 19, 33, 68
Margret, 18
Margrett, 27
Mary, 33
Rachel, 35
Richard, 33, 80
Ruth, 37
Sarah, 35
Susanah, 48
Thomas, 21, 33, 73
William, 15, 16, 19
HOLLON, Janes, 13
HOLLOND,
Elizabeth, 13
Francis, 13
Margret, 13
Sarah, 13
HOLLYDAY, Sarah, 25
HOLYDAY, William, 14
HOOD, Anne, 36
Elenor, 36
James, 46
William, 36

HOOKER, Benjamin, 12
Damaris, 12
Jacob, 17
Joan, 1, 12
Joanna, 1
Mary Ann, 1, 12
Samuel, 19
Sarah, 13, 14, 16, 19
Thomas, 1, 12, 13, 16, 19, 67
Umphrey, 13, 16
HOPKINGS,
Elizabeth, 25
Gerrard, 25
Margaret, 25
HOPKINS, ---, 24, 38, 39
Ann, 9, 48, 49, 50, 89, 92
Anna, 38, 39
Annamary, 41
Anne, 49
Basil Brooke, 91
Benjamin, 43
Cassandra, 43
Cathrine, 43
Catty, 10
Deborah, 10, 49, 91
Elisha, 8, 10, 39, 41, 42, 43, 44, 45, 46, 48, 49, 50, 91
Elisha Hall, 41
Eliza, 90
Elizabeth, 4, 7, 8, 9, 11, 22, 24, 25, 26, 34, 36, 37, 38, 39, 40, 41, 42, 43, 44, 45, 46, 48, 49, 50, 51, 76, 84, 85, 88, 89, 91, 92
Evan, 9, 48, 49, 51
Ezekiel, 8, 36, 38, 84, 92
Garard, 20
Garr:, 19
Garrard, 35, 36, 38, 39, 40, 41, 42, 43, 50, 51
Gerard, 20, 30, 43, 46, 49, 79, 88, 90
Gerd., 22, 23, 24
Gered, 30

Gerr:, 17, 19
Gerrard, 4, 7, 8, 11, 17, 18, 22, 24, 25, 26, 27, 28, 29, 30, 31, 32, 33, 34, 35, 36, 37, 38, 40, 41, 43, 44, 46, 48, 49, 50, 51, 69, 82
Gerrard R., 89
Gerrd., 20, 21, 22, 23
Hanah, 50
Hannah, 8, 10, 44, 50, 88, 90, 91, 92
Hannah Moore, 46
Hannee, 11
Henrietta, 89
Henrietta Ann, 91
Henry, 48
Hesther, 92
Isaac, 50
Isaac Gray, 11, 88
Isaac Howel(l), 10, 11, 48, 88, 91
Isaiah B., 92
J---, 38
Joanna, 38
Johannah, 40, 41
John, 4, 35, 36, 38, 41, 42, 43, 46, 49, 51, 85
John Snowden, 91
Johns, 8, 9, 10, 11, 34, 35, 36, 37, 38, 39, 41, 42, 43, 48, 49, 80, 81, 82, 90, 92
Joseph, 4, 8, 10, 11, 25, 26, 28, 29, 36, 37, 38, 39, 41, 42, 43, 44, 45, 46, 48, 49, 50, 78, 88
Joseph Janney, 90
Joshua, 10
Leonard, 29
Mahlon, 90
Margaret(t), 4, 7, 8, 11, 18, 19, 20, 22, 23, 24, 25, 26, 27, 28, 29, 30, 31, 32, 33, 34, 35, 36, 43, 44, 45, 46, 48, 49, 50, 82, 88, 89, 90
Margarit, 35
Margret, 42, 43, 46
Margrett, 43

INDEX

Maria, 48, 50
Mary, 8, 11, 25, 34, 35, 36, 37, 38, 39, 41, 43, 48, 49, 50, 51, 83, 88, 89, 90, 92
Nicholas, 41, 43
P. H., 46
Patience, 11, 45, 46, 48, 49, 88, 91
Phil H., 46
Philip, 7, 8, 29, 30, 33, 34, 35, 38, 39, 42, 43, 45, 46, 48, 49, 50, 79, 82, 84, 90, 92
Philip H., 48
Phillip, 4, 29, 31, 35, 36, 44, 49
Phillr:, 50
Priscilla, 11
Prisillah, 88
Rachel, 8, 9, 36, 37, 38, 39, 41, 43, 50, 51, 92
Rebecah, 43
Richard, 4, 7, 8, 36, 38, 39, 40, 41, 42, 43, 44, 45, 46, 48, 49, 50, 84, 89, 92
Richard Snowden, 91
Sam, 46
Samuel, 4, 7, 8, 11, 37, 39, 41, 42, 43, 44, 45, 46, 48, 49, 50, 83, 88, 90
Samuel Snowden, 89, 91
Sarah, 8, 11, 35, 36, 43, 48, 50, 51, 82, 88, 89, 90, 91, 92
Susanna, 42
Susannah, 92
Thomas Snowden, 91
William, 4, 46, 48
HORN, Margaret, 17
Sarah, 17
HORNE, Constant, 75
Sarah, 69
HOUGH, John, 47
Joseph, 48
Robert, 48
HOWARD, John, 40, 50
Sarah, 40

HOWELL, Catharina, 43
Hannah, 43
Isaac, 43, 48
Jacob, 43
Patience, 43, 48
Samuel, 43
HOZIER, Henry, 58
Mary, 58
HUCHENS, ---, 16
Elizabeth, 17
HUCHINS, Mary, 20
HUGHES, Benjamin, 43, 45, 50, 92
Caroline, 92
Edward, 43, 92
Elizabeth, 92
Hannah, 50, 92
Hesther, 92
Isaiah B., 92
James Williams, 92
John, 92
Mary, 92
Mordicai B., 92
HUMPHREY, Hannah, 43
HUMPHRY, Jane, 43
HUNT, Elizabeth, 61, 64, 65
Job, 43, 61, 65
Jobe, 75
John, 64, 65
Margaret, 43
Mary, 61, 65
Orton, 65
Philip, 65
Priscilla, 65
Sarah, 61
Thomas, 64, 65, 77
William, 65
HURLE, John, 13
HUSBAND, Herman, 83
Rachel, 46
HUSBANDS, Susan, 46
HUTCHEN, Francis, 21
HUTCHENS, Elizabeth, 20
Fras., 22

M---, 21
Sussanah, 22
HUTCHINGS, Sarah, 19
HUTCHINS, Elizabeth, 14, 17, 18, 62
Fran:, 19
Frances, 25
Francis, 13, 14, 20, 24, 62
Frans., 25
Fras., 20
John, 20, 70
Margaret, 14
Mary, 3, 13, 20, 68, 73
Priscilla, 72
Prisilla, 20
Richard, 62
Sarah, 71

-I-
IJAMS, John, 32
Plummer, 32
William, 36
ISHAM, James, 32

-J-
JACKSON, Isaac, 49
John, 22
Joseph, 47, 49
July, 49, 51
Ralph, 15
Ruth, 22
JANNEY, Hannah, 49
John, 49
Joseph, 49
Mahlon, 37, 47
Rebeckah, 49
Sarah, 37
Susan, 50
JEANES, Ann, 35
JENINGS, Edmond, 35
Samuel, 19
JENKINSON, Hanah, 33
Hannah, 30, 78
JIAMS, William, 36
JOHNE, Ann, 30
Richard, 30
JOHNES, Abraham, 15

105

Ann, 28
Elizabeth, 15
Rebekah, 26
JOHNS, ---, 20, 24
Abra., 22, 24, 26, 29
Abraham, 14, 25, 28, 53, 58, 59, 60, 65, 66, 72, 78, 80
Abram., 21
Ann, 23, 25, 26, 35, 40, 62, 64, 79, 85
Ann Thomas, 64
Anne, 31, 54, 60, 61, 83
Aquil(l)a, 20, 21, 33, 53, 58, 61, 65, 72, 78
Benjamin, 33, 34, 39, 42, 54, 61, 62, 66
Betsey, 42
C---, 42
Eliza, 61
Elizabeth, 14, 17, 19, 20, 21, 22, 24, 25, 26, 28, 29, 39, 40, 41, 53, 58, 59, 61, 62, 63, 64, 65, 66, 73, 79, 83
Hosier, 38
Isaac, 20, 21, 22, 23, 24, 25, 26, 27, 29, 30, 53, 54, 60, 61, 63, 64, 74, 78, 79
Jacob, 60
Jane, 65
Joseph, 59, 65, 77
Kensey, 21, 22, 23, 25, 26, 27, 28, 34, 35, 39, 40, 53, 61, 62, 72, 75
Kinsey, 20, 42, 66
Margaret(t), 19, 20, 21, 34, 35, 58, 59, 64, 65, 69, 73, 83
Margrett, 53
Mary, 21, 26, 39, 42, 43, 58, 59, 62, 64, 66, 73, 83
Philip, 64
Pricilla, 25
Prisa., 22, 23
Priscilla, 20, 21, 28, 33, 53, 59, 65, 70, 83
Rachel, 33, 54, 62, 66

Rebecka, 58
Rebeckah, 76
Rebekah, 26
Ri., 36
Richard, 13, 14, 15, 17, 18, 20, 21, 22, 23, 24, 25, 26, 27, 28, 29, 30, 31, 34, 35, 36, 53, 58, 59, 60, 61, 62, 64, 65, 66, 67, 72, 73, 76, 78, 79, 81, 83
Samuel, 60, 62, 80
Sarah, 59
Susanah, 41
Susanna, 35, 40, 43
Susannah, 40
Thomas, 65
William, 64
JOHNSON, Heneritta, 49
Joseph, 38
Robert, 14
Samuell, 28
Thomas, 38
JONES, ---, 24
Abraham, 37
Elizabeth, 18
Griffith, 18
Joane, 18
Joseph, 18, 84
Mary, 23
Morgan, 42
Prisler, 42
Rachel, 37
Richard, 20, 21
Ruth, 18, 70, 78
Sam, 18
Sarah, 23, 42, 59
Thomas, 36
JORDAN, Dorothy, 39
John Morton, 40
Joseph, 28

-K-
KEYS, Elizabeth, 69
KIDD, Margaret, 14, 19
KINGSBURY, Elizabeth, 19
KINSEY, Isaac, 50, 51

James, 51
Mary, 50
Sarah, 51
KNIGHTON, Elizabeth, 13
Mary, 14
KNOTT, Ann, 46, 47, 48, 49
Thomas, 46

-L-
LAKE, Daniel, 45, 46
LAMAR, John, 32
LAMBART, Ann, 14
LAMBOT, Ann, 14
LANE, Dutton, 16, 17, 18
Peshe:, 19
Richard, 23
Sam, 17
Samuel(l), 14, 17, 18, 21, 23, 49
Sarah, 18, 19, 20, 21, 23, 24, 25, 32
Thomas, 31
LARKIN, John, 15
LARKING, John, 13
LATTEN, Richard, 14
LAURENCE,
Benjamin, 4, 67, 69
Elizabeth, 4
John, 4
Levin, 4
Lucey, 69
Margarett, 4
Rachel, 4
Sophia, 4
LAVILE, John, 40
LAVISH, John, 42
LAWRANCE,
Benjamin, 25
Rachel, 25
LAWRENCE,
Benjamin, 15, 17, 18, 22, 23, 24, 51
Elizabeth, 13, 16, 17, 51
Rachel(l), 19, 22, 24, 26
William, 16
LAY, Frainces, 29
LEACH, John, 21

INDEX

LEATHERINGTON, Benjamin, 16
LEEDS, John, 25
LELALAND, Joshua, 41
LETTLE, Honer, 14
LETTON, Richard, 14
LEVISH, Jane, 42
LEWEN, Elmer, 41
  Richard, 71, 77
LEWES, Richard, 77
LEWIN, Mary, 20
LEWING, Eleanor, 42
LEWIS, Elizabeth, 27
  Richard, 27
LINCECOM, Jane, 14
  Thomas, 14
LINGAN, Thomas, 34
LINTHICOM, Hezekiah, 19
LINTHICUM, Deborah, 29
  Giden, 29
  Leon, 29
  Thomas, 29
LINTHYCOMBE, Deborah, 20
  Hezekiah, 20
LISTON, Ann, 48
  Joseph, 48
LITTELL, Elizabeth, 59
  Thomas, 59
LITTLE, Thomas, 72, 77
LIVIRB, Jane, 42
LLOYD, Deborah, 19
LOCKED, Elizabeth, 19
LOCKS, Sarah, 28
LOCKWOOD, Elizabeth, 13, 15, 16, 19, 20
  Robert, 15
LOTHERINGTON, William, 27
LOUDON, Elizabeth, 49
LOVELL, William, 23, 74

LOWDEN, Elizabeth, 50
LOWES, Tubman, 35
LOYD, Charles, 14
LYLES, Margery, 37
  Prisciler, 38
  Zach., 37
LYON, Benjamin, 50
  James, 42
  Rachel, 42
  Robert, 51

-M-
MACCUBBIN, James, 35
MACCUBIN, Zachariah, 31
MACKALL, Sarah, 40
MACKEMBINE, Mary, 27
MCKIM, John, 51
  Mary, 51
MCPHERSON, Daniel, 48
  Isaac, 48
  William, 48
MACUBBINE, Zacha., 25
MAGRUDER, Ann, 84
MANNER, Ospon, 32
MARIARTEE, Rachell, 69
MARRIARTE, Edward, 17
  Honer, 17
  Rachel, 17
MARSSEY, Sarah, 78
MARTAIN, Francis, 48
MARTIN, John:, 19
MARYARTY, Honour, 14, 15
  Margaret, 14
MASON, George, 39
  John, 46
MASSEY, Aquil(l)a, 29, 32, 35, 81
  Charles, 37
  Jonathan, 29, 34
MASSY, Aquilla, 77

MATHER, Christopher, 16, 19
MATHEW, Christopher, 16
MATHEWS, George, 44, 45
  Margret, 38
MATHIAT, George, 48
MATHIOT, George, 46
  John, 46
MATTHEWS, Edward, 34
  George, 34
  Margaret, 83, 85
  Oliver, 37
  Samuel, 43
MATTHIOTT, Ruth, 48
MAXWELL, Anthony, 40
MEAR, Rebecca, 16
MEARES, Hanna, 69
  Hannah, 51
  John, 56
  Sarah, 51, 56, 69
  William, 51
MEARS, Elizabeth, 14
  William, 67
MENDENALL, Thomas, 48
MEREDITH, Samuel, 40
MEREWETHER, Reuben, 40
MERITON, John, 15
MERRICK, Elizabeth, 44
MERSEY, Ann, 34
MIDELMORE, Frances, 32
MILES, Elizabeth, 5
  John, 27, 28
  Rachell, 32
  Ruth, 5
  Sarah, 5, 27, 49, 77
  Thomas, 5, 16, 17, 18, 21, 23, 27, 28, 32, 33, 37, 70, 74
MILLER, Robert, 51

Sarah, 49
MITCHEL, John, 46
MITCHELL, Burges, 22
Mord., 22
MOALE, John, 14
MOONE, M., 13
MOOR, Mord., 15
MOORE, Ann, 47, 92
  Asa, 47, 91
  Caleb, 92
  Chals:, 33
  Charles, 38
  Deborah, 5, 6, 20, 21, 22, 23, 76
  Elizabeth, 6, 7, 47
  Hannah, 6, 33, 38, 81
  Heather, 6
  Hesther, 6
  M., 15, 16, 23
  M:, 22
  Margaret, 7, 26, 29, 33
  Mary, 6, 7, 26, 28, 29, 33, 38, 49, 91
  Mord., 18, 24
  Morda., 17, 18, 20, 21, 22, 33
  Mordecai, 5, 6, 7, 25, 33, 70, 72
  Rachel, 6, 33
  Richard, 7, 20, 28, 29, 33, 72
  Robert, 46
  Safrettar, 33
  Samuel Preston, 7, 81
  Saphreateon, 33
  Thomas, 33, 38, 47, 49, 50, 51, 81, 91
MOORES, Sarah, 14
MOORS, Sarah, 13
MORE, Ann, 37
  Mordica, 80
  Mordicai, 13
MORGAN, Elizabeth, 40
  Thomas, 42
MORRAY, Jo:, 19
  Keia, 19
MORRIS, George
  Anthony, 39

Samuel C., 39
Susanna, 77
MORTHLAND, Sarah, 51
MOSS, John, 33
MULIKIN, Margaret, 40
MULKLIKIN, Martha Hall, 50
MULLIKEN, Margret, 42
MURDOCK, Jeremiah, 22
MURRAY, Ruth, 27
  Sarah, 7
  Zipporah, 19
MURRY, James, 15, 26, 71
  Jemima, 71
  Jemina, 26
  Keziah, 71
  Melchizadick, 77
  Melchizdeck, 26
  William, 43
  Zeporah, 71

-N-
NAIMBY, John, 40
NEEVES, Sarah, 18
NEIGHBOR, Mary, 16
NELLIS, Hannah, 74
NEVES, Sarah, 70
NEWMAN, John, 24
  Jona., 24
NICHOLAS, Beal, 38
NIGHTON, Mary, 13
NORMAN, George, 35
NORRIS, Ann, 11
  Edward, 25, 27
  Elizabeth, 11, 21
  Hanah, 21
  Isaac, 19
  John, 11, 21
  Joseph, 25
  Mary, 42, 48, 85
  Mary Ann, 11
  Robert, 11, 39, 40, 85
  Sarah, 11, 21, 39, 41, 74
  Thomas, 11, 36, 39, 42, 48, 72, 84

William, 40, 42, 84

-O-
ODELL, Sarah, 43
OGG, Allesander, 42
  Susanna, 42
OGLE, Margaret, 85
  Samuell, 33
ORTON, Elizabeth, 58
  Henry, 58, 67
  Mary, 58
OWEN, Elioner, 35
  Griffith, 19
OWING, Mary, 34
OWINGS, Ann, 45
OXLEY, Joseph, 85

-P-
PABCOAST, William, 44
PACA, Aquila, 25
  Drucilla, 32
  Martha, 32
  Pricilla, 32
  Susanah, 24
  William, 38, 39
PAIRPOINT, Cha:, 32
  Francis, 80
  Frans:, 32
  Henry, 32
  Joseph, 32
  Sidney, 32
PANCOAST, Abigail, 44
  Adin, 44
  Caleb, 44
  John, 44
  Mary, 44
  Robert, 44
  Sarah, 44, 85
PARAN, Jane, 40
  Moses, 40
  Richard, 40
PARDO, Berenton, 52
  Darrington, 52
  Hester, 52
  Hesther, 14
  John, 14, 52, 67
  Joseph, 52
  Louse, 52

INDEX

Lucy, 52
Mary, 52
Peter, 52
Rebecka, 52
Sarah, 52
Susanah, 52
PARDOE, John, 56, 68, 69
Joseph, 68
Lucy, 26
Sarah, 56, 68
PARIS, Joseph, 34
PARISH, Ann, 24
John, 27
Maru, 25
Mary, 24, 31
Sarah, 27
William, 27
PARKER, George, 33
Hannah, 69
Mary, 40
PARKES, Hannah, 69
PARRAN, Samuel, 40
PARRISH, Clare, 17
Edward, 17, 20, 21, 22, 24, 25, 27
Elizabeth, 21, 22, 28, 73
John, 17, 22, 27, 28, 69, 76
Mary, 21, 22
S---, 28
Sarah, 22, 27, 72
William, 17, 27
PARROT, Gabrill, 14
PARROTT, Elizabeth, 69
PATRICK, Elizabeth, 48, 49
PAYTON, Catherine, 36
PEACH, Mary, 47, 50
Samuel, 44, 45, 46, 47
PEAD, Ann, 33
PEARPOINT, John, 79
PEARSON, Mary, 43
Thomas, 42, 43
PEIRPOINT, Ann, 44, 51
Deborah, 44, 51
John, 32, 44

Walter, 51
PEISLEY, Mary, 36
PEMBERTON,
Charles, 40
Israel, 39
Joseph, 39, 40
PENNINGTON,
Isaac, 73, 74
Joseph, 73, 74
PERDUE, Henry, 33
Richard, 33
PERIPOINT, Joseph, 51
PERNALL, Richard, 13
PHELYS, Elizabeth, 14
PHILIPS, George, 16
Samuel, 16
PICKETT, John, 70
PIERPOINT, Ann, 48
Anne, 45
Barsheba, 45
Benedict, 45
Bershaby, 45
Deborah, 44, 45, 46, 48
Faithful, 44
Henry, 44, 45, 46
John, 45, 46, 48
Joseph, 44, 45, 46, 48
Nicholas, 45
Samuel, 44
PIERPONT, Charles, 32, 81
Francis, 32
John, 32
Sidney, 32
PILES, Richard, 33
William, 33
PLEASANT,
Henneritta, 49
PLEASANTS, Ann
Thomas, 39
Elizabeth, 83
James B., 46
John, 37
Mary, 83
Robert, 37, 82
Samuel, 40
Sarah, 47
Thomas, 37, 46, 83

PLUMBER,
Abraham, 83
Elizabeth, 83
Jerrom, 80
Joseph, 81
Rachel, 82
Ruth, 80
Sarah, 82
Thomas, 81
PLUMMER, Abener, 41
Abraham, 10, 37, 38, 40, 41, 42, 83
Ann, 11, 33, 37, 38
Ann Thomas, 88
Anna, 10, 37, 38, 41
Cassander, 10
Chs., 32
Elizabeth, 10, 22, 23, 27, 28, 32, 37, 38, 83
Francis, 32
Gab., 32
George, 22, 27, 33
Gerd., 50
Gerrard, 10, 48, 88
Ibeg., 33
James, 22, 27, 28, 32
Jemima, 37
Jer., 32
Jerom, 10, 22, 27, 28, 32, 33, 34, 48, 88
Jerrom, 63, 65, 66, 80
Jery, 50
Johannah, 10, 88
John, 10, 11, 22, 27, 32, 39, 40, 41, 42, 43, 63, 65, 88
Joseph, 10, 11, 33, 37, 41, 88
Joseph P., 88
Ma., 32
Maria, 48
Mary, 10, 33, 34, 35, 36, 37, 38, 39, 41, 63, 65, 88
Micajah, 27, 28, 32
Phebe, 27
Philemon, 22, 27
Priscilla, 27
Prisiller, 33
Rachel, 10, 37, 82

Ro--a, 28
Ruth, 10, 32, 33, 80
Samuel(l), 10, 27, 32, 33, 37, 41, 77
 Sarah, 10, 28, 33, 37, 41, 42, 82
 Susana, 37
 Susanna, 40, 41
 Susannah, 10
 Thomas, 10, 22, 27, 28, 33, 38, 81
 Ursula, 10, 37, 38, 41
 Yate, 40
 Yates, 32, 33, 37
POLTNEY, Thomas, 48
PORIE, Mart., 48
POULTNEY, Elizabeth, 46
 Thomas, 46
PRATHER, John Smith, 32
PRESLY, Elizabeth, 16
PRESTON, John, 17, 18, 20, 71
 Margaret, 29, 72
 Samuel, 29, 68
 Thomas, 20, 21, 22, 23
 William, 72
PRICE, Benjamin, 25
 Elizabeth, 20, 71
 Ezebn., 25
 John, 28
 Mary, 20, 25, 75
 Mordecai, 20, 25, 28
 Mordicai, 20, 77
 Sarah, 28, 77
 Stephen, 20, 21
 Steven, 75
PURNELL, Mary, 15, 16
 Richard, 15, 16

-R-
RADRIFFE, Mahlon, 13
RAMSAY, John, 34
RANDALL, Thomas, 19

RANSOLD, Francis, 40
RAWLINGS, Ann, 24, 26, 27, 28, 56
 Anne, 55
 Aron, 20, 24, 25
 Aron:, 19
 Daniel, 37, 55, 56, 76
 Daniell, 67
 Elizabeth, 55
 Isaac, 55
 Jona., 32
 Mary, 55, 56
 Moses, 25
 Richard, 32
 Susana, 21
RAWLINS, Susanna, 29
RAY, George, 50
REACH, Henry, 44
READ, Dennis, 48
 Jacob, 45, 51
 Larkin, 45
RENDELL, John, 31
RESTON, John, 15, 18
REVETS, Thomas, 27
RHOADS, Samuel, 40
 Sarah, 40
RICH, Benjamin, 51
 Sarah, 51
RICHARDON, Thomas, 30
RICHARDSON, ---, 29, 38
 Ann, 8, 34, 35, 37, 81
 Ann Thomas, 8, 12, 43
 Anne, 8
 Daniel(l), 3, 7, 9, 12, 13, 14, 15, 17, 18, 20, 21, 23, 24, 25, 26, 27, 28, 29, 30, 31, 32, 33, 34, 35, 36, 82
 Deborah Snowden, 12
 Elizabeth, 1, 3, 5, 6, 7, 8, 11, 12, 13, 14, 15, 16, 17, 18, 19, 20, 21, 22, 30, 31, 32, 36, 38, 39, 74, 81, 85
 Hannah, 7, 37, 38
 J., 26, 30

 Job, 38
 John, 3, 5, 21, 22, 24, 43
 John Thomas, 8, 12
 Joseph, 1, 3, 4, 5, 8, 11, 12, 13, 14, 15, 16, 17, 18, 19, 20, 21, 22, 23, 24, 25, 26, 27, 28, 29, 30, 31, 32, 33, 34, 35, 36, 37, 38, 39, 40, 41, 42, 43, 71, 76
 Joseph Hill, 38
 Joshua, 25
 Laurana, 20, 72
 Lauriana, 20
 Leurania, 3
 Lucretia, 84
 Mar., 18, 19
 Margaret(t), 3, 6, 9, 11, 15, 17, 18, 19, 20, 21, 22, 23, 24, 25, 26, 27, 28, 29, 30, 31, 32, 34, 82
 Margret, 18, 25, 36
 Margrett, 27, 31
 Mary, 5, 8, 11, 12, 17, 23, 28, 30, 31, 34, 43, 78, 81
 Milcah, 38, 84
 Nath., 30
 Nathan, 3, 6, 7, 26, 28, 30, 31, 32, 33, 34, 38, 79
 Phillip, 5, 32
 Rebecca, 30, 39
 Rebeckah, 31, 32
 Rebekah, 8, 12, 28, 31, 32, 33, 34, 35, 36, 37, 38, 39, 40, 41, 42, 43
 Richard, 3, 5, 6, 8, 9, 11, 12, 22, 23, 25, 26, 27, 28, 29, 30, 31, 32, 33, 34, 35, 36, 37, 38, 39, 41, 42, 43, 46, 79, 84
 Ruth, 23, 25
 Samuel(l), 3, 5, 6, 21, 22, 23, 24, 25, 26, 27, 28, 29, 35, 37, 38
 Samuel Elliott, 11
 Sarah, 3, 4, 5, 20, 21, 22, 23, 24, 25, 26, 27, 28, 31, 32, 35, 37, 77, 80, 83

INDEX

Sop--, 17
Sop:, 15
Sophia, 1, 3, 6, 13, 14, 15, 16, 17, 18, 21, 22, 23, 35, 74
Sophia Elizabeth, 12
Sopphira, 1
Thomas, 3, 6, 28, 30, 31, 32, 33, 36, 37, 38, 39
Will, 16
William, 1, 3, 5, 6, 7, 8, 11, 12, 13, 14, 15, 16, 17, 18, 19, 20, 21, 22, 23, 24, 25, 26, 27, 28, 29, 30, 31, 32, 33, 34, 37, 47, 74, 80, 84
RIGBIE, Casandra, 30
  Casna., 24
  Cassandra, 26, 28
  Elizabeth, 21, 23, 24, 75
  James, 83
  John, 24
  Nat., 26, 30
  Nathan, 24, 75
  Nathn., 26
  Sarah, 39
RIGGS, Elisha, 37
  John, 37
  Thomas, 37
RINGGOLD, Mary, 40
  Thomas, 40
ROBERS, Priscilla, 29
ROBERSON, Samuell, 78
ROBERT, Allen, 40
ROBERTS, Allen, 42, 64
  Ann, 77
  Elizabeth, 26, 56, 64, 71, 76
  Hugh, 64
  Isaac, 56, 64, 80
  Jane, 56
  Kensey, 56
  Margaret, 56
  Mary, 85
  Patience, 56
  Pris:, 18
  Prisa., 20
  Priscilla, 21, 26, 56
  Richard, 40, 56, 64, 85

Robert, 17, 18, 19, 20, 21, 23, 24, 26, 27, 28, 56, 64, 70, 71, 73, 75
  Ruth, 32
ROBERTSON, Ann, 10, 40, 50, 63
  Anna, 37, 40, 41, 42
  Daniel(l), 34, 36, 37, 63, 66, 67, 82
  Elenor, 42
  Elizabeth, 10, 28, 34, 36, 41, 42, 48, 50, 51, 63, 66, 67, 78
  Georg, 36
  George, 39, 40, 41, 63, 66, 82, 83
  Hannah, 67
  Isaac, 67
  Joseph, 10
  Margarett, 66
  Mary, 10, 39, 40, 41, 42, 47, 63, 67
  Rachel, 40, 41, 63
  Rebecca, 10
  Richard, 10
  Samuel, 10, 34, 35, 36, 38, 39, 40, 41, 42, 47, 49, 50, 63, 66, 67
  Sarah, 28, 36, 47, 49, 50, 63, 66, 78, 82
  Susanah, 50
  Susanna, 50, 66
  Thomas, 47, 49
  William, 10, 36, 39, 40, 41, 42, 46, 51, 63
ROBINSON, Danel, 18
  Daniel(l), 4, 70
  Elizabeth, 4
  Samuel, 4
  Sarah, 4, 51
ROBISON, Daniel, 70
ROCKHOULD, Thomas, 19
ROGERS, Samuel, 35
  Sarah, 45
ROORER, Mathew, 15
ROPER, Robert, 19
ROSENQUEST, Alexander, 25
  Hanah, 24, 25
ROSS, Thomas, 81

ROYSTON, Abell, 51
  Able, 21
  George, 14, 16, 51, 52, 68
  John, 51
  Rebeckah, 51
RULEY, Elizabeth, 38, 39
  John, 38, 39
  Mary, 38
  Michael, 38
  Prisiler, 38
  Prissilla, 36
  Thomas, 33
RULY, Priscilla, 83
RUSILL, Mary, 49
RUSSEL, Hannah, 46, 47
  John, 47
  Mary, 47
RUSSELL, Hannah, 47
  John, 44, 45, 47
  Mary, 44, 47, 49
  Sarah, 44, 47, 49
  Thomas, 43, 44
RUTLAND, Jane, 24

-S-
SADERS, Henry, 50
SALKELD, John, 17, 18
SALMON, Thomas, 16
SAMPLE, Robart, 14
SANDERS, Elizabeth, 36, 39
  Henry, 36, 84
  James, 32
  Sarah, 36, 39
SAPPINGTON, Polly, 46
SARSON, Edward, 2
  Elizabeth, 2
  Hannah, 2
  Mary, 2, 14
SAUL, John, 74
SAUNDERS, Robert, 20
SAWELL, Ellinor, 59
  Mary, 59
  Peter, 59

Ursilla, 59
SCHOFIELD, Rachel, 45, 47
SCHOLFIELD, Isaacar, 47
SCOTT, Ann, 44
  Benjamin, 44
  Richard, 44
  William, 44
SCOTTE, John, 17
SCRIVENER,
  Benjamin, 14
  Grace, 14, 15
SELBY, Edward, 13
SELMAN, Ann, 43
  Elizabeth, 43
  Johnathan, 43
  Jont., 43
  Margret, 43
  William, 43
SERSON, Mary, 14
SEWELL, Usila, 77
SHARP, Peter, 24, 28
  William, 67, 68
SHIPLEY, James, 44
  Susana, 44
SHIPPEN, Ann, 19
  Edward, 19
  Joseph, 19
SHOMAKER, Charles, 48
SHOOTER, Ann, 18
SHORT, Ann, 16
SHORTER, Ann, 18
SIMMONS, John, 29
  Margarett, 29
  Richard, 77
SIMONS, Thomas, 52
SKINNER, Arthur, 42
  Fredick, 42
SKIPWITH,
  Cassabdra, 16
  Cassandra, 1, 16
  Elizabeth, 1, 2, 12, 14
  George, 1, 2, 12
  Gorg, 2
SLOPER, Elizabeth, 13, 67
SMALL, Benjamin, 75
  Elizabeth, 76

SMITH, ---, 16, 20
  Abigail, 40
  Abraham, 85
  Alce, 15, 16
  Alece, 14
  Alice, 15, 16
  Alles, 17
  Alse, 13, 14
  Althea, 39
  Casn., 24
  Cassandra, 24, 26, 76
  Daniel, 85
  Eleanor, 23
  Elizabeth, 14, 15, 16, 17, 18, 20, 21, 26, 28, 29
  Hannah, 85
  Isaac, 85
  Jacob, 85
  Jane, 47
  Joseph, 13, 20, 22, 23, 25, 40, 72, 85
  Joshua, 25
  Laurana, 23
  Laurania, 26
  Levy, 85
  Lurania, 22
  Luranie, 25
  Margaret, 3, 14, 81
  Margret, 13
  Mary, 13, 15, 16, 20, 23, 25, 68
  Mordecai, 84
  Nat., 18
  Nat:, 18
  Nath:, 19
  Nathan, 14, 15, 16, 18, 20, 21, 26, 32, 79, 85
  Rachel(l), 16, 85
  Samuel, 30, 48
  Sarah, 13, 14, 15, 21, 23
  Seth, 85
  Susana, 22
  Sussana, 21
  Thomas, 13, 14, 15, 16, 17, 18, 19, 21, 23, 25, 26, 28
  Walter, 13
  William, 81
SNODEN, Mary, 19

SNOWDEN, Ann, 41, 42
  Caroline, 91
  Deborah, 29, 77
  Elizabeth, 11, 20, 23, 25, 26, 28, 29, 31, 35, 41, 42, 44, 46, 50, 77, 82, 85, 89, 90, 94
  Hannah Moore, 46
  Henneritta, 44, 48, 50
  Hennrietta, 49
  Henrietta, 46
  Henry, 38
  Isaac, 91
  James, 91
  John, 35, 37, 38, 39, 40, 41, 42, 44, 45, 46, 89, 94
  John P., 91
  Joseph, 31, 89, 90
  Martha, 89
  Mary, 16, 19, 20, 21, 23, 24, 29, 35, 44, 78, 89, 93
  Mary Ann, 90
  Patience, 11, 90
  Philip, 11, 44, 45, 46, 48, 90, 94
  Philip Thomas, 91
  Phillip, 49, 50
  Rebecca, 89
  Richard, 16, 19, 20, 22, 23, 24, 25, 27, 28, 29, 31, 35, 36, 38, 39, 40, 41, 42, 72, 75, 89, 90, 93
  Sam, 46
  Samuel, 11, 35, 37, 38, 39, 40, 41, 42, 43, 44, 45, 46, 48, 49, 50, 85, 89, 90, 94
  Samuel Hopkins, 49
  Sarah, 46, 48, 49, 50, 89
  Thomas, 35, 37, 39, 40, 41, 42, 44, 46
  William, 91
SOMERFIELD,
  Hannah, 73
  Ralph, 22, 73, 76
SPARROW, ---, 17
  Elizabeth, 14, 15
  Sa., 18

INDEX

Sara, 17
Sarah, 15, 16, 17, 18, 19, 20, 21, 22, 23, 24, 25, 75
Sol, 17
Solloman, 13, 14, 16
Sollomon, 24
Solo:, 19
Soloman, 14
Solomon, 14, 15, 16, 17, 18, 20, 21, 22, 23, 24, 25, 26, 27, 29, 30
Soph, 17
Sophia, 18
Thomas, 14, 15, 16, 21
SPENCER, Adam, 35
Isaacar, 47
SPIGG, Osborn, 32
Thomas, 32
SPRIGG, Edward, 33, 34, 36
Elizabeth, 6, 33, 34, 35, 36, 39, 43
Henrietta Sarah, 6
Margaret, 6
Mary, 84
Osborn, 32
Rebeckah, 6
Richard, 6, 36, 38, 39
Sophia, 6
Thomas, 32, 33, 34, 36, 39, 40, 43
SPRIGGS, Thomas, 6
STABLER, Caleb Bentley, 89
Deborah, 49, 50, 89
Edward, 89
James, 89
Thomas Pleasants, 89
William, 49, 50, 51, 89
William Henry, 89
STEDMAN, Benjamin, 44, 45
Phebe, 44, 45
STERLING, James, 33
STEUART, William, 39
STEVEISON, Jam:, 19
STEWARD, Anna, 36, 37, 40
Betsey, 41

Elizabeth, 39
John, 27, 39, 42, 77
Sarah, 30, 40, 41, 42
Stephen, 39, 40
STEWART, Anna, 65
Elizabeth, 65
John, 31, 65
Mary, 44
Sarah, 31, 65
Stephen, 65, 81
Steven, 65
Susanna, 39
STOCKETT, Samuell, 26
Thomas, 19, 26
STODDERT, James, 16
STONE, James, 42
STORK, Robert, 73, 74
Tabitha, 73
STRINGFELLOW, E., 31
SUDERS, Henry, 50
SULLIVAN, John, 50
Mary, 49
SULLIVIN, Mary, 47
SUMERFIELD, Hanah, 23
Ralph, 22, 23
SUMMERFIELD, Hannah, 26
SUVY, Elizabeth, 16
SYMPSON, Mary, 33

-T-
TAGART, John, 46
TAILLER, Elizabeth, 13
TAILOR, Thomas, 17
TALBOT, Edward, 20
Elizabeth, 13, 16, 18
John, 17, 18, 71
Rachel, 84
TALBOTT, Abraham, 57
Ann, 66
Benjamin, 40, 41, 42, 66
Cassander, 4
Cassandra, 29, 30, 78
Daniel, 40, 42, 56, 57, 84

David, 41, 42
Ed., 13, 18, 19
Edward, 1, 13, 14, 16, 18, 20, 22, 24, 31, 32
Elizabeth, 1, 14, 15, 16, 18, 19, 20, 21, 23, 24, 25, 26, 32, 40, 42, 56, 57, 66, 70, 72
George, 57
John, 4, 13, 14, 18, 19, 20, 21, 22, 23, 24, 25, 29, 30, 31, 33, 34, 36, 37, 40, 41, 42, 56, 57, 66, 82, 85
Joseph, 40, 41, 42, 66
Lucey, 79
Lucy, 30, 31
Margaret, 34, 82
Mary, 4, 21, 24, 30, 31, 40, 41, 42, 57, 66, 79
Peggy, 66
Prudence, 32
Rachel, 66
Richard, 1, 56
Samuel, 66
Sarah, 15, 56, 57
Sophia, 56
Susanna, 66
Thomas, 56
TALER, Elizabeth, 14
TANEHILL, Andrew, 21
TANNER, Nath., 27
TASKER, Ann, 33
Anne, 33
Benjamin, 33
TAYLER, Joseph, 44
Rachel, 44
Richard, 28
TAYLLER, Richard, 13
TAYLOR, Elizabeth, 15
Jonathan, 17
Joseph, 44
Richard, 27
Thomas, 77
TEAD, Ann, 33
TEALL, Ann, 45
TENCH, Margarett, 14, 15

THOMAS, ---, 16, 34
  Ann, 7, 9, 23, 25, 26, 27, 28, 29, 30, 31, 34, 35, 38, 39, 40, 41, 43, 44, 45, 46, 78, 86, 87
  Deborah, 47, 48, 50, 88, 94
  Deborah Elizabeth, 11
  Elizabeth, 3, 7, 17, 21, 23, 24, 31, 34, 35, 37, 41, 42, 43, 49, 50, 51, 75, 82, 86, 87, 88
  Evan, 35, 36, 37, 38, 39, 41, 42, 43, 44, 45, 46, 47, 49, 50, 51, 86, 94
  Even, 35
  Frederick A., 94
  Frederick Augustus, 11, 88
  Henney, 50
  Hennrietta, 48
  Henrietta, 49, 87
  Henritta, 51
  Henry, 39, 47, 87
  John, 3, 7, 18, 20, 24, 25, 27, 28, 29, 31, 34, 35, 36, 37, 38, 39, 40, 41, 42, 43, 44, 45, 46, 47, 49, 50, 51, 77, 82, 87
  John C., 48
  Margaret(t), 7, 30, 31, 32, 44, 46, 47, 49, 50, 80, 87
  Margarett E., 88
  Margret, 37, 38, 41, 42, 43
  Margrett, 37, 41
  Maria, 50
  Mary, 3, 7, 9, 11, 15, 16, 17, 18, 19, 20, 21, 22, 23, 24, 25, 26, 27, 28, 29, 30, 31, 32, 34, 35, 37, 40, 44, 45, 48, 49, 50, 73, 75, 81, 82, 86, 87, 88, 93, 94
  Mary Ann, 40, 42
  P., 31, 34
  Philip, 3, 7, 9, 18, 20, 24, 25, 28, 34, 35, 36, 37, 38, 39, 40, 41, 42, 43, 45, 46, 47, 51, 77, 79, 82, 86, 93
  Philip E., 86
  Philip William, 39
  Phillip, 19, 27, 36, 76
  Rachel, 41, 43, 46, 50, 51, 86
  Richard, 7, 11, 34, 35, 36, 37, 38, 39, 43, 44, 46, 47, 48, 49, 50, 51, 87, 88, 94
  Roger Brooke, 88
  S., 41
  Salley, 51
  Sally, 50
  Sam, 18
  Samuel(l), 3, 7, 9, 13, 15, 16, 17, 18, 19, 20, 21, 22, 23, 24, 25, 26, 28, 30, 31, 34, 35, 37, 38, 39, 41, 42, 43, 44, 45, 46, 47, 49, 50, 68, 78, 82, 86, 87, 93, 94, 46
  Sarah, 3, 7, 11, 13, 16, 17, 18, 19, 23, 35, 38, 45, 46, 47, 48, 49, 50, 71, 87
  Sarah B., 88
  Thomas, 11, 50
  Will, 37
  William, 31, 32, 34, 35, 37, 40, 46, 47, 49, 50, 87
  Witt, 37
THOMPSON, Edward, 35
  Israel, 34, 81
  John, 38, 67
  Samuell, 14
THOMSON, John, 67
THORNBURGH,
  Deborah, 51
  Elizabeth, 51
  Joseph, 51
  Margarett, 51
  Phebe, 51
  Sally, 51
  Thomas, 51
THORPE, George, 19
TIDINGS, Charity, 19
  John, 19
  John:, 19
  Richard, 19
TIMMONS, John, 29
  Margarett, 29
TINCH, Thomas, 15
TIPPLE, William, 35
TISON, Isaac, 51
TOLBUT, Edward, 16
TOMASS, Mary, 14
TONGUE, Elizabeth, 40
  Thomas, 40
TOUNGE, Thomas, 40
TOWGOOD, Josias, 19, 21
  Mary, 19, 21
TRASEY, Ann, 13
TRAYHORN,
  Rebecca, 83
TROTH, Elizabeth, 24
  Henry, 73, 76
  William, 73
TUCKER, Rebecca, 84
TURNER, Elijah, 50
  Thomas, 70
TYDINGS, Charity, 13
  John, 71
TYSON, Elisha, 46, 51
  Esther, 46
  Isaac, 46, 51
  Jacob, 46
  Jesse, 46
  Lucretia, 51
  Mary, 51
  Nathan, 46

-U-
UNDERWOOD,
  Hannah, 46

-V-
VREILY, Elizabeth, 13

-W-
WALKER, Abraham, 45
  Ann, 62
  Arnold, 41
  Elizabeth, 34

INDEX

George, 28, 62
Hannah, 81
Isaac, 80
Jane, 62, 73
John, 62
Robert, 22
Sarah, 62, 80
William, 62, 73, 74, 80
WALLACE, Charles, 38
WALLIS, Abraham, 30, 61
  Ann, 61, 78
  Arthur, 61
  Constant, 61
  Frances, 61, 73, 84
  John, 36
  Mary, 61
  Samuel(l), 30, 36, 61, 69, 73, 78, 79
WALTERS, Elizabeth, 19
WAMAN, Edmund, 20
  Leonard, 20
WARD, Ann, 42
  Edward, 33
  Elizabeth, 36, 42, 84, 93
  Elliner, 76
  James, 42
  John, 36, 38, 84
  Mary, 42
  Robert, 14, 36, 38, 41, 42
  Sarah, 36, 38, 83
  Sarah E., 93
  William, 42, 93
  Yate, 93
WARDE, John, 84
WARFIELD, Anna, 44
  George F., 45
  Joshua, 37
  Ruth, 36
WARING, ---, 34
  Basil, 32
  Elizabeth, 35
WARMAN, Fr., 33
WARREN, Thomas, 27
WARRING, Sampson, 69

WARTERS, Elizabeth, 31
WARTNABY, Elizabeth, 24
WASON, Frances, 19
  Francis, 20
WASSON, Thomas, 25
WATERHOUSE, William, 45
WATERS, Ann, 40, 41
  Arnold, 40, 42
  Artridge, 38, 40
  Charity, 42
  Edward, 44, 45, 46, 48, 49
  Elizabeth, 4, 17, 18, 20, 21, 30, 32, 34
  Gulielma Maria, 49
  Hanah Moor, 50
  Hanah More, 49
  Ignatius, 50
  Jacob, 40, 49, 50
  Jane, 31
  John, 4, 21, 37, 49, 50
  Josephas, 42
  July, 48
  Littleton, 33, 78
  Margaret(t), 4, 18
  Margret(t), 21, 41
  Mary, 4, 17, 18, 19, 42, 50, 71
  Mordecai, 33
  Nat., 39
  Nathan, 38
  Rachel, 30
  Richard, 35
  Robert, 40
  Samuel, 17, 19, 22, 31, 33, 38, 40, 42, 46, 49, 50, 82
  Samuell, 18, 37, 79
  Sarah, 33
  Stephen, 44
  Steven, 48
  Susanah, 41
  Susanna, 41, 66
  Susannah, 41
  Thomas, 42
  William, 4, 21
WATKINS, ---, 31
  Ann, 31, 36

Gass., 36
  Joseph, 31
  Sarah, 31
WATTERS, Edward, 46
  Elizabeth, 4, 25, 26
  Henry, 46
  John, 4
  Joseph, 4
  Margaret, 73
  Stephen, 46
  William, 4
WATTS, Bartholemy, 13
WAYMAN, Ann, 29
  Edmund, 29
  Leonard, 24, 29
  Mary, 29
WEBB, Elizabeth, 69
  John, 69
  Levicey, 69
  Lucey, 69
  Mary, 14, 68
  Richard, 69
WEBILL, Elizabeth, 46
WEBSTER, Elizabeth, 66
  Isaac, 37, 83
  John, 31, 32, 79
  Lucy, 79
  Margaret(t), 32, 83
  Mary, 4, 32, 79
  Sarah, 79, 84
WEEMS, John, 34
WELCH, Beniamen, 20
  Elizabeth, 29, 78
  Richard, 30
WELLS, Eliner, 32
  Johns, 42
  Sarah, 28, 32
WELSH, Benjamin, 17, 19, 21, 24, 25
  Elizabeth, 15, 25, 27
  John, 15, 24
  Mary, 15
  Rachel(l), 24, 29
  Richard, 15, 26
  Robert, 26
  Sarah, 15

Silveser, 15
Thomasin, 22
WESH, John, 22
WESTGARTH,
  George, 24
WEYMAN, Dorcas, 20
  Leonard, 20
WHELY, Elizabeth, 14
WHICHCOTE,
  Benjamin, 25
WHITE, Benjamin,
  27, 28, 32
  Elizabeth, 22, 23, 27,
  28, 74, 77
  Guy, 28
  Joseph, 81
  Samuel(I), 23, 27, 28,
  32, 37, 47
  Sarah, 23, 75
WIGG, Richard, 15,
  17, 25, 28
WILKINSON, ---, 38
  Ann, 34, 64
  Anna, 34, 64
  Elizabeth, 34, 57, 64, 77
  Henry, 33, 57
  John, 33, 34, 57, 58, 64, 78
  John Benjamin, 34, 64
  Mary, 34, 35, 36,
  38, 39, 57, 64, 84
  Orton, 57, 58
  Philip, 28
  Phillip, 57
  Priscilla, 57
  William, 57
WILLAMES, Joseph, 14
WILLCOX, Joseph, 18
WILLEX, Joseph, 18
WILLIAMS, Agness, 45
  Ennion, 44, 45, 46, 48, 51
  Esther, 49
  Hanah, 48
  Hannah, 45, 46, 51
  Hester, 47, 48
  Isaac, 44
  Lyda, 44

Lydia, 45, 46
  Mary, 45, 46
  Phebe, 32
  Susanna, 41
WILLOBEE, Sarah, 17
WILLS, Peter, 24
WILLSON, Benkid, 82
  Jo., 18
  John, 13
WILLUMES, Joseph, 13
WILMOTE, John, 19
WILSON, Benjamin, 44
  Benkid, 43
  Cassandra, 43
  Elizabeth, 41, 55, 82
  Frances, 55
  Hannah, 13
  Henry, 37, 40, 42, 43, 80
  James, 55
  Jo., 21
  John, 13, 21, 39, 55, 74
  Joseph, 55
  Josiah, 55
  Margaret, 43, 55, 71, 85
  Margret, 42
  Mary, 55
  Moses, 13
  Priscilla, 43
  Rachel, 32, 41, 43
  Samuel, 41
  Sophia, 55
  Thomas, 55
  William, 32, 41, 42, 74, 80, 81
WISH, Elizabeth, 30
WITCHELL, Jean, 14
  Mary, 15, 20, 21, 23, 24, 25, 29
  Nor., 14
  Thomas, 14, 15
WITHELL, Mary, 19
WOARD, Robert, 14
WOODDEN,
  Elizabeth, 15, 16
  John, 15
WOODEN, Elizabeth,
  20, 21, 24, 25, 26, 29, 30

WOODING,
  Elizabeth, 22, 23, 26, 28
WOOLDING,
  Elizabeth, 15
WOOTTON, Turner, 25
WORD, Ivanna, 14
WORTHINGTON,
  John, 41
WRIGHT, Charles, 58
  Elizabeth, 58
  John, 58
  Joseph, 58
  Mary, 58
  Samuel, 58
  Sarah, 58
  Thomas, 50, 51, 58
WYNN, Martha, 15
  Sydney, 15
  Thomas, 15

-Y-
YARNALL,
  Elizabeth, 85
YATES, Joseph, 30
  Joshua, 38
YOUNG, Ann, 21, 54, 55, 74
  Anna, 54, 70
  Arthur, 54, 55, 70, 72, 73
  Constance, 22, 78
  Constant, 55
  Constn., 23
  Elizabeth, 55, 75
  Faith, 13
  Frances, 54, 69
  Mary, 55, 72
  Peter, 54
  Rachel, 55
  Rebekah, 39
  Samuel, 15
  Sarah, 55

-Z-
ZACHARY, Loyd, 26
ZINKES, Anthony, 49
ZIRKES, Anthony, 49

Other books by the author:

A Closer Look at St. John's Parish Registers [Baltimore County, Maryland], 1701-1801

A Collection of Maryland Church Records

A Guide to Genealogical Research in Maryland: 5th Edition, Revised and Enlarged

Abstracts of the Ledgers and Accounts of the Bush Store and Rock Run Store, 1759-1771

Abstracts of the Orphans Court Proceedings of Harford County, 1778-1800

Abstracts of Wills, Harford County, Maryland, 1800-1805

Baltimore City [Maryland] Deaths and Burials, 1834-1840

Baltimore County, Maryland, Overseers of Roads, 1693-1793

Bastardy Cases in Baltimore County, Maryland, 1673-1783

Bastardy Cases in Harford County, Maryland, 1774-1844

Bible and Family Records of Harford County, Maryland Families: Volume V

Children of Harford County: Indentures and Guardianships, 1801-1830

Colonial Delaware Soldiers and Sailors, 1638-1776

Colonial Families of the Eastern Shore of Maryland Volumes 5, 6, 7, 8, 9, 11, 12, 13, 14, and 16

Colonial Maryland Soldiers and Sailors, 1634-1734

Dr. John Archer's First Medical Ledger, 1767-1769, Annotated Abstracts

Early Anglican Records of Cecil County

Early Harford Countians, Individuals Living in Harford County, Maryland in Its Formative Years Volume 1: A to K, Volume 2: L to Z, and Volume 3: Supplement

Harford County Taxpayers in 1870, 1872 and 1883

Harford County, Maryland Divorce Cases, 1827-1912: An Annotated Index

Heirs and Legatees of Harford County, Maryland, 1774-1802

Heirs and Legatees of Harford County, Maryland, 1802-1846

Inhabitants of Baltimore County, Maryland, 1763-1774

Inhabitants of Cecil County, Maryland, 1649-1774

Inhabitants of Harford County, Maryland, 1791-1800

Inhabitants of Kent County, Maryland, 1637-1787

Joseph A. Pennington & Co., Havre De Grace, Maryland Funeral Home Records: Volume II, 1877-1882, 1893-1900

Maryland Bible Records, Volume 1: Baltimore and Harford Counties

Maryland Bible Records, Volume 2: Baltimore and Harford Counties

Maryland Bible Records, Volume 3: Carroll County

Maryland Bible Records, Volume 4: Eastern Shore

Maryland Deponents, 1634-1799

Maryland Deponents: Volume 3, 1634-1776

Maryland Public Service Records, 1775-1783: A Compendium of Men and Women of Maryland Who Rendered Aid in Support of the American Cause against Great Britain during the Revolutionary War

Marylanders to Carolina: Migration of Marylanders to North Carolina and South Carolina prior to 1800

Marylanders to Kentucky, 1775-1825

Methodist Records of Baltimore City, Maryland: Volume 1, 1799-1829

Methodist Records of Baltimore City, Maryland: Volume 2, 1830-1839

Methodist Records of Baltimore City, Maryland: Volume 3, 1840-1850 (East City Station)

More Maryland Deponents, 1716-1799

More Marylanders to Carolina: Migration of Marylanders to North Carolina and South Carolina prior to 1800

More Marylanders to Kentucky, 1778-1828

Outpensioners of Harford County, Maryland, 1856-1896

Presbyterian Records of Baltimore City, Maryland, 1765-1840

Quaker Records of Baltimore and Harford Counties, Maryland, 1801-1825

Quaker Records of Northern Maryland, 1716-1800

Quaker Records of Southern Maryland, 1658-1800

Revolutionary Patriots of Anne Arundel County, Maryland

Revolutionary Patriots of Baltimore Town and Baltimore County, 1775-1783

Revolutionary Patriots of Calvert and St. Mary's Counties, Maryland, 1775-1783

Revolutionary Patriots of Caroline County, Maryland, 1775-1783

Revolutionary Patriots of Cecil County, Maryland

Revolutionary Patriots of Charles County, Maryland, 1775-1783

Revolutionary Patriots of Delaware, 1775-1783

Revolutionary Patriots of Dorchester County, Maryland, 1775-1783

Revolutionary Patriots of Frederick County, Maryland, 1775-1783

Revolutionary Patriots of Harford County, Maryland, 1775-1783

Revolutionary Patriots of Kent and Queen Anne's Counties

Revolutionary Patriots of Lancaster County, Pennsylvania

Revolutionary Patriots of Maryland, 1775-1783: A Supplement

Revolutionary Patriots of Maryland, 1775-1783: Second Supplement

Revolutionary Patriots of Montgomery County, Maryland, 1776-1783

Revolutionary Patriots of Prince George's County, Maryland, 1775-1783

Revolutionary Patriots of Talbot County, Maryland, 1775-1783

Revolutionary Patriots of Worcester and Somerset Counties, Maryland, 1775-1783

Revolutionary Patriots of Washington County, Maryland, 1776-1783

St. George's (Old Spesutia) Parish, Harford County, Maryland: Church and Cemetery Records, 1820-1920

St. John's and St. George's Parish Registers, 1696-1851

Survey Field Book of David and William Clark in Harford County, Maryland, 1770-1812

The Crenshaws of Kentucky, 1800-1995

The Delaware Militia in the War of 1812

Union Chapel United Methodist Church Cemetery Tombstone Inscriptions, Wilna, Harford County, Maryland

CPSIA information can be obtained at www.ICGtesting.com
Printed in the USA
BVOW06s1958181015

422971BV00013BA/297/P